YORK NOTES

OTHELLO

WILLIAM SHAKESPEARE

NOTES BY REBECCA WARREN

The right of Rebecca Warren to be identified as Author of this Work
has been asserted by her in accordance with the Copyright,
Designs and Patents Act 1988

YORK PRESS
322 Old Brompton Road, London SW5 9JH

PEARSON EDUCATION LIMITED
Edinburgh Gate, Harlow,
Essex CM20 2JE, United Kingdom

Associated companies, branches and representatives throughout the world

First published 1998
New editions 2003 and 2012
This new and fully revised edition 2015

10 9 8 7 6 5

ISBN 978-1-4479-8225-8

Illustration on page 86 by Alan Batley
Phototypeset by Carnegie Book Production
Printed in China by Golden Cup

Photo credits: © iStock/frentusha for page 6 bottom / Lance Bellers/Shutterstock for page 7 middle/ © iStock/cawcaw for page 8 bottom / © iStock/TonyBaggett for page 10 middle/ © iStock/Kazakov for page 12 middle / EMJAY SMITH/Shutterstock for page 13 bottom / © iStock/Heijo for page 14 bottom / © iStock/Tarek El Sombati for page 15 bottom / Anneka/Shutterstock for page 16 middle / © iStock/Yuri_Arcurs for page 17 middle / Adisa/Shutterstock for page 18 bottom / Kiselev Andrey Valerevich/Shutterstock for page 19 top / Kostyantyn Ivanyshen/Shutterstock for page 20 middle / Sugarless/Shutterstock for page 21 bottom / FooTToo/Shutterstock for page 22 bottom / © iStock/BrianAJackson for page 23 bottom / © iStock/duncan1890 for page 24 bottom / Dziurek/Shutterstock for page 25 top / PANORAMA MEDIA TASHKENT/Shutterstock for page 26 bottom / © iStock/MariaBrzostowska for page 28 top / © iStock/dlewis33 for page 29 bottom / VICTOR TORRES/Shutterstock for page 30 top / hacohob/Shutterstock for page 31 bottom / Eric Isselee/Shutterstock for page 32 middle / fluke samed/Shutterstock for page 33 middle / © iStock/GlobalP for page 34 bottom / Dan Kosmayer/Shutterstock for page 35 bottom / © iStock/Michal Krakowiak for page 36 bottom / KatyKing27/Shutterstock for page 37 middle / © iStock/Lagui for page 38 middle / Suppakij1017/Shutterstock for page 39 top / Zvonimir Atletic/Shutterstock for page 40 bottom / Sibrikov Valery/Shutterstock for page 41 top / © iStock/Zauberschmeterling for page 42 bottom / nednappa/Shutterstock for page 43 middle / © iStock/Sadeugra for page 44 bottom / oksana2010/Shutterstock for page 45 bottom / © iStock/Heijo for page 46 top / Viorel Sima/Shutterstock for page 46 bottom / Gianni Dagli Orti/The Art Archive/Alamy for page 49 middle / © iStock/Yuri Arcurs for page 50 top / Linus/Shutterstock for page 50 bottom / Kiselev Andrey Valerevich/Shutterstock for page 52 top / Aleksminyaylol/Shutterstock for page 54 top / cinemafestival/Shutterstock for page 55 bottom / Dudaeva/Shutterstock for page 56 top / Surkov Dimitri/Shutterstock for page 58 top / sniegirova mariia/Shutterstock for page 59 middle / © iStock/Ceneri for page 60 top / © iStock/oeil for page 61 top / Surachai/Shutterstock for page 62 middle / maximult/Shutterstock for page 63 middle / © iStock/imagedepotpro for page 65 bottom / Refat/Shutterstock for page 66 top / Matej Kastelic/Shutterstock for page 67 bottom / SJ Watt/Shutterstock for page 69 top / © iStock/IakovKalinin for page 71 middle / Curioso/Shutterstock for page 72 bottom / isak55/Shutterstock for page 73 bottom / Mariusz Szczygiel/Shutterstock for page 74 middle / Sylvie Corriveau/Shutterstock for page 76 bottom / Olga_i/Shutterstock for page 77 top / © iStock/montreehanlue for page 78 top / Art man/Shutterstock for page 79 middle / © iStock/3drenderings for page 81 bottom / © V&A/Alamy for page 82 top / Dudaeva/Shutterstock for page 82 bottom / Martin Bache/Alamy for page 83 bottom / David M. Benett/Getty Images for page 84 bottom / kamiwro/Shutterstock for page 87 bottom / LanKS/Shutterstock for page 88 bottom / © iStock/satori13 for page 89 middle / lassedesignen/Shutterstock for page 90 bottom / wavebreakmedia/Shutterstock for page 107 middle

CONTENTS

PART FIVE: CONTEXTS AND INTERPRETATIONS

PART SIX: PROGRESS BOOSTER

PART SEVEN: FURTHER STUDY AND ANSWERS

HOW TO USE YOUR YORK NOTES TO STUDY AND REVISE *OTHELLO*

These Notes can be used in a range of ways to help you read, study and revise for your exam or assessment.

Become an informed and independent reader

Throughout the Notes, you will find the following key features to aid your study:

- **'Key context'** margin features: these widen your knowledge of the setting, whether historical, social or political. This is highlighted by the AO3 (Assessment Objective 3) symbol to remind you of its connection to aspects you may want to refer to in your exam responses.
- **'Key interpretation'** boxes (a key part of AO5): do you agree with the perspective or idea that is explained here? Does it help you form your own view on events or characters? Developing your own interpretations is a key element of higher-level achievement in A Level, so make use of this and similar features.
- **'Key connection'** features (linked to AO4): whether or not you refer to such connections in your exam writing, having a wider understanding of how the play, or aspects of it, links to other texts or ideas can give you new perspectives on the text.
- **'Study focus'** panels: these help to secure your own understanding of key elements of the text. Being able to write in depth on a particular point or explain a specific feature will help your writing sound professional and informed.
- **'Key quotation'** features: these identify the effect of specific language choices – you could use these for revision purposes at a later date.
- **'Progress booster'** features: these offer specific advice about how to tackle a particular aspect of your study, or an idea you might want to consider discussing in your exam responses.
- **'Extract analysis'** sections: these are vital for you to use either during your reading or when you come back to the text afterwards. These sections take a core extract from a scene and explore it in real depth, explaining its significance and impact, raising questions and offering interpretations.

Stay on track with your study and revision

Your first port of call will always be your teacher, and you should already have a good sense of how well you are doing, but the Notes offer you several ways of measuring your progress.

- **'Revision task'**: throughout the Notes, there are some challenging, but achievable, written tasks for you to do relevant to the section just covered. Suggested answers are supplied in **Part Seven**.
- **'Progress check'**: this feature comes at the end of **Parts Two** to **Five**, and contains a range of short and longer tasks which address key aspects of the Part of the Notes you have just read. Below this is a grid of key skills which you can complete to track your progress, and rate your understanding.
- **'Practice task'** and **'Mark scheme'**: use these features to make a judgement on how well you know the text and how well you can apply the skills you have learnt.

The text used in these Notes is the Arden edition, 1995.

A02 PROGRESS BOOSTER

You can choose to use the Notes as you wish, but as you read the play it can be useful to read over the **Part Two** summaries and analysis in order to embed key events, ideas and developments in the **narrative**.

A02 PROGRESS BOOSTER

Don't forget to make full use of **Parts Three** to **Five** of the Notes during your reading of the play. You may have essays to complete on genre, or key themes, or on the impact of specific settings, and can therefore make use of these in-depth sections. Or you may simply want to check out a particular idea or area as you're reading or studying the play in class.

A01 PROGRESS BOOSTER

Part Six: Progress Booster will introduce you to different styles of question and how to tackle them; help you to improve your expression so that it has a suitably academic and professional tone; assist you with planning and use of evidence to support ideas, and, most importantly, show you three sample exam responses at different levels with helpful AO-related annotations and follow-up comments. Dedicating time to working through this Part will be time you won't regret.

Othello is the first Moor who is a **tragic** hero in Jacobean drama. The first Moorish protagonists on the English stage appeared in George Peele's *The Battle of Alcazar* (*c*. 1591). Muly Mahamet, a dark-skinned Moor, is a scheming usurper, while his uncle, the rightful king Abdelmelec, is a fair-skinned Moor who is portrayed sympathetically. Peele's play was anti-Spanish and pro-Moroccan because of its historical context. The Spanish Armada was defeated in 1588, and Elizabeth I attempted to form an alliance with Moroccan Sultan Ahmad al-Mansur in the 1590s.

OTHELLO: A SNAPSHOT

Othello's enduring appeal

Othello is one of Shakespeare's most frequently performed plays and has had a successful stage history since it was first performed in the early 1600s. The play's enduring popularity can be accounted for in several ways. The two central male roles are challenging for actors and compelling for audiences. Othello's psychological complexity and the tight focus on his relationships with Desdemona and Iago exert what Norman Sanders has called a 'relentless emotional grip' on the audience. The Machiavellian villain Iago is a figure of psychological complexity too. Critics have debated his characterisation for centuries, trying to pin down his motives and account for his evil.

For the seventeenth-century theatre-goer the Italianate setting of *Othello* would have also made the play intriguing. Italy was frequently used by Jacobean dramatists who wished to explore themes related to appearance and reality, corruption and sexual decadence. The contrasting emotions experienced by the characters – passion, hatred, jealousy, envy – are as compelling today as they would have been for the seventeenth-century audience.

Othello's success also lies in its emphasis on a universal theme – love – which resonates in any age. For many this play is, in G. R. Elliott's words, 'the world's supreme secular poem of "human love divine"'. Othello is one of the greatest lovers in dramatic literature. There is something truly grand about the passions by which he is swayed. Othello and Desdemona's marriage is characterised by mutual commitment and romance, and this makes its destruction deeply tragic. The play exerts a hold on our emotions because of the intensity of the central couple's emotions.

Othello remains popular because the 'noble Moor' is both a traditional and a unique tragic hero. Many would argue Othello is brought down by **hubris**, a kind of blind pride which afflicts many Jacobean tragic **protagonists**. But Othello is also unusual: he is the first black hero to be represented on stage. Shakespeare's portrayal of xenophobia and racial stereotypes – and the subversion of these stereotypes – make this tragedy as relevant today as it was in the seventeenth century.

Shakespeare and the writing of *Othello*

Shakespeare wrote thirty-seven plays between the late 1580s and 1613, as well as contributing to plays by other dramatists. Two actors from Shakespeare's company collected together thirty-six of Shakespeare's plays, including *Othello*, for publication in the first collected edition of his plays, known as the First Folio, in 1623. (*Pericles* was not included in the First Folio.) Shakespeare's career was highly successful. He made enough money to buy land around Stratford-upon-Avon, as well as a large house in the town.

The primary source Shakespeare used when writing *Othello* was the *Hecatommithi*, a collection of tales by the Italian writer Giambattista Cinzio Giraldi. In Giraldi's story the Moor and his wife (Disdemona) live happily together in Venice for some time before the Ensign (who falls in love with the Moor's wife) persuades him that Disdemona has been unfaithful with Cassio, a captain. Together the Moor and his Ensign plan to kill Disdemona. The Ensign commits the murder, bludgeoning Disdemona to death with a stocking filled with sand. The ceiling is then collapsed on the body to make the death look like an accident. The Moor denies his part in the murder and is sent into exile, where he is killed by Disdemona's kinsmen. The Ensign continues his life of crime, eventually dying as a result of the torture inflicted on him in prison.

Shakespeare stuck to Giraldi's tale closely, although there are significant differences between this story and *Othello*. Shakespeare compresses the timescale to heighten the emotional impact of events and makes use of two contrasting locations. He introduces the characters of Roderigo and Brabantio (Desdemona's father) and the war between the Turks and Venetians. The lust of the Ensign in Giraldi's tale is replaced by the personal and professional jealousy of Iago, providing thematic continuity. Interestingly, Shakespeare makes Emilia an unwitting aid to her husband. In Giraldi's story the Ensign's wife is fully aware of her husband's villainy but is too frightened to speak out.

Shakespeare's theatre

When Shakespeare arrived in London in the early 1590s, there were flourishing theatres and companies of actors waiting for him. His company performed at James Burbage's Theatre in Shoreditch, the first permanent theatre in England, until 1596, and used the Swan and Curtain until moving into their own new theatre, the Globe, in 1599.

Attending the theatre in Shakespeare's day was very different from modern theatre-going. Performances took place during the daytime and in the open air, and so the audience and the actors were always aware of each other. Shakespeare's theatre was a communal experience, enjoyed by a range of social classes. Wealthier spectators sat in covered galleries, but 'groundlings' could stand and watch for a penny. Audiences were less polite than they are today. People came in late, interrupted, joined in and sometimes even got on to the stage.

Theatrical conventions were very different. All female roles were played by boys. Plays were preceded and followed by jigs and clowning, and the pace of the drama was much faster than we are used to. There were no intervals between acts, and very little in the way of props or scenery which needed changing. It is thought that Shakespeare's plays were performed in around two hours.

Study focus: Key issues in *Othello*

A02

- **Conflict and love** Shakespeare deliberately chooses a military man as the tragic lover in *Othello*, drawing our attention to the themes of conflict and love from the first scene. The marriage of Othello and Desdemona provokes very strong reactions in Act I. Some characters oppose the match (Brabantio) while others accept it (the Duke).
- **Race** Objections to Othello's marriage and the negative descriptions of the hero in Act I draw our attention to the theme of race. The Elizabethans were often prejudiced against foreigners and had particular fears about marriages between black men and white women. They commonly believed that the offspring of such unions would be monsters. The black man had long been associated with the devil in art and literature. In the Renaissance many Christians viewed Moors with suspicion because they considered them heathens, like the Turks. There had been a long-standing conflict between the Muslim Ottoman Empire (the Turks) and the Catholic maritime states of Europe, which sought to hold on to their territories – including Cyprus – in the Mediterranean and prevent the expansion of the Ottoman Empire. As a Moor, Othello would thus have been associated in the Elizabethan mind with a range of ideas and events which provoked anxiety.
- **Gender roles and power** The assertive heroine Desdemona, who chooses her own husband and refuses to be parted from him, draws our attention to gender roles and power in *Othello*. Desdemona's deception of her father also alerts us to the difference between appearance and reality, upon which Iago's evil scheming depends. Ultimately, in spite of her bravery and defence of her own virtue, like so many women in Elizabethan drama, Desdemona does not have the power to determine her own fate; it lies in the hands of the men who abuse her.

A03 **PROGRESS BOOSTER**

In Giraldi's tale the Moor is taken back to Venice, where he is tortured and refuses to confess to his crimes. In *Othello* it is Iago who refuses to speak at the end of the play, while Othello commits suicide to atone for his sins. Try thinking about the dramatic significance of the changes Shakespeare made to his source.

A03 **KEY CONTEXT**

In Shakespeare's London there were between five and eight theatres open at any one time. Audience figures were very large, with 18,000 to 24,000 people visiting the theatre each week.

A03 **KEY CONTEXT**

Christian traditions of the Renaissance suggested that Africans were descendants of Noah's son Ham, who was cursed by his father. Thus, it held that they were an accursed race. This tradition partly accounts for the kind of racial prejudice expressed by Roderigo and Iago in *Othello*.

SYNOPSIS

Act I

Othello: The hero driven by love

The Moor Othello, a respected general, has secretly married a wealthy Venetian aristocrat, Desdemona. Her father, Brabantio, is informed of this (on the night of the marriage) by Roderigo, who had hoped to marry Desdemona himself. Brabantio goes in search of Othello and then makes his way to the senate where he accuses Othello of bewitching his daughter. Brabantio's accusations are proved false when Othello and Desdemona explain how they fell in love. The Duke of Venice tries to reconcile Brabantio to his daughter's marriage but the angry father disowns Desdemona. The senate sends Othello to defend Cyprus from a Turkish invasion. Desdemona asks to be allowed to accompany her husband. She is put in the care of Othello's ensign, Iago. Iago's wife, Emilia, is to be Desdemona's lady-in-waiting.

Iago: The villain driven by revenge

Iago is an embittered man, who is angry because Othello has not given him a promotion that he believes is due to him. A young Florentine soldier, Cassio, has been made lieutenant over him. Iago seeks to revenge himself on both Cassio and Othello, and has already made trouble for Othello; it was he who persuaded Roderigo to inform Brabantio of Desdemona's elopement in the first scene.

Act II

Personal and political conflict in Cyprus

The action moves to Cyprus. The threat of military invasion is removed when the Turkish fleet is destroyed in a storm, which Othello, Desdemona and Iago pass through safely. There is a night of festivities to celebrate the destruction of the Turkish fleet and the marriage of Othello and Desdemona. The newly-weds seem secure in their love. However, while there is no longer a military conflict, there is a new threat to the couple's happiness: Iago. Roderigo has been persuaded to follow Desdemona to Cyprus. Iago has promised to help him woo Desdemona, making Roderigo believe that she will soon tire of Othello. Iago now makes Roderigo believe that Cassio is his rival for Desdemona's affections. On the night of the celebrations Iago goads Roderigo into challenging Cassio, whom he has plied with drink. A fight ensues. Cassio is disgraced and Othello dismisses him from his post. Iago tells Cassio that his best chance of winning back Othello's good opinion lies in asking Desdemona to plead for him. Iago plans to persuade Othello that Desdemona has committed adultery with Cassio. Iago claims to have personal motives for his revenge on Cassio and Othello. He claims that they have both cuckolded him by having sexual relations with Emilia.

Act III

Othello: The hero is driven by jealousy

Iago persuades Othello that Desdemona is in love with Cassio and has committed adultery with him. He contrives proof of this, making use of a handkerchief belonging to Desdemona, which he claims has been found in Cassio's bedchamber. In fact, the handkerchief was passed on to Iago by Emilia, who picked it up when Desdemona dropped it. Although he is reluctant to believe his wife unchaste, Othello becomes convinced that Desdemona is a whore and is seized by overpowering jealousy. He vows to seek revenge on Desdemona and Cassio by killing them. Iago promises to help him. Desdemona is frightened by Othello when he questions her about the handkerchief and lies about what has happened to it. She is unaware of the danger she is in by continuing to plead for Cassio. Cassio gives the handkerchief to his mistress, Bianca.

Act IV

Iago: The villain's poison destroys Othello's mind

Iago continues to torment Othello with insinuations about Desdemona and Cassio fornicating. Othello is so overwhelmed that he falls down in a fit. While he is writhing on the ground, Iago creates another opportunity to 'prove' Desdemona is a whore. He persuades Othello to observe him talking to Cassio. Unable to hear what is being said, Othello believes that Cassio is laughing about committing adultery with Desdemona. Bianca returns the handkerchief to Cassio, convinced that it was given to him by another woman and thus that it proves has been unfaithful. Othello observes what happens between Cassio and Bianca and believes that this is evidence of Desdemona's adultery. Othello decides to poison his wife, but Iago suggests smothering her in the marital bed instead. Desdemona is abused physically and verbally in Act IV. Othello refuses to believe her or Emilia's protestations of Desdemona's innocence. Othello calls Desdemona a whore and strikes her in front of Lodovico, who has arrived with a letter from the Venetian senate. Othello has been recalled to Venice and Cassio is to govern in Cyprus. Desdemona asks Emilia to put her wedding sheets on her bed and sings a melancholy song about a woman forsaken in love.

Act V

The tragic denouement: Love is destroyed

Othello has asked Iago to kill Cassio. Iago again persuades Roderigo to assist him but the attempt on Cassio's life does not go as planned. Iago wounds Cassio himself and then kills Roderigo. Iago believes removing Roderigo will ensure his safety, but he does not know that Roderigo was carrying letters outlining Iago's evil schemes. These letters are discovered in the final scene. Gripped by jealousy, Othello smothers Desdemona in her bed. She dies protesting her innocence. Emilia comes to inform Othello of the attack on Cassio and finds her mistress dying. Desdemona refuses to blame Othello for her murder. Emilia calls out for help. Montano, Gratiano and Iago come running in to find out what has happened. Othello is taken prisoner. Iago's plots are revealed, largely by Emilia, who is killed by her husband for speaking the truth. Iago attempts to escape but is captured and brought back under arrest. He refuses to explain why he has plotted against Othello. Othello realises his terrible folly. He is prevented from killing Iago and turns his weapon on himself. He dies, full of remorse, on the bed next to Desdemona. Cassio is made governor of Cyprus and Iago is led away for torture.

A05 KEY INTERPRETATION

In *Othello* (1997), E. A. J. Honigmann claims that *Othello* is 'the most unbearably exciting' of Shakespeare's **tragedies**. What details of the plot do you think led him to say this?

A05 KEY INTERPRETATION

Caryl Phillips says Othello's love of Desdemona 'is the love of a possession. She is a prize, a spoil of war'. To what extent do you agree with this interpretation?

A03 KEY CONTEXT

It is possible that Shakespeare may have been influenced by the interests of James I when he chose to write *Othello*. James was fascinated by Turkish history and wrote a poem about the famous sea battle which occurred at Lepanto in the Ionian Sea in October 1571. A coalition of Christian forces, including the Republic of Venice, defeated the main Turkish fleet. When Shakespeare wrote *Othello* James was the new patron of Shakespeare's acting company, the King's Men.

ACT I SCENE 1

Summary

- Roderigo is unhappy with Iago for failing to promote his marriage to Desdemona, who has secretly married Othello.
- Iago says that Othello has promoted an inexperienced soldier, Michael Cassio, over him, and that he hates Othello and wants revenge on him.
- To cause trouble, Iago urges Roderigo to wake up Brabantio and inform him of his daughter Desdemona's elopement.
- Brabantio discovers that Desdemona is not in her room. Calling for weapons, he sets out to locate Desdemona and Othello.

Analysis

Conflict and the tragedy of Othello

From the beginning of *Othello* the scene is set for conflict. The topic under discussion in the opening lines (marriage) seems of little political significance. However, Shakespeare **juxtaposes** Roderigo's failure to marry Desdemona with Iago's failure to gain promotion, making it clear that private, domestic issues and the public, professional world will collide in *Othello*. The scene ends with an indication that this is not a purely domestic drama. Brabantio arms himself and rouses his neighbours to help him hunt down Othello. He is making his daughter's elopement a public, political affair. The audience realises that the marriage of Othello and Desdemona is going to be at the heart of the conflict in the play. Act I Scene 1 also includes references to the Venetian conflict with the Turks over Cyprus, the setting where Othello's mind and marriage will be destroyed.

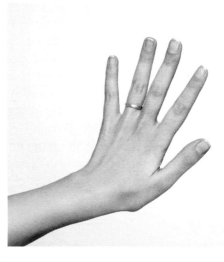

KEY CONNECTION A04

In the 1952 Orson Welles film production, the play opens with the funeral procession of Desdemona and Othello. Iago is seen suspended in a cage, his eyes glinting wickedly. This opening suggests the tragic inevitability of the events that occur. Check Act I Scene 1 for words or events that **foreshadow** a tragic outcome.

KEY CONTEXT A03

Venice had a more rigid class structure than England at the time *Othello* was written. The nobility and 'common people' were very distinct from one another. We see evidence of Iago's class envy early in the play when he complains about how promotion goes by 'preferment'. As a man who had risen in society himself, Shakespeare would have understood Iago's resentment.

A02

Progress booster: Deception and deceit

Deception emerges as a key theme. It is established in two ways. Firstly, there are the deceptions that occurred before the events of the play began. Roderigo was deceived into believing he could win Desdemona's hand in marriage. Brabantio has been deceived by both Desdemona and Othello. Iago deceived himself when he believed he would be promoted. Secondly, there is the language of deceit which Iago uses. Iago says that he admires men who make 'shows of service on their lords' (line 51). His reputation as a dutiful subordinate is deceptive; Iago says openly 'I am not what I am' (line 64). Notice how Shakespeare has structured the play in such a way that the audience will question the difference between appearance and reality from the start.

The language men use to define women

The ways in which the male characters discuss women reveal the **patriarchal** context of the play. Iago sneers that Cassio is 'A fellow almost damned in a fair wife' (line 20). This casual sexism helps to establish Iago's misogyny, which he will use to infect Othello's mind. The **imagery** also makes it clear that the male characters view women as their possessions. Iago shouts to Brabantio, 'Look to your house, your daughter, and your bags!/ Thieves, thieves!' (lines 79–80).

Brabantio believes Desdemona has subverted the natural order by eloping. Her decision to choose her own husband is 'treason of the blood' (line 167). The image of Desdemona in 'the gross clasps of a lascivious Moor' (line 124) makes it plain that her 'revolt' (line 132) is outrageous not just because Desdemona has deceived her father, but also because she has chosen a Moor. Perhaps because it is too alarming to believe that Desdemona is a willing bride, Brabantio suggests his daughter is a passive victim. Her 'youth and maidhood' have been 'abused' by Othello and his love potions (lines 170–1). This idea reflects the Renaissance stereotype of the black man as cunning sexual predator.

First impressions of the villain

Iago reveals his villainy early on. He seems to have a clear motive for causing Othello harm. Iago tells Roderigo he is bitter because of the way 'Preferment goes by letter and affection/ And not by the old gradation' (lines 35–6). Iago feels Othello has cheated him out of a promotion that was his due. However, should the audience trust what Iago says? Iago stresses that he only follows Othello to 'serve my turn upon him' (line 41).

Iago is good at getting himself out of trouble, or avoiding it altogether: he leaves the stage just as Brabantio discovers Desdemona has gone, knowing that it is 'not meet nor wholesome to my place,/ To be produced' (lines 143–4). The language Iago uses here is a good example of the **irony** that the audience will come to associate with him. Neither his words nor his actions in this scene have been 'wholesome'. There are other examples of **dramatic irony** that centre on Iago in this scene. Roderigo fails to see that a man who admits he is a selfish fraud might be using him and Brabantio is unaware of the truth of his words to Iago, 'Thou art a villain!' (line 116). By the end of Act I Scene 1, Shakespeare has established Iago as a powerful, manipulative figure, who instigates and stage-manages chaos efficiently.

The tragic hero

Because we do not see him, and he is not referred to by name, Othello is a mysterious figure at this stage. Shakespeare has structured the scene to draw the audience's attention to the role rumour is to play in events. Everything we learn about Othello is second hand. Should we dismiss it as gossip? Iago says Othello is a self-satisfied and bombastic speaker (lines 11–13), who gets his way with the senate in order to promote his own favourites. However, Iago also admits that Othello is an effective soldier, relied on by the Venetian senate (lines 145–51).

Revision task 1: Iago's motives — A02

Make brief notes on what you have learned about Iago's motives for revenge against Othello and Cassio by the end of this scene. Write about:

- Why he has grudges against Othello and Cassio.
- Whether Iago's motives are plausible.

A05 KEY INTERPRETATION

Dr Johnson took a very dim view of Iago. He said that 'the character of Iago is so conducted, that he is from the first scene to the last hated and despised'. Do you think that this is how Shakespeare intended the audience to react to Iago? Are there other ways of responding to Iago?

A05 KEY INTERPRETATION

Many critics have said that the most important theme in *Othello* is jealousy. Notice how quickly Shakespeare establishes the theme. Iago is jealous of Cassio, and Roderigo feels jealous of Othello for 'beating' him to Desdemona.

A02 PROGRESS BOOSTER

Analyse how Shakespeare creates dramatic interest and tension in the first scene through the characterisation of Iago. Until Brabantio appears Iago dominates the scene, speaking the most lines. This is a pattern that is repeated throughout the play. Because we are given access to the villain's thoughts so early, are we being seduced into colluding with evil?

EXTRACT ANALYSIS

Act I Scene 1 lines 81–138

A heated exchange between Iago, Roderigo and Brabantio occurs immediately after Iago has informed Roderigo that he hates Othello, and follows the Moor only to 'serve my turn upon him' (I.1.41). We see here how successfully Iago manipulates the way characters perceive each other. He displays this skill throughout the play. Although this is the very first scene and only eighty lines in, the ensign has already succeeded in prejudicing Roderigo's view of Othello's marriage. This is so he can obtain Roderigo's assistance. He wants Roderigo to 'Call up her [Desdemona's] father', 'poison his delight' (I.1.66–7) and 'Plague him with flies' (I.1.70). Iago's use of **metaphors** associates him with poison, corruption and disease throughout the play. Shakespeare has begun to prepare us for the poisoning of Othello's mind, which occurs in Act III.

The location of Act I Scene 1 is significant. It is night-time, and the two levels of the stage used (Brabantio at the window, Iago and Roderigo concealed in the darkness of the street below) signifies disruption and confusion. Brabantio's physical security (his house) is threatened, as well as his peace of mind. Iago refers to Desdemona's elopement using a verb that signifies an assault on Brabantio's property; the old man has been 'robbed' (line 84). Roderigo's descriptions of Desdemona's movements add to the atmosphere of disorder, and establish the danger of Venice at night. 'At this odd-even and dull watch o' the night' Brabantio's daughter has been transported to the 'gross clasps of a lascivious Moor'. We know that the social

order has been threatened by the elopement because Desdemona has been taken away from her home in darkness, and by 'a knave of common hire, a gondolier' (lines 121–4).

When he first appears Brabantio assumes the role of angry **patriarch**. We know he is powerful because he speaks of 'my spirit and my place' (line 102). When he says to Roderigo 'My daughter is not for thee' (line 97), we know that Brabantio looks upon Desdemona as a possession. This idea follows on neatly from the earlier use of 'robbed'. Brabantio dismisses Roderigo in a commanding tone at line 95 and is offended by Iago's mode of address, asking 'What profane wretch art thou?' before insulting him as a 'villain' (lines 113–16). Brabantio's social position is undermined in this scene, not just by the 'wheeling stranger' who has eloped with his daughter (line 134), but also by Iago's impudent words and Roderigo's description of Desdemona's 'gross revolt' (line 132). Another reason we know that Brabantio's authority is subverted is because his utterances contain questions as well as threats, and his words increasingly show he is alarmed. Instead of directing his social inferiors, Brabantio finds himself acting in response to them.

Roderigo follows Iago's instructions throughout Act I Scene 1. He speaks politely to Brabantio, reinforcing our sense of the father's important social position. The terms in which Roderigo describes Desdemona's elopement, and in particular Othello, echo the negative descriptions of the Moor earlier in the scene. The **images** Roderigo employs focus on the unnatural quality of the match and Desdemona's disobedience. This marriage is a subversion of the natural order. Roderigo is a representative of Venetian society, one of the 'curled darlings'

(I.2.68) Desdemona has rejected. His **xenophobic** view of her marriage is one that Brabantio can understand. As we see later in the first act, Brabantio views his daughter's marriage as an incomprehensible rejection of everything she has known. Brabantio's death from grief later in the play will be directly attributed to the sorrow he feels about Desdemona's 'gross revolt.'

Iago speaks a different language from the other two male characters. He is crude and mocking. Iago's descriptions of Othello, which we would now view as racist, are a key part of the negative black stereotype that is being created. Iago's references to 'an old black ram', 'a Barbary horse' and 'the beast with two backs' (lines 87, 110, 115) reinforce the idea that Desdemona has made an unnatural match and cast Othello in a repugnant role as lustful predator. Iago's imagery suggests race and sex are going to be important issues in *Othello*. The reduction of the Desdemona–Othello match to bestial sexuality is typical of Iago, who is associated with unpleasant animal imagery throughout the play. However, we might already feel that the imagery here tells us more about Iago's character than it does about Othello's because we are aware of Iago's hatred. Earlier Iago said he wants revenge on the Moor, so we know he is an untrustworthy villain.

We also realise that Iago is persuasive and self-confident. He answers Brabantio back and forces his own interpretation of events on him, a pattern that will be repeated when he poisons Othello's mind in Acts III and IV. It is Iago's crude comments which really capture Brabantio's attention in this scene. Act I Scene 1 also reveals Iago's ability to improvise, which is a key aspect of his characterisation throughout the play. He sets the pace and controls the drama. It was his idea to wake Brabantio and he gets the result he wanted; an angry father, appalled by what he hears.

This is an exchange of contrasts and discord which sets the scene for the events that follow. The contrasts are reflected in the imagery and setting, which establish a number of themes and ideas that are going to be important in *Othello*: social disruption, class and power, delusion and knowledge, male and female sexuality and black and white. The rather chaotic feel signifies that disruption has already occurred and we know that the marriage of Othello and Desdemona is going to be the focal point for future disruption because Iago, Roderigo and Brabantio react to it so strongly and describe it in such negative terms. We are also aware of the difference between Desdemona and her husband: she is the 'white ewe' (line 88) while Othello is the 'black ram'. Desdemona has been stolen, but we also know she has given herself away because she has chosen to elope secretly. Venice – a civilised place associated with power, prosperity and order – has been assaulted by a 'wheeling stranger' (line 134). We wonder how the tension that has been set up in this scene will be resolved, particularly the evident dislike and disdain the three characters feel for Othello.

A02 PROGRESS BOOSTER

In his tragedies, Shakespeare often leads up to the first entrance of his **tragic** protagonist with a scene focusing on minor characters or a subplot. Analyse the impact that this has on the audience of *Othello*. When we hear Iago's crude words about his 'master', are we inclined to be prejudiced against Othello – or against his disloyal servant?

A05 KEY INTERPRETATION

For a **New Historicist** discussion about the way Shakespeare portrays race in the play, see an essay on *Othello* by Frances Dolan, 'Revolutions, Petty Tyranny and the Murderous Husband' in Kate Chedgzoy (ed.), *Shakespeare, Feminism and Gender* (2001).

A05 KEY INTERPRETATION

The actor Dominic West, who played Iago in 2011, described *Othello* as 'a sexual competition between him [Iago] and Othello' (BBC Radio 4, *Front Row*, 23 December 2011). Do you find this view helpful when considering the relationship between Othello and Iago, and Iago's relationship with Desdemona?

ACT I SCENE 2

Summary

- Iago warns that Brabantio may use his influence to have Othello arrested and his marriage dissolved.
- Othello is confident that his services to the state, his reputation and his royal breeding make him a suitable match for Desdemona.
- Cassio brings a message from the Duke, who urgently requires Othello's presence at a meeting of the Venetian council. On the way there Othello and his soldiers are accosted by Brabantio and his followers.
- Othello commands the men to put away their weapons and denies Brabantio's accusations of bewitching Desdemona.
- Brabantio decides to go to the council meeting too, so that the Duke can be informed of Othello's treachery.

Analysis

Othello's conflict

Two **images** in this scene highlight the conflict that Othello faces. On the one hand, he is a successful soldier, used to leading armies, as his command to Brabantio's followers makes clear: 'Keep up your bright swords, for the dew will rust them' (line 59). On the other hand, having married, he has now his 'free condition/ Put into circumscription and confine' (lines 26–7). The audience may wonder how Othello will combine his conflicting roles as military man and lover-husband. What do you make of the fact that the military image Othello uses is poetic, while the language he uses to describe his marriage suggests entrapment?

First impressions of Othello

In contrast to the characters we have seen so far, Othello speaks with a measured calm in **blank verse** in this scene. Othello and Iago are polar opposites: one seeks to resolve conflict while the other revels in it. Iago does his best to stir up trouble when he tells Othello that Brabantio has spoken against Othello in 'scurvy and provoking terms' (line 7), but Othello is unworried. Two brief statements, 'Let him do his spite' (line 17) and 'I must be found' (line 30), suggest he is ready to face the consequences of his actions. When he is accused of evil enchantment Othello pleads for calm and says it is not time to fight (lines 81–3).

Othello's quiet confidence and sincerity about his love for Desdemona are attractive. Othello is not the pompous man Iago described in Act I Scene 1. In spite of his secret marriage, he says he prefers to be open about his actions (lines 30–2). Othello is also brave, dignified and authoritative, as shown by his handling of Brabantio and his followers. We may accuse him of pride when he speaks of his services to the state and insists that his 'parts … title, and … perfect soul' (line 31) will 'manifest me rightly' (line 32), but we understand that his reputation has been attacked. By making Othello so different from the version of him described by Iago, is Shakespeare challenging his audience to accept the Moor as a noble, worthy man?

Study focus: The language of insults

A02

The coarse imagery Iago used in Act I to describe the sexual union of Othello and Desdemona continues. Iago makes a crude joke when he tells Cassio that Othello has 'boarded a land carrack' (line 50). By using a **metaphor** of piracy Iago is degrading Othello, and echoing Brabantio's accusation that he is a 'foul thief' (line 62). Brabantio adds to his earlier insulting comments about enchantment. Othello is 'a practiser/ Of arts inhibited' (lines 78–9). The 'foul charms' he has used to bewitch Desdemona are 'gross'. As if it were not demeaning enough to accuse Othello of practising black magic, Brabantio also makes a racial insult. He cannot believe that Desdemona would 'Run from her guardage to the sooty bosom/ Of such a thing as thou' (lines 70–1). This negative language dehumanises Othello. Will the audience side with the deceived father or the victim of his verbal assault?

A03 **KEY CONTEXT**

Iago's use of 'land carrack' has a double-meaning, either a treasure ship or a slang term for a prostitute.

Cassio's first appearance

Just as we will compare the real Othello with Iago's version of him, so we will want to see if Cassio is the inexperienced fool Iago portrayed him as in Act I Scene 1. In his first speeches Cassio comes across as trustworthy and reliable. He delivers his urgent summons from the Duke in a way which makes it clear the Cyprus mission is very important. However, Othello has not taken Cassio into his confidence about his marriage: he acted alone when he eloped. Does this mean there is a distance between the two soldiers? The most significant feature of Cassio's presentation in this scene is his failure to understand Iago's sexual joke about Othello's marriage at line 50. His puzzlement suggests Cassio does not share Iago's crude sense of humour, thus distancing him from the villain at this stage. This appears **ironic**, however, as Iago will cast Cassio in the role of seducer in the next scene.

A03 **KEY CONTEXT**

Brabantio suggests the world has been turned upside down by Othello's marriage to Desdemona in the rhyming couplet that closes the scene. In Jacobean tragedy, references to the subversion of the 'natural' order are used to warn the audience that there is trouble ahead.

Key quotation: The language of love

A02

Othello defends his love for Desdemona simply and clearly, stating: 'I love the gentle Desdemona' (line 25).

- This is the first sincere reference to love in the play.
- Othello's positive view of his relationship with Desdemona is in conflict with the way it is perceived by others.
- 'Gentle' is a pun which means both kind-hearted and of noble birth. By stressing that Desdemona is 'gentle', does Shakespeare reinforce or undermine our view of Othello as a deserving romantic hero?

A04 **PROGRESS BOOSTER**

If you are asked to comment on the portrayal of the male lovers and husbands in *Othello*, you could start by considering the ways in which the male characters differ in their attitudes to women when they first appear in Act 1. Then you could chart the ways in which Roderigo, Cassio and Othello 'deteriorate' under Iago's influence, to the point where they speak, think and act like him. Do they become abusive and destructive lovers because of Iago's influence, or does Shakespeare suggest the patriarchal context of the play is to blame?

ACT I SCENE 3

Summary

- Othello is told to prepare for war against the Turks after their invasion of Cyprus.
- Brabantio repeats his accusations of witchcraft against Othello.
- Othello recounts the history of his relationship with Desdemona and she is brought to the council chamber to confirm Othello's words; the Duke urges Brabantio to reconcile himself to the marriage.
- Desdemona asks to be allowed to accompany her husband on his military campaign and Othello places her in Iago's care.
- Brabantio warns Othello against trusting Desdemona.
- Iago says he will help Roderigo seduce Desdemona and cuckold Othello.

Analysis

Othello on trial

Othello faces a great deal of opposition in this scene. He is effectively put on trial in the council chamber when he is forced to defend his character and his actions. When Desdemona backs him up and refuses to be parted from him, we know that Othello has one steadfast ally. However, in spite of the Duke's support, his trials are not over. Shakespeare has structured this scene so that discussions move back and forward between love and war, showing that Othello will constantly be pulled in different directions.

Othello's military skill is established by repeated references to him as 'valiant' early in the scene, while Desdemona's refinement and femininity are emphasised. Iago sneers that Desdemona is a pampered and delicate 'super-subtle Venetian' (line 357), while Othello is 'an erring barbarian' (line 356). Because of their differences, we may wonder whether Othello and Desdemona are a good match. However, Othello is confident that love and war can be combined. An audience may doubt this. Othello has had little experience in matters of the heart. He needed prompting to woo Desdemona. And Othello is a mature man, coming late to love, while Brabantio suggests his daughter is not much more than a girl.

Study focus: The language of love

An analysis of the language Othello and Desdemona use when describing their love for each other is revealing. Othello says that Desdemona 'loved me for the dangers I had passed/ And I loved her that she did pity them' (lines 168–9). Desdemona was seduced by Othello's story-telling powers, while the Moor was enchanted by the Venetian's sympathetic response to his history: 'She gave me for my pains a world of sighs' (line 160). Later in this scene Desdemona says that she 'saw Othello's visage in his mind' (line 253). There is no question of their deep sincerity, but an audience might wonder whether Othello and Desdemona fell in love with an **image** or idea of the other. Look closely at the other speeches about love in Act I Scene 3. Are the lovers too idealistic?

KEY CONTEXT A03

By 1603 when Shakespeare came to write *Othello*, Venice had been employing paid mercenaries and freelance generals like Othello – who had their own armies – to protect the wealth of the city for quite some time. It was a cosmopolitan place, where personal advancement was possible, in spite of the rigid and hierarchical social structure that existed.

PROGRESS BOOSTER A02

You need to show an excellent understanding of the way Shakespeare uses language and other dramatic techniques. Commenting on 'honest' and 'honesty', which are key words in the play, is a good way of showing your understanding of **irony** in *Othello*. In Act I Scene 3, Othello twice refers to Iago's honesty (lines 285 and 290).

Desdemona as daughter and lover

Consider carefully your first impressions of Desdemona, who is commented on as daughter and lover by her father and husband in this scene. Take into account the conflicting views that the characters and critics have of her. Some critics see her as a victim, while others believe she is partly responsible for what happens to her. In this scene she clearly makes choices for herself.

There is a contradiction in what Brabantio tells us about his daughter, and the young woman we see. How are we to reconcile the image of a 'maiden never bold;/ Of spirit so still and quiet that her motion/ Blushed at herself' (lines 95–7) with Othello's description of Desdemona as 'half the wooer' (line 176)? How would Shakespeare's audience have reacted to the idea of a woman choosing her own husband and teaching him how to win her heart (see Othello's speech at line 129)?

Think about how an actress playing Desdemona should deliver the lines she addresses to her father, the Duke, and her husband. Desdemona seems to speak assertively to her father when he rejects her. She challenges Brabantio when she declares 'I am hitherto your daughter. But here's my husband' (line 184). She also refuses to stay with her father while Othello is away at war. However, Desdemona accepts male authority at the same time that she subverts it. She speaks of transferring her duty and obedience from her father to her husband, just as her mother did. But there is another contradiction to consider. Desdemona claims she is a submissive wife ('My heart's subdued/ Even to the very quality of my lord', lines 251–2) but also demands the right to accompany Othello to Cyprus ('I did love the Moor to live with him … Let me go with him', lines 249–60).

Iago the revenger

Iago speaks in fast-moving **prose** when outwitting Roderigo, suggesting he is thinking on his feet. Alone on stage, Iago returns to **blank verse**, demonstrating his ability to manipulate his style to suit his audience and purposes. At the start of his **soliloquy** he has not decided how he is going to proceed with his revenge. A few lines later Iago has the outline of a subtle plan. He delights in his quick wits, suggested by the way he thinks aloud, 'let me see now' (line 391). For 'mere suspicion' (line 388) he will destroy Othello's marriage and disgrace Cassio. It is **ironic** that Iago will fabricate a rumour that Cassio is 'too familiar' (line 395) with Desdemona as revenge for the rumour that he was cuckolded.

A05 KEY INTERPRETATION

Caryl Phillips has remarked on Othello's lack of confidence as a wooer, pointing to two lines: 'It was my hint to speak' (I.3.143) and 'Upon this hint I spake' (I.3.167). Phillips says that Othello 'feels constantly threatened and profoundly insecure'. To what extent do you agree that Othello is an insecure lover?

A05 KEY INTERPRETATION

Iago tells us there is a rumour that Othello has slept with his wife Emilia (lines 68–71). Is this a plausible reason for revenge and does anyone else corroborate Iago's story? For Iago's **characterisation** as 'motiveless malignity', see Coleridge's comments in John Wain (ed.), *Othello* (1971).

A03 KEY CONTEXT

The Elizabethans used the term 'black' to refer to a range of skin colours; anyone of non-European background might be described as 'black' by Shakespeare's contemporaries during the Renaissance. For the early audiences of *Othello*, the hero's skin colour would have signified Othello is an outsider. They may well have seen him as someone alienated from society.

ACT II SCENE 1

Summary

- The Turkish fleet is destroyed by a storm, but all the characters arrive safely in Cyprus.
- Iago dislikes the courteous way Cassio greets Emilia.
- Othello is overjoyed to be reunited with Desdemona.
- Iago persuades Roderigo to provoke Cassio into losing his temper in the hope of discrediting him.
- Iago reiterates his desire to have revenge on Othello and Cassio. He suspects them both of cuckolding him.

Analysis

The Cyprus setting and the storm

The principal characters are now isolated in the 'warlike isle' (line 43) of Cyprus, removed from the orderly social and political scene of Venice. The storm **foreshadows** the passions that will be unleashed in this new setting and we might also see it as being related to Othello and his violent emotions. Indeed, Othello is associated with sea **imagery** throughout the play (see **Part Four: Language**). Or we may see the storm as representing Iago, whose violence it reflects. The storm is also a device by which Shakespeare can dispose of the Turkish threat, which is no longer necessary to the plot. The external threat (the Turks) is replaced by the internal threat (Iago).

The storm serves other purposes. While it rages, the soldiers cannot see clearly what is happening and are full of fear, enabling Shakespeare to **mirror** the confusion of Act I Scene 1. Montano's concern for Othello's safety indicates his respect for 'the warlike Moor' (II.1.27) and reinforces our esteem for him. **Ironically**, Othello, who is looked upon as Cyprus's saviour, will prove as destructive as any tempest. Equally ironically, Iago, who will destroy Othello's happiness, arrives in Cyprus a week earlier than expected because the storm has helped his progress. It seems that fortune is favouring Iago. Symbolically, Iago lands before Othello, suggesting he will be in charge in this new setting. A final irony to consider: the marriage of Othello and Desdemona is destroyed in the birthplace of the goddess of love, Aphrodite.

Study focus: Ominous signs

An audience might be concerned that the tone and content of Desdemona's impudent speeches during her conversation with Emilia and Iago seem very different from Othello's romantic speeches. Does this difference foreshadow the couple's doom?

Iago the predator

Shakespeare sets Iago in direct opposition to Othello and Cassio in this scene. Because a **soliloquy** by Iago closes the scene, we know the villain will triumph. The differences between Othello and Iago are clear: Othello's speeches are generous and joyful, while Iago is full of hatred and contempt for the Moor's 'constant, loving, noble nature' (line 287). Personal and professional jealousy dominates Iago's soliloquy. His admission of 'love' (line 289) for Desdemona is intriguing. Should we believe Iago is in love with Desdemona? Perhaps not. Iago immediately redefines his feeling as 'lust' (line 290), 'partly led to diet my revenge' (line 292). Iago wants Othello to suffer the same torment that rages inside him. Would you agree that there is an undertone of competitive racism in Iago's soliloquy? He cannot accept that Desdemona, an aristocratic white woman, has chosen a black soldier.

When talking to the other characters Iago takes on the role of plain-speaking soldier. Ironically, Desdemona and Emilia are amused by Iago's cynical attitude towards women. We might view his crude delineation of the female character as a sign of Iago's narrow and twisted nature. Unlike Othello, who takes delight in his wife's presence, Iago can only see women as false, inferior creatures.

Cassio's gallantry is in contrast to Iago's misogyny. Cassio greets Desdemona like a courtier, 'O, behold,/ The riches of the ship is come on shore:/… Hail to thee, lady!' (lines 83–5). Later he takes Desdemona by the hand. He is also gracious to Emilia. Cassio and Iago are opposites in other ways too. Cassio mocks Iago when he says to Desdemona, 'you may relish him more in the soldier than in the scholar' (lines 165–6). Cassio is also clearly proud of his own 'breeding' (line 98) and good manners, while Iago is 'profane' (worldly and crude, line 164). However, the audience knows that Cassio's 'courtesy' (line 175) will be used against him when Iago says he'll 'have our Michael Cassio on the hip' (at his mercy, line 303). This image makes Iago's predatory nature clear.

A02

Progress booster: Othello as a lover

If you are commenting on Othello as a lover, you should pay particular attention to the language that he uses to describe his love for Desdemona in this scene. Compare his words here with the way he describes his courtship in Act I and how he speaks to and about his wife in later scenes, when his love is polluted by Iago. Make sure you can write about how the language of love changes in *Othello*.

A02
Revision task 2: A loving reunion with Desdemona

Make brief notes about what you have learned about Othello's love for Desdemona when he is reunited with her in Cyprus. Write about:

- How Othello responds when he is reunited with Desdemona.
- What his comments about his love for Desdemona reveal about him.

A05 KEY INTERPRETATION

E. A. J. Honigmann ('Introduction', *Othello*, 2001) comments that Iago is a seductive character, who is able to get the audience to collude with him. Because 'his victims lack humour, Iago appeals to us as more amusing' than the other characters. Shakespeare's 'dramatic perspective compels us to see with his eyes, and to share his "jokes". His humour also makes him seem cleverer than his victims.' Is this how you view Iago in Act II Scene 1?

A05 KEY INTERPRETATION

Writing in 1697, Thomas Rymer dismissed Desdemona as a 'silly Woman' whose virtue was suspect. Rymer was offended by Desdemona's vulgar conversation with Iago, commenting that Desdemona was behaving like 'any Countrey Kitchin-maid with her Sweet-heart'. Do you think Desdemona is silly and vulgar in this scene?

EXTRACT ANALYSIS

Act II Scene 1 lines 138–99

The reunion between Othello and Desdemona should be a moment of great happiness, but Iago's presence casts a dark shadow over it. Iago's crude **asides** undermine the couple's joy. While they anxiously await Othello's arrival, Iago acts the role of bluff soldier to divert Emilia and Desdemona. Ironically, the sentiments he expresses when he jokes with the female characters are close to the misogynistic opinions he offers in his **soliloquies**. Is Iago so clever, so in control, that he can even get away with pretending to pretend? Desdemona and Cassio do not really take Iago seriously in this scene. He is a source of amusement to them. The audience knows better. We realise that Iago should be feared, and his asides provide an alarming running commentary. The **imagery** Iago uses establishes his deadly power. He speaks gleefully of spinning a 'web' to 'ensnare as great a fly as Cassio' (lines 168–9). It is **ironic** that Cassio mocks Iago at line 165, for we know that it is his social and professional inferior who is in control. Indeed, Iago intends to use Cassio's gallantry and sophistication against him.

Iago will also succeed in misconstruing the playful sexuality that Desdemona displays when she says to Emilia, 'O, most lame and impotent conclusion!' (line 161). An audience might feel uncomfortable about Desdemona participating in this exchange, but Shakespeare deliberately stresses her sexuality for several reasons. Firstly, Desdemona's physical attraction to Othello establishes the hero's innocence of witchcraft, and helps us see the couple as a good match. We need to understand how – as Iago puts it – 'well tuned' Desdemona and Othello are (line 198). This makes the collapse of their marriage truly tragic. Secondly, Desdemona's sexuality is important to the plot. Iago's evil designs rely on Desdemona's sexual attractiveness. Thirdly, Desdemona's confidence and quick wits, shown in her questions at lines 139 and 159, are an important part of her appeal. These qualities will be used against the heroine when Iago makes Desdemona's speech seem unreliable and dishonest. There is a cruel irony in the fact that Desdemona warns Emilia playfully about believing what Iago says; it is she who needs to beware of Iago's words. It is also ironic that Iago's description of 'a deserving woman' (lines 148–58) comes to suit Desdemona perfectly in Acts IV and V, when the heroine displays a submissive character.

Although the other characters do not take Iago's misogyny seriously, we do. As Iago's plots evolve, they rely on the heartless manipulation of Desdemona, Emilia and Bianca. Iago also influences the way in which the other male characters think of and respond to these women. However, the audience will question what Iago says about the female sex. Although she has disobeyed her father, Desdemona displays none of the negative traits Iago describes in this scene, and as the drama unfolds we realise that women are victims rather than fools in *Othello*. Interestingly, the discussion about female faults contains irony that eventually works against Iago, who says that he can only stand a quiet woman who will 'ne'er disclose her mind' (line 156). At the end of the play Iago's villainy is revealed when Emilia refuses to be silent.

Iago does not simply have a low opinion of women; he also wants to degrade them. This idea emerges in Iago's soliloquy at line 284. Iago's reference to 'clyster-pipes' at line 176 is crude. Throughout *Othello*, Iago employs similar vulgar images to describe female sexuality. We know from his earlier descriptions of Desdemona as a 'land carrack' (I.2.50) and his impudent chat with Cassio in Act II Scene 3 that Iago cannot think of the heroine as possessing any real worth. Desdemona's love for Othello is so inexplicable to Iago that he has to dismiss it as lust. However, although we want to reject Iago and his crude world view, the villain keeps drawing us back to him. He butts in, whispers, invites us to collude with him and see through his eyes. We don't hear what Desdemona and Cassio say at line 167, so we are compelled to listen to Iago's interpretation of their conversation. This is precisely what Iago does to all the characters in this play; he forces them to accept his version of events.

It is a measure of Iago's power that he is able to undermine a loving reunion. When they meet in Cyprus, Othello and Desdemona's kisses suggest the erotic strength of their love. We know just how powerful Othello's emotions are because his first thought is for his 'fair warrior' (line 179). It gives Othello 'wonder great as my content/ To see you here before me'; Desdemona is his 'soul's joy' (lines 181–2). Othello's love and the delight he feels in his marriage are moving. However, even before Iago makes his snide and threatening aside of lines 197–9, we are aware that there is a worrying undercurrent. Othello says – innocently – 'I fear/ My soul hath her content so absolute/ That not another comfort like to this/ Succeeds in unknown fate' (lines 188–91). Othello thinks that he is at the height of happiness, but also mentions an 'unknown fate', hinting unknowingly at the **tragedy** that awaits him. Notice the negativity that creeps into Othello's words. In his next speech he says that his happiness 'is too much joy' (line 195). Desdemona rejects this idea, but perhaps Othello's words undermine the power of the kisses that follow and **foreshadow** the tragedy to come.

The sea **metaphor** Othello employs to describe the happiness he feels at lines 183–7 is also worrying. Othello suggests that he would be prepared to come through terrible dangers so long as he had Desdemona to greet him. We wonder how he will rise to the challenge of a battle in his personal life because we know he is already overwhelmed by his feelings for Desdemona, and we also know Iago is plotting to destroy the intense faith he has in his wife. Thus even Othello's joy adds to the tension of this scene.

A05 KEY INTERPRETATION

E. A. J. Honigmann, ('Introduction', *Othello*, 2001) makes interesting comments about Iago as a source of humour in the play. He says that Iago's humour 'either intends to give pain or allows him to bask in his sense of his own superiority ... very rarely is it at his own expense'. Honigmann notes that in Act II Scene 1, 'we see Iago at his most playful'. However, we also see the darker side of Iago here. Honigmann adds, 'the impression that he *simply* enjoys himself, having fun and being sociable, is overshadowed by our awareness that he "crowds" his companions, and then suddenly cancelled when he reveals, in soliloquy, that he hates the social games he took part in.'

ACT II SCENE 2

Summary

- Peace is restored in Cyprus.
- There is to be a night of revels to celebrate the destruction of the Turkish fleet and Othello's marriage.

Analysis

War and love

War and love are **juxtaposed** once again, as they have been throughout the play. The herald's joyful proclamation marks a return to civil order. This is **ironic**, because in the very next scene Iago will disrupt the peace, and Cyprus will become the location of drunken street fighting. Notice that war is mentioned before love in the herald's speech, a reversal of what happened in the previous scene, when Othello greeted Desdemona before Montano, putting love before war. Shakespeare is reminding us that Cyprus is a dangerous place.

The public festival planned is intended primarily to celebrate the 'perdition' (line 3) of the Turkish fleet. Othello, however, has decided that the celebration of peace should become a celebration of his marriage. The herald stresses Othello's generosity when he says 'there is full liberty of feasting … till the bell have told eleven' (lines 9–10). Iago will take advantage of Othello's generosity in order to start his own campaign of destruction.

Progress booster: Dramatic techniques **A02**

You need to be able to comment on Shakespeare's dramatic methods to achieve a good AO2 mark. Watch out for examples of irony and foreshadowing that prepare the audience for trouble ahead. For example, in this scene the herald's proclamation is both ironic and an example of foreshadowing. The audience infers that Othello's marriage is under threat because love is linked to war. Look out for other examples throughout the play.

ACT II SCENE 3

Summary

- Iago is put in charge of the festivities and Desdemona and Othello leave to consummate their marriage.
- Iago persuades Cassio to join in the carousing and undermines Cassio's reputation by telling Montano that Cassio is a drunkard.
- Roderigo antagonises Cassio, a fight ensues and Othello dismisses Cassio from his post.
- Iago advises Cassio to seek Desdemona's help on his behalf.
- Iago intends to persuade his wife, Emilia, to promote Cassio's cause with Desdemona while he poisons Othello's mind.

Analysis

Reputation

The theme of reputation dominates this scene. Two characters lose control and diminish their reputations. Cassio ruins his in a drunken brawl. Othello undermines his reputation as a cool-headed commander by losing his temper. Conversely, Iago enhances his reputation as an honest, conscientious soldier and helpful friend. He has masterful self-control in this scene and is able to control others, for example Roderigo's actions and Cassio's drinking. Iago also controls how others see events. He convinces Montano that Cassio is unfit for his job. More subtly, he increases Othello's disgust at Cassio by seeming reluctant to criticise him. Iago's words are just as devastating as Cassio's actions in destroying the lieutenant's reputation. At the end of the scene Iago moves on to his next victim. By destroying Desdemona's reputation the villain will be able to destroy Othello's sanity, marriage and honour.

Love degraded

The consummation of the marriage of Othello and Desdemona is interrupted by brawling and degraded by Iago's coarse discussion with Cassio about Desdemona. As a result the audience knows that their love is not secure. Ominously, Othello has to leave his marriage bed to deal with the fight. Iago makes a number of disrespectful comments about Desdemona. He focuses on her sexuality. She is 'sport for Jove' and 'full of game' (lines 17, 19). These are **images** of lust, not love. Cassio describes her attractions in a positive way: she is 'fresh and delicate', 'modest', 'perfection' (lines 20, 23, 25). Shakespeare presents these two versions of Desdemona to foreshadow the choice Othello will have to make. Will he choose to believe his love is a faithful wife or a whore? Iago thinks it will be easy to destroy the marriage because Othello is 'so enfettered to her love' (line 340) that Desdemona can 'play the god/ With his weak function' (lines 342–3). There is disgust in these images. To Iago, love is weakness.

A02

Study focus: Othello's anger

This scene is a turning point in the play. Othello's loss of temper is a sign that he is no longer master of himself. 'My blood begins my safer guides to rule' (line 201) he says, trying to discover the cause of the fight. Othello is ruled now by passion rather than judgement. His swift dismissal of Cassio is proof of this: 'never more be officer of mine' (line 245). Cassio doesn't get to defend himself. Othello also sounds vindictive. 'I'll make thee an example' (line 247) he says when he realises that Desdemona has been 'raised up' (line 246) by the brawl. Othello's **idiom** is changing. His measured style now includes oaths – 'Zounds' (line 203) – suggesting Othello's loss of control.

Iago: Stage director and accomplished actor

Iago directs this scene from the start. He skilfully manages a large cast of characters and the events which he has set in motion. A convincing actor, Iago also changes roles in order to manipulate his victims. He reassures Cassio that he must not give up hope, playing the part of friend and adviser. This is the same tactic he has used with Roderigo, who does exactly what he's told by Iago, entering and exiting on cue throughout Act II Scene 3. With Othello, Iago is an 'honest' (line 6) dependable soldier. We see the effectiveness of Iago's manipulation in the fact that at the start of the scene he acted under Cassio's orders, but by the end he is Othello's right-hand man.

Roderigo: Victim or villain?

Roderigo plays a minor role in *Othello*, but has a key part in this scene. Up to now he has been thematically significant as a failed lover. Now Roderigo is structurally important as Iago's first victim. He started the play a wealthy landowner, but has now spent most of his money and been 'exceedingly well cudgelled' in a fight (line 361). In some productions Roderigo is played for comedy, to contrast with Othello's tragic downfall. However, Roderigo's intentions and actions are villainous: he wants to cuckold Othello and helps to destroy Cassio's career. But everything Roderigo does is stage-managed by Iago, who tells him where to go, what to do, and when to do it. When Iago dismisses Roderigo at the end of the scene we see how insignificant he really is: 'Away, I say, thou shalt know more hereafter:/ Nay, get thee gone' (lines 376–7).

A01

Key quotation: The imagery of poison

- Iago is confident that he can manipulate Othello's thoughts. In his **soliloquy** he says: 'I'll pour this pestilence into his ear' (line 351).
- Iago uses the **imagery** of poison which fits his role as villain. His use of a definite statement here shows Iago has confidence in his powers of verbal persuasion.
- The sentence structure makes it clear Othello is to be the passive recipient of his 'pestilence' and that Iago is in control.
- The sound patterning (alliteration of the 'p' and sibilance of the 's') used in this line about poisoning adds emphasis and intensity to Iago's plan, heightening the tension for the audience.

ACT III SCENES 1 AND 2

Summary

- Cassio hires some musicians to serenade Othello and Desdemona, but Othello sends a clown to pay the musicians to leave.
- Iago says he will divert Othello's attention so that Cassio can speak to Desdemona alone and Emilia agrees to help.
- Othello sets out to inspect the fortifications in the town with Iago at his side.

Analysis

Emilia's role

Emilia is Iago's stooge (his puppet) in Scene 1. She comes on stage after Iago, suggesting that her movements and actions have been directed by him, and that she does what her husband tells her. Emilia's support for Cassio is appealing. However, we know that she is unknowingly helping her husband and not Cassio when she agrees to take him to speak to Desdemona. It is ominous and **ironic** that Emilia reports that Othello and Desdemona have already been discussing – perhaps even arguing about – Cassio.

Study focus: Ominous irony

There are two further ominous ironies in the first scene of Act III. In Shakespeare's *Twelfth Night* the nobleman Orsino calls music 'the food of love'. Here, like the previous night's brawl, the music intrudes on the private time for Othello and Desdemona. Othello's dislike of the music may also suggest he is a barbarian, since an appreciation of music was thought to be the sign of a civilised and cultured mind. There is another example of irony involving Iago. Cassio could not be more wrong about 'kind and honest' (line 41) Iago, who is working against Cassio in this scene. The audience might also see it as ironic that Iago talks openly to Cassio about deceiving Othello – 'I'll devise a mean to draw the Moor/ Out of the way' (lines 37–8) – in order to show how loyal he is to Cassio's cause.

Iago's malign influence is extended

Act III Scene 2 is as ironic as the previous scene. While the innocent Othello is absorbed in military matters, his personal affairs are being steadily undermined (we assume that Cassio will take this opportunity to speak to Desdemona, thus falling into the trap that Iago has laid for him). This very short scene neatly encapsulates one of Iago's key methods of manipulation. Iago presents himself as a faithful and helpful servant. He speaks respectfully to Othello, calling him 'my good lord' (line 4) and doing Othello's bidding when he is sent off to deliver letters. Like Cassio in the previous scene, Othello believes he is being assisted by Iago.

A02 PROGRESS BOOSTER

In order to show your understanding of Shakespeare's dramatic methods, you need to consider the way in which irony is used throughout *Othello*. How do the examples of the word 'honest' in Act III Scene 1 add to your understanding of Shakespeare's use of irony in the play?

A04 KEY CONNECTION

In the ominous clues they contain about the villain's ability to get others to act in ways directed by him, the first two scenes of Act III prepare us for Iago's assault on Othello in Act III Scene 3, the central scene in the play.

ACT III SCENE 3

Summary

- Desdemona pleads with Othello to reinstate Cassio.
- Iago poisons Othello's mind against Cassio, hinting that he has committed adultery with Desdemona, and Othello begins to doubt Desdemona's love and becomes jealous.
- Desdemona drops her handkerchief, which Emilia picks up and gives to Iago.
- Othello demands proof of Desdemona's adultery.
- Iago describes how Cassio called out for Desdemona in a dream and has been seen wiping his beard with the handkerchief.
- Othello asks Iago to kill Cassio and he promotes Iago.
- Othello intends to kill Desdemona.

KEY CONTEXT (A03)

During the **Renaissance** people believed that you could tell whether someone was good or evil by observing their outward appearance. For example, physical defects such as birthmarks could be proof that you were a witch. Because he looks honest, Iago is able to conceal his villainy.

Analysis

Thinking, seeing and knowing

The **imagery** of thinking, seeing and knowing demonstrates how Iago poisons Othello's mind so effectively. Othello is first made suspicious when Iago draws attention to Cassio's exit early in the scene: 'I cannot think it/ That he would steal away so guilty-like/ Seeing you coming' (lines 38–40). Notice how Iago comments on what looks like physical evidence. He has started to interpret events for Othello, a tactic he uses repeatedly. By refusing to share his thoughts, Iago makes Othello desperate to know what they are. Othello's irritation builds, shown in the way his commands, which are at first simply direct ('Show me thy thought', line 119) become angry ('By heaven, I'll know thy thoughts!', line 164). Iago says he is reluctant to speak because his thoughts are 'vile and false' (line 139), leading Othello to assume the worst and jump to false conclusions.

Othello's false belief in Desdemona's treachery is also reflected in images of seeing and knowing. Othello says to Iago, 'If more thou dost perceive, let me know more' (line 243). Notice how Iago's perception is relied on, that there is evidence already and 'more' to find. We know that Othello's thoughts have been successfully infected when he asks Iago to 'set on thy wife to observe' Desdemona (line 244). Othello is no longer 'well tuned' with his wife, but with Iago. Iago even instructs Othello to spy on Desdemona, suggesting the villain's increasing power over his victim.

Othello's agony in the last part of the scene is reflected in images of seeing and knowing. He demands, 'What sense had I of her stolen hours of lust?/ I saw't not, thought it not' (lines 341–2). The final images that relate to seeing lead Othello to thoughts of murder. Iago wonders if Othello would like to witness Desdemona's adultery with Cassio. Iago makes the suggestion in the crudest and most graphic terms: 'Would you, the supervisor, grossly gape on?/ Behold her topped?' (lines 398–9). Earlier in the scene Othello was secure in his wife's love, declaring, 'she had eyes and chose me' (line 192). The once confident husband now believes he is a cuckold and has been deceived by his wife.

A02

Study focus: Proof

Does Othello 'give in' to jealousy too easily? Perhaps not. Iago's 'proofs' are many, varied and plausible. His reinterpretation of prior events is persuasive. Cassio was a go-between when Othello and Desdemona were courting, so he had an opportunity to get to know Desdemona. Desdemona deceived her father, so might well be deceiving Othello. Iago reminds Othello that he is a naive outsider who does not understand the 'country disposition' (line 204) of Venetians. Iago presents himself as an expert with superior knowledge about the behaviour of Italian women, implying that his judgement can be trusted. Iago points out that Desdemona rejected a number of suitable partners before marrying Othello. He suggests that it is only natural therefore that she should be 'recoiling to her better judgement' (line 240) and feeling attracted to Cassio. Iago also makes up compelling stories. Cassio's sexual dream is a fabrication, as is the tale of Cassio wiping his beard with the handkerchief. However, Iago's lies seem like truths because he has the handkerchief in his possession, 'ocular proof' to support his version of events (line 363).

Love and war

Love becomes war in this scene. In Act I, Othello was under attack from Brabantio, but he had allies on the Venetian council, and was united with Desdemona. Now he is alone, and feels as if he is being assaulted from all sides. Desdemona blurs the boundaries between domestic and public life when she intercedes for Cassio, making Othello uncomfortable. **Ironically**, Othello does not want to hear his wife's words, and asks to be left alone, suggesting that he is beginning to see Desdemona as an enemy rather than an ally. Equally ironically, just as Othello begins to feel at odds with Desdemona, Iago speaks to him using the language of love: 'My lord, you know I love you' (line 119). This scene is a battle between Desdemona's true love and Iago's false love. Because it is Iago whose voice Othello wishes to listen to, we know that true love will be defeated by false words.

Othello's words about love are troubling even before Iago's poison takes hold. When Desdemona leaves, Othello says, 'perdition catch my soul/ But I do love thee! and when I love thee not/ Chaos is come again' (lines 90–2). Othello is in the grip of emotions that he cannot handle, even before he becomes overwhelmed by jealousy. Is marriage proving too much for him? Notice the two negative abstract nouns that **foreshadow** tragedy: 'perdition' and 'Chaos'. It is ironic that Othello should use these words at this point in the play. By the end of this scene, Othello will be consumed by dark and chaotic thoughts, and he will be planning a murder which he fears will damn his soul.

A02

Study focus: A false love

The ritual that closes this scene shows that Iago's false 'love' has triumphed. Othello and Iago kneel and join together in the 'bloody business' (line 472) of revenge. Iago swears allegiance to 'wronged Othello's service' (line 470) in a **parody** of the wedding vow Desdemona made to Othello. There is a horrible irony here. Othello is now united with his enemy, as we know from his words to Iago, 'I am bound to thee for ever' (line 217). When Othello begins to discuss killing Desdemona, we know that the first battle in the war for his mind has been won.

A04 KEY CONNECTION

In Oliver Parker's 1995 film, Iago is driven by malice, but there is also a definite suggestion of homoerotic love. When Iago delivers the line 'I am your own forever' (line 482), he embraces Othello tightly, and tears appear in his eyes. In the final scene, Othello fatally wounds Iago, who crawls on to the bed to lie at his dead general's feet, where he himself dies.

A03 KEY CONTEXT

Notice the way in which Iago raises the topic of 'Good name in man and woman' (line 158) before he reveals his 'suspicions' about Desdemona and Cassio. This reminds us of the importance of masculine honour in Renaissance society. A wife's chastity was part of her husband's honour. A woman's good name was important in Shakespeare's society. Court records for York c. 1600 show that 90 per cent of defamation cases involving female plaintiffs involved the woman's sexual reputation.

The handkerchief

The handkerchief plays an important role in this scene. In Desdemona's hands it is a symbol of love and faithfulness. Desdemona offers to bind Othello's aching head with it, showing wifely concern. However, Othello will not be comforted, and his rejection of the handkerchief is a sign that he is starting to reject Desdemona. In her anxiety, Desdemona does not realise that she has dropped her handkerchief, which is picked up by Emilia. Emilia informs us that the 'napkin' (line 294) was Desdemona's first gift from Othello and that Iago has been pestering her to steal it. Iago is delighted when Emilia gives him the handkerchief but refuses to tell her how he will use it. Now the handkerchief becomes a sinister object. In Iago's hands it is a symbol of abuse and the misuse of power. Iago won't give it back even when Emilia says that Desdemona will 'run mad' (line 321) when she realises it has gone. Later in the scene Iago turns the handkerchief into false proof of adultery. The love token then becomes a symbol of destruction.

Progress booster: Structure and pace

AO2

This is a long scene but on stage it moves swiftly. The pace suits Iago. He needs his poison to work quickly. The pace and structure create a sense of claustrophobia: Othello enters and exits twice but, wherever he turns, he cannot escape Iago's foul words and his own foul thoughts. The way in which the dialogue is structured is significant. During most of the scene there is one-to-one dialogue between Othello and Iago, and Iago comes to dominate: he speaks more words and has more turns than Othello. We will notice how Iago and Othello finish each other's lines, showing that Othello is moving closer to Iago and away from Desdemona. Notice how the structure of this scene **mirrors** the structure of Act II Scene 3. In the earlier scene Iago used Roderigo as his stooge. Here the 'fall guy' is Desdemona. Roderigo was physically hurt. In this scene, Desdemona's reputation is wounded. Look out for other structural parallels as you read the play.

PROGRESS BOOSTER **AO2**

A close analysis of the way in which Shakespeare uses the handkerchief to create meaning would enable you to show your understanding of the dramatist's methods. If you referred to the cultural significance of handkerchiefs in the Renaissance, you would be working towards fulfilling the AO3 criteria.

Silence and submission

In this scene the female characters' voices are silenced. Neither Desdemona nor Emilia is listened to. Both submit to their husbands. Emilia gives Iago the handkerchief because he wants it. Her reluctant submission is a sign of danger to come. It **foreshadows** Emilia's silence about the handkerchief in Act III Scene 4, when she unwittingly propels Desdemona towards tragedy. Like Emilia, Desdemona does what she is told. She defends Cassio, but says to Othello before she leaves, 'What e'er you be, I am obedient' (line 89). Desdemona's submission foreshadows the way in which she will accept responsibility for her own death.

What makes Othello vulnerable?

There are several reasons why Othello is vulnerable. Firstly, he is inexperienced in dealing with conflict in his private life, as demonstrated by his uneasy exchanges with Desdemona. Othello's headache is a symbol of his discomfort. Secondly, as we know from Act II Scene 3, Othello is swift to anger. His resolution is a weakness now. 'No: to be once in doubt/ Is once to be resolved' he tells Iago (line 182). Such decisiveness makes Iago's evil work easier for him. Othello introduces the subject of Desdemona himself when he is warned in general terms about jealousy, also sees things from extreme positions. Desdemona can only be a perfect, submissive wife or a 'whore'. 'She's gone, I am abused' he declares at line 271.

Valerie Traub has suggested that Othello is vulnerable because he internalises Iago's negative view of black men, which undermines his sense of self. In this scene, under Iago's influence, Othello starts to consider the differences between himself and Desdemona as problematic. Othello speaks of his weak merits as a husband. He is 'black … declined/ Into the vale of years' (lines 267–70). The once confident lover, proud of his royal lineage, military career and fitness as a husband, is slowly being diminished.

Othello the revenger

The change from noble soldier and romantic hero to jealous revenger is signalled when Othello returns to the stage at line 332. Othello's words are increasingly violent, showing his degradation (see line 362), and he also grasps hold of Iago. This example of physical violence foreshadows the violence he will use against Desdemona. Othello says he does not know what to believe: 'I think my wife be honest, and think she is not' (line 387). However, the violent **images** he uses indicate that Iago is winning: he speaks of 'Poison, or fire, or suffocating streams' (line 392) and then begins to curse, 'Death and damnation! O!' (line 399). At this point Othello's speech begins to break down, signifying the disruption in his mind. The oaths are another example of the 'Iagoisation' of Othello's speech. Othello's words become more disjointed, his thoughts more wild and bloody (see lines 449–53 and 456–65). Othello's most arresting line is the ferocious, 'I'll tear her all to pieces!' (line 434). At the end of the scene Othello speaks like the villain of a **Jacobean revenge tragedy** when he says he will withdraw to 'furnish me with some swift means of death/ For the fair devil' (lines 480–1).

Revision task 3: Iago's poisoning of Othello's mind **A02**

Make brief notes about what you have learned about the way Iago poisons Othello's mind in this scene. Write about:

● The ideas and arguments Iago uses.
● Whether Othello gives in to Iago's poison too easily.

A03 **KEY CONTEXT**

Handkerchiefs were important signifiers of status and wealth in Renaissance Europe. Karen Newman relates the story of a fifteenth-century Venetian who was fined and sentenced to eighteen months' imprisonment after taking a lady's handkerchief. Newman says 'possession of a lady's handkerchief was considered proof of adultery' (see 'Femininity and the Monstrous in *Othello*', in Smith (ed.), *Shakespeare's Tragedies* (2004).) We can see why Othello places so much emphasis on the handkerchief he gives Desdemona.

A05 **KEY INTERPRETATION**

Caryl Phillips remarks that Othello's line 'she had eyes and chose me' (II.3.193) reveals Othello's 'gross insecurity'. Do you agree? He also says that the 'fatal mistake' Othello makes is 'to question his own judgment'. Do you agree that this is the cause of Othello's downfall?

A03 **KEY CONTEXT**

According to **Aristotle**, the tragic hero should not be entirely good or evil. Instead, he should possess a fatal flaw, which will incite pity and fear in the audience. Critics are divided about Othello. Some feel that he is a noble man brought down by a devil, while others think he is too easily moved to jealousy. Based on your reading of this scene, what do you think?

ACT III SCENE 4

Summary

- Desdemona asks the clown to inform Cassio that she has pleaded for him.
- She is uneasy about losing the handkerchief.
- She tries again to promote Cassio's cause.
- Othello is angry with Desdemona because he believes she has lost the handkerchief.
- Cassio's mistress, Bianca, is annoyed with Cassio because he has not visited her recently; he gives Bianca Desdemona's handkerchief, saying he found it in his bedchamber.

Analysis

Desdemona the victim

This unhappy scene focuses on Desdemona. She is not only her husband's and Iago's victim. Here she is also at the mercy of the clown, whose riddling shows how words can be misconstrued. Desdemona's powerlessness **mirrors** her position in the previous scene. In spite of her lies to Othello about the loss of the handkerchief, an audience is likely to sympathise with Desdemona. She is bullied by Othello but does not appreciate the danger she is in when she tries to return to the subject of Cassio. She is understandably alarmed by Othello's description of the handkerchief and his repeated requests to see it. We can understand Desdemona's falsehood here; surely she is simply seeking not to anger Othello further?

Desdemona is abused by Emilia and Cassio too. Emilia knows what has happened to the handkerchief but fails to defend or help her mistress. In spite of knowing Othello is angry, Cassio selfishly accepts further offers of help from Desdemona. By the end of the scene we will feel that generous and true-hearted Desdemona is as troubled and isolated as Othello, but more vulnerable because she is a woman. Her vulnerability is indirectly alluded to in Emilia's **metaphor** about food. Emilia tells Desdemona that men soon tire of women: 'They are all but stomachs [appetites], and we all but food' (line 105). She adds that men 'eat us hungerly, and when they are full/ they belch us' (lines 106–7). This **image** of vomiting suggests the danger that Desdemona is in; she will be eaten up and destroyed.

Study focus: Liars and deceivers

The lies Iago told in the previous scene lead directly to the deceptions here, all of which are linked to the handkerchief. Othello interrogates Desdemona about it, but fails to share his suspicions openly. Instead, Othello tells what might be considered lies about the handkerchief in that the yarns he spins about the handkerchief's origins are contradictory. Desdemona also panics and resorts to lies, claiming she still has the handkerchief. Emilia lies when she says she does not know where it is. Bianca believes she has been deceived by Cassio when he gives her the handkerchief. Although he tells the truth about how he got it, Cassio is still deceitful. He sends Bianca away because he doesn't want to be seen 'womaned' (line 195), yet he is happy for Desdemona to work for him behind the scenes.

KEY CONTEXT **A03**

Shakespeare's use of the name 'Bianca', meaning 'white' and thus signifying purity and decency, appears ironic, given her role as a courtesan. However, Bianca is not the typical corrupt courtesan of Renaissance drama; her love for Cassio is genuine and honest, so in fact her name is well matched to her role.

KEY INTERPRETATION **A05**

Thomas Rymer, an early negative critic of *Othello*, suggested that the 'ado', 'stress' and 'passion' caused by the loss of the handkerchief was implausible. Rymer mocked Shakespeare's use of the prop by saying, 'the Handkerchief is so remote a trifle, no Booby … could make any consequence from it'. To what extent do you agree?

A magic symbol

The handkerchief is now loaded with ominous significance, and the whole plot hangs on it. It represents different things to different characters. To Othello, the handkerchief symbolises Desdemona's honour. The mythic qualities that Othello endows it with represent the Moor himself. The 'magic in the web' (line 71) of the handkerchief represents the 'magic' of Othello and Desdemona's marriage, which has been destroyed by Iago. For Desdemona, the handkerchief is no longer a love token. Instead, it is a frightening object which is linked to discord. The strawberries woven into the handkerchief might represent Othello's passion, or Desdemona's blood, which will be spilt. For Emilia, the handkerchief is a test of her loyalty. She has chosen her husband over Desdemona. Cassio treats the handkerchief as carelessly as he treats Bianca. It is a symbol of how Cassio is a user and abuser of women, not unlike Iago. For Iago, the handkerchief is a symbol of his evil power.

Jealousy

Emilia introduces the subject of Othello's jealousy. Her comments enable us to appreciate how much faith Desdemona has in Othello. We learn that we can rely on Emilia's judgement, in spite of her lies. Emilia rightly guesses that Othello is eaten up with jealousy, which she defines as 'a monster/ Begot upon itself, born on itself' (lines 161–2). In succeeding scenes we will see how true these words are. The exchange between Cassio and Bianca shows us another example of amorous jealousy. Like Desdemona, Bianca has to be satisfied with the treatment she receives from the man she loves; she is powerless to change or direct Cassio. Notice the way in which repetition of the word 'jealous', a noticeable feature of the previous scene, is replaced by repetition of the word 'angry'. Iago's triumph is emphasised by his references to Othello's anger (lines 133, 135, 138). Iago has the power to control the hero's moods now. Othello's anger is a result of his growing jealousy. Arguably, all of the jealousy we see here can be traced back to Iago's jealousy of Cassio and Othello.

Key quotation: Othello's treatment of Desdemona (A02)

- Othello asks Desdemona to give him her hand. He says, 'Give me your hand. This hand is moist, my lady' (line 36).
- This command shows Othello physically marking the beginning of his interrogation of Desdemona.
- Othello sees the moistness of Desdemona's hand as proof of her lechery. Othello's 'palm reading' can be linked to his pagan ancestry, revealing that he is moving away from the Christian values he adopted.
- Shakespeare is **foreshadowing** Othello's comments about the magic qualities of the handkerchief. The focus on Desdemona's hand here also foreshadows the heroine's fate in a darkly ironic way. In Act V, convinced of her lechery, Othello uses his hands to smother Desdemona.

(A04) KEY CONNECTION

Critics have compared Othello to characters who appear in the Romance genre. His wooing of Desdemona with fantastic tales of his past and his travels and, in this scene, his insistence on the magical properties of the handkerchief suggest this. Shakespeare was to write several Romances at the end of his career: *Pericles*, *Cymbeline*, *The Winter's Tale* and *The Tempest*.

(A02) PROGRESS BOOSTER

Shakespeare uses the dramatic technique of mirroring in *Othello* to create contrasts and cohesion within the play. Watch out for examples of mirrored events and scenes which you can comment on to demonstrate your understanding of structure and themes for AO2. Here you might consider Bianca's jealousy and anger, and how they mirror Othello's.

(A04) KEY CONNECTION

You may want to compare Othello's interrogation of Desdemona in this scene with the interrogation by the senate Othello faced in Act I Scene 3. In Act I Othello and Desdemona defended each other and their love. Here, the interrogation is uneasy and unequal. Othello has all the power, while Desdemona has no choice but to obey her husband's commands. We can see how Iago has distanced the lovers from each other.

ACT IV SCENE 1

Summary

- Iago torments Othello with crude **images** of Desdemona's infidelity and references to the handkerchief, leading to Othello falling down in a fit.
- Iago tells Othello to withdraw so that he can have a conversation with Cassio, and he questions Cassio about Bianca.
- Seeing Desdemona's handkerchief in Bianca's hand and believing Desdemona must have given it to Cassio as a love token, Othello vows to murder his wife.
- Venetian visitors bring news that Cassio is to replace Othello.
- Othello strikes Desdemona.

Analysis

Violence and madness

This scene is one of verbal and physical violence, **foreshadowing** the end of the play. Othello gradually becomes overwhelmed by violent thoughts. When Othello falls down in a violent fit, Iago's description of him makes Othello sound like a wild beast. Othello's first thought after spying on Cassio is violent: 'How shall I murder him, Iago' (line 167). He says he would like Cassio to endure an agonising death. The conversation moves to methods of murdering Desdemona. Two come from Othello. He will 'chop her into messes' (line 196) or poison her. Iago suggests strangulation. Is it a sign of madness that Othello accepts this suggestion as 'justice' (line 206)? The verbal violence leads to physical violence as Othello strikes Desdemona. Foreshadowing her grace and dignity in death, she responds passively: 'I will not stay to offend you' (line 246).

Study focus: Iago in control   **A02**

Iago controls Othello completely. There is **irony** in his reference to his poisoning as 'medicine' (line 45). Iago's methods are a sadistic repetition of those he used in Act III Scene 3. Iago commands Othello's imagination, conjuring up distressing images of infidelity. He plays devil's advocate when he suggests that Desdemona's honour is hers to give away as she chooses. Iago keeps Othello focused on the handkerchief. Eventually he brings on Othello's fit when he jests about Cassio in Desdemona's bed, 'With her, on her, what you will' (line 34). The casual brutality of these words shows how much Iago enjoys his power. Notice that Iago uses Othello's name when he is in his trance. The villain no longer speaks to his victim with respect.

Iago's revenge

Iago's control extends to Cassio in their crude discussion about Bianca. Watching this 'play within a play' is uncomfortable. Every word Cassio speaks is infected with Iago's crude world view. Iago is so much the master of events that he even chooses how Desdemona dies when he next speaks to Othello. Iago says it will be best to strangle her in the bed she has 'contaminated' (line 205). There is a horrible irony in Iago, who is the source of infection in this play, using this word. But why does Iago want Desdemona and Cassio dead? It is not simple sadism. They must die before Othello decides to question them. In Act III Scene 3, Othello threatened Iago with death – 'woe upon thy life!' (line 369) – if he could not prove Desdemona to be a whore. Iago's choice of strangulation for Desdemona suits the manipulator's **characterisation**. By having her smothered in her marriage bed Iago is replacing the loving ritual of consummation with a cruel ritual of strangulation.

Othello's degradation

Othello's fit is a symbol of his degradation. He is degraded by Iago, but he also degrades himself. His speech style and use of imagery reflect this. Many of Othello's speeches are full of disjointed sentence structures. It is also noticeable that later in the scene Othello uses **prose**, signalling his debasement. Early on, when he is tormented by a theoretical discussion about whether it is possible for man and woman to be 'Naked in bed … and not mean harm' (line 5), Othello uses Christian imagery: 'The devil their virtue tempts, and they tempt heaven' (line 8). Later he speaks of Desdemona being 'damned tonight' (lines 178–9). Othello still has a moral code. However, his speeches are also full of savagery and egotism. 'I will chop her into messes! Cuckold me!' he roars (line 197). The final words he barks at Desdemona are brutal: 'Hence, avaunt!' (line 260).

Othello's degradation is also signified by the way he follows Iago's commands. He becomes Iago's puppet. We will remember how Iago controlled Roderigo's entrances and exits when Othello is sent to spy on Cassio. During Iago's play within the play Othello is a pathetic bystander, making helpless comments: 'Look how he laughs already!' (line 110). His lines show how he has been reduced: 'So, so, so, so: they laugh that win' (line 123). This gloating is worthy of Iago. However, the audience knows that it is Iago who will have the last laugh, not Othello.

In spite of the verbal violence, there is much **pathos** in this scene. We sense Othello's pain as he works up to killing Desdemona. He cannot bear the loss of his 'sweet woman' (line 176). Consider this key line: 'But yet the pity of it, Iago – O, Iago, the pity of it, Iago!' (lines 192–3). Othello is torn between thoughts of his wife's sweetness and her treachery. This battle continues for some time, and even after he has decided to kill her 'this night', Othello is worried that Desdemona's 'body and beauty' will 'unprovide my mind again' (lines 202–3).

Further degradation occurs after the Venetian visitors arrive. Othello slips quickly into oaths and savagery. 'Fire and brimstone!' (line 233) he exclaims when he discovers he is to be replaced as governor of Cyprus by Cassio. It seems as if Cassio has supplanted Othello not only in his bed, but also in his military role. We know that Othello has reached rock bottom and destroyed his honour when he strikes Desdemona. This shameful act humiliates everyone. Othello's rude treatment of Lodovico in accusing him of wanting to sleep with Desdemona also reveals how far the hero has fallen (see line 252). His exit line, 'Goats and monkeys!' (line 263), is a long way from the eloquent rhetoric of Act I.

A04 **KEY CONNECTION**

In Oliver Parker's 1995 film, Iago's control of Othello is demonstrated when the ensign locks his master behind bars. It is from this cell that Othello overlooks Iago's conversation with Cassio. The camera occasionally offers the audience Othello's view of events, framed by the bars. We can see how trapped and powerless he is.

A05 **KEY INTERPRETATION**

For a discussion of the importance of the handkerchief and its qualities, see Robert B. Heilman's *Magic in the Web: Action and Language in 'Othello'* (1956).

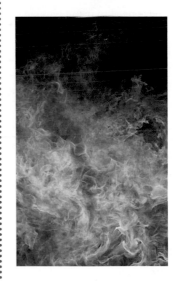

Key quotation: Iago's infection of Othello **A02**

Iago torments Othello about the handkerchief. Othello wishes he could forget it: 'O, it comes o'er my memory/ As doth the raven o'er the infectious house' (lines 20–1).

- The plague reference reminds us that Iago is still infecting Othello with poison.
- He is utterly relentless and completely focused.
- Notice how passive Othello is; the sentence structure suggests his mind is being acted upon. He is no longer in control of his thoughts.
- Croaking ravens were thought to be birds of ill omen, so the imagery here foreshadows the tragic outcome for Othello once his peace of mind is destroyed.

ACT IV SCENE 2

Summary

- Othello questions Emilia but does not believe her when she says Desdemona is true to him.
- Othello confronts Desdemona, trying to get her to confess she has committed adultery, but Desdemona defends her honour.
- Believing that she has assisted Desdemona in her wantonness, Othello offers Emilia money and leaves in disgust.
- Desdemona appeals to Iago for help.
- Iago persuades Roderigo to help in his plot to kill Cassio.

Analysis

Othello's war with himself

Othello's struggle to reconcile the warring emotions of love and jealousy is dramatised through his use of contrasting **images** in this scene. Othello says that 'The fountain' (line 60) of his pure love has been polluted, becoming 'a cistern, for foul toads/ To knot and gender [copulate] in' (lines 62–3). Turning to Desdemona, Othello wonders how she can look so 'lovely fair' while being a 'weed' (line 68). Othello now looks 'grim as hell' (line 65) when faced with the 'rose-lipped cherubin' Desdemona (line 64). These images suggest how much under Iago's influence Othello is. His repetition of the words 'whore' and 'strumpet' indicates how far Othello is removed from the noble hero of the first two acts, even if he still speaks poetically and with a measured tone at times (see lines 48–65). Othello's speech is peppered with vile images even when he is eloquent. The insults he offers Desdemona and Emilia as he leaves make it hard to view Othello with much sympathy at this moment. He is a verbal as well as a physical bully.

The word 'whore' was the most common term of abuse used to insult women in seventeenth-century England. The word had multiple meanings. For example, it could be used to refer to a professional courtesan or a woman who was dissolute and of bad character. When Othello uses the word to abuse his wife he is degrading his wife publicly to shame her. But Othello degrades himself too: a wife's good reputation was an integral part of a man's honour.

Yet an audience must sympathise. Desdemona's presence is painful to Othello. When Desdemona defends herself he tries – rather weakly – to send her away. As he leaves he speaks to her contemptuously: 'I cry you mercy then,/ I took you for that cunning whore of Venice/ That married with Othello' (lines 90–2). Notice the way in which Othello dramatises himself using the third person. What is happening is so painful that he has to distance himself from what he is saying. This helps Othello to justify his words and actions. We will see this tendency again later in Act V.

Study focus: Truth and lies

A02

Iago has abused the word 'honest' so much that no other character can use it without suspicion falling on them. Both women insist Desdemona is 'honest' and are denounced as liars. We see how far Othello has sunk when he fails to believe either Desdemona or Emilia. They both tell the truth and are abused for it. Emilia's role is similar to Iago's in Act I. However, Emilia is a true rather than a false servant. She defends Desdemona's honour. She is absolutely correct that an 'eternal villain' has slandered her mistress (line 132). For her truthful, plain speaking, Emilia is paid off as if she were a brothel keeper. For her honesty, Desdemona is called a whore. Iago has infected Othello so successfully that he misconstrues every true word he hears. Othello turns the truth into lies in this scene.

The trial of Desdemona

If Othello is suffering, so is his wife. Desdemona is put on trial in this scene. She has become a figure of great **pathos**. It is horribly **ironic** that Desdemona kneels first to Othello, the man who will destroy her physically, and then to Iago, the man who has destroyed her reputation. Desdemona is bewildered by her husband's treatment of her. She asks, 'What horrible fancy's this?' (line 27), revealing her fear of Othello. Desdemona tells him plaintively, 'I understand a fury in your words/ But not the words' (lines 32–3). Her words show that Desdemona and Othello no longer 'speak the same language'.

Desdemona's speeches emphasise her innocence and misery. She asks what 'ignorant sin' she has committed (line 71). She says she's 'a child to chiding' (line 116) and cannot bring herself to use the word 'whore'. Notice Desdemona's humility and generosity in this scene. She does not say that Othello is wrong to chide her, just that he could have done it 'with gentle means' (line 114). Desdemona says earnestly that she still loves Othello and will continue to do so however unkindly he treats her; she still calls Othello 'my noble lord' (line 66) and looks for excuses for his behaviour. Desdemona hopes to 'to win my lord again' (line 151), but we know she cannot win because the person she asks to help her (Iago) is – ironically – her deadly enemy.

Key quotation: Emilia's role as defender of Desdemona

A02

Emilia castigates Othello for believing Desdemona is false. She says, 'Remove your thought, it doth abuse your bosom' (line 14).

- Emilia's open defence of Desdemona prepares us for the role she will play in Act V Scene 2 when she reveals Othello's crime.
- Emilia's disapproval reminds us how far Othello has fallen.
- Ironically, Emilia does not realise Othello's thoughts have been abused – by Iago.

Revision task 4: The darker side of love

A02

Make brief notes on what you have learned about the way in which Othello treats Desdemona in this scene and how she responds to him. Write about:

- The way in which Othello interrogates and intimidates Desdemona.
- What Desdemona's responses to Othello's behaviour show about her feelings for him.

A05 PROGRESS BOOSTER

It is important to incorporate critics' views. You could use a critic's view to introduce your own point of view, such as: 'Many critics, including Leavis, perceive Othello's **hamartia** as jealousy. While I agree that Othello becomes jealous, it can be argued that there are other factors that lead to his tragic end, for example pride and naivety.'

A05 KEY INTERPRETATION

G. K. Hunter has said that Othello becomes 'a tragedy of the loss of faith'. Do you agree with this assessment? To what extent do you agree that loss of faith is the cause of Othello's downfall?

A05 KEY INTERPRETATION

For comments about the female characters as victims, see Lisa Jardine's chapter on *Othello* in *Still Harping on Daughters* (1983).

ACT IV SCENE 3

Summary

- Othello sends Desdemona to prepare for bed.
- Emilia says she wishes Desdemona had never met Othello, but Desdemona says she still loves her husband.
- Desdemona is unable to dismiss a melancholy song from her mind and sings it.
- The women discuss female infidelity.

Analysis

Two wives

In this scene, the audience is invited to compare the two female characters and their views about men and love. Like her husband, Desdemona is a romantic. Love means everything to her. Now that she believes she no longer has Othello's love, she is lost and melancholy. Desdemona seems unworldly, especially compared with the down-to-earth Emilia. But this is appropriate. Shakespeare is emphasising Desdemona's innocence and the lost romance of her marriage.

Like her husband, Iago, Emilia has a cynical view of human relationships and has a pragmatic approach to sin. Unlike Desdemona, who cannot believe that women can ever be unfaithful to their husbands, Emilia suggests adultery is a 'small vice' (line 69). However, we know Emilia is actually a virtuous woman because she says she would not commit adultery for 'a joint-ring' (a promise of marriage, line 72). In Renaissance society, the wedding ring was a symbol not just of marriage, but also of the wife's chastity, reminding us of the double standards of Shakespeare's time, when codes of sexual conduct for men and women were very different. Emilia takes chastity seriously, as her outrage at Othello's accusations against Desdemona show. It is important that we see Emilia as a virtuous woman if she is to be Desdemona's defender after death. It is appropriate that a woman accuses and condemns Desdemona's masculine abusers.

Emilia offers a realistic – if rather pessimistic – description of marriage. Many of her ideas will strike a chord with a modern audience used to gender equality. It may seem strange that Shakespeare gives so much time to a discussion of sexual politics in a scene which is a pre-death ritual, but giving Emilia a powerful voice in this scene is dramatically significant. Emilia is to become the voice of the audience. She will express the audience's horror in Act V when Othello's crime and Iago's lies are revealed. The audience will contrast the relationship between Desdemona and Emilia with the relationship between Othello and Iago. Unlike Iago, Emilia is a true servant who works hard to support her mistress.

Study focus: Bad omens

A02

There are several bad omens in this scene. Desdemona is engaged in the ritual of undressing, but instead of preparing for her wedding night, she is preparing for her death bed. Desdemona is full of foreboding. She mentions winding sheets, her eyes itch, she is drawn to Barbary's melancholy song of death. Her lines often seem fatalistic. She says, 'All's one … how foolish are our minds!' (line 21). It does not matter ('all's one') what she does, she cannot change Othello's 'foolish' mind about her. Barbary's song contains references to two trees which are ominous. In *Romeo and Juliet*, Romeo is found wandering in a sycamore grove, suggesting the tree can be associated with forsaken love. In western Scotland sycamores were planted for a sinister purpose. The barons used them to hang their enemies from. The willow was a more traditional symbol for lost or unrequited love.

A04 KEY CONNECTION

In Shakespeare's *Hamlet*, the tragic heroine, Ophelia, like Barbary, goes mad when her lover Hamlet rejects her. Ophelia drowns, having fallen out of a willow tree into the water when the branch she was sitting on broke. Love and madness are often linked together in Renaissance drama.

The Willow song and weeping

Othello and Desdemona have been driven to tears in Act IV. Both have wept – unwittingly – because of Iago's evil influence. Othello has been in mourning for his marriage and his own and his wife's lost innocence. Desdemona has wept because she has lost her love. The mind of Othello has been destroyed and Desdemona is shortly to be tortured, her life snuffed out. It is therefore fitting that the play should be structured so that this quiet scene of sorrow, punctuated by the melancholy willow song, should come at this point. The willow song expresses the meaning of Desdemona's name (ill-starred) and **foreshadows** her terrible fate.

Desdemona's mother had a maid, Barbary, who died singing the willow song which 'expressed her fortune' (line 27). There are clear parallels here with Desdemona. The words of the song refer to accusations of unfaithfulness, reminding us of the heroine's terrible predicament. In the willow song the 'poor soul' sits weeping by the water (line 39). She is able to soften the stones in the 'fresh streams' (line 43). However, unlike the woman in the song, Desdemona has been unable to soften Othello's hard heart with her tears. We learn that the woman in the song 'murmured her moans' (line 43) as she lay by the water. Desdemona will murmur and moan on her death bed as she lies dying.

Progress booster: Symbolism

A02

There are strong undercurrents beneath the surface of *Othello* and unlocking Shakespeare's use of symbols and **metaphors** is key to appreciating the play's meanings. The willow song and the handkerchief are obviously key symbols. Watch out for other symbols that you can link to these and comment on.

ACT V SCENE 1

Summary

- Following Iago's instructions, Roderigo tries to wound Cassio but instead Roderigo is wounded by Cassio.
- As Iago steps in and stabs Cassio in the leg, Othello hears cries, believes Cassio has been killed, and is spurred on to his own revenge.
- Lodovico and Gratiano come out when they hear the commotion and attend to the wounded Cassio.
- Iago kills Roderigo.
- Bianca appears. Iago accuses her of involvement in a plot to kill Cassio.
- Roderigo's body is discovered and Iago sends Emilia to inform Othello and Desdemona of what has happened.

Analysis

Iago improvises

As in the first scene of the play, we are in a street at night when the action of Act V begins. Iago still seems to be in control, in spite of Roderigo's uneasiness about killing Cassio. The **image** Iago uses to describe Roderigo at line 11 reminds us of the villain's arrogance. Roderigo is simply a 'young quat' (pimple or boil, line 11). And when Iago has finished with Roderigo, 'he must die' (line 22). Iago's ruthlessness and lack of respect for human life prepare us for the violence and brutality of Act V. This scene **mirrors** two others. The confusion and mistaken identities remind us of the storm scene. The street brawling recalls the drunken fight between Cassio and Roderigo on the night of the wedding celebrations. On all three occasions, Iago got the result he wanted. Will he succeed again?

There are signs that Iago will prevail. The action moves swiftly, making a marked contrast with the previous scene. We know that Iago needs events to unfold rapidly if his treachery is to remain hidden. However, Iago is forced to become personally involved in the action, wounding Cassio in an underhand way when Roderigo fails to hit his target. But we see Iago's mastery of the situation when he stabs Roderigo. The violent death of Desdemona's failed suitor **foreshadows** the deaths of much nobler victims in the final scene.

Iago's motives

What motives does Iago offer us in this scene? He has two reasons for wanting Cassio murdered. Firstly, Cassio 'hath a daily beauty in his life/ That makes me ugly' (lines 19–20). Iago cannot bear human virtue in any form and seeks to destroy it. This is a psychological motive. Secondly, Iago needs to kill Cassio for practical reasons. Othello may 'unfold' him to Cassio (line 21). Iago's security is threatened. In spite of his assurance, Iago's urgent final **aside** indicates the danger he is in. Iago repeats an idea that he expressed at the beginning of the scene (see lines 4 and 128–9). The events of this night will make or mar his fortunes. It is appropriate that Iago should use the language of gambling. It might be argued that Iago's closing lines should be delivered in an exultant tone. Even at this critical moment the villain relishes his own evil.

Study focus: Settings

You need to demonstrate a good understanding of the way in which settings are used for AO2 (which covers the ways in which meanings are shaped in the text). For example, you could choose to look at the ways in which the night-time settings for the opening and closing scenes of the play mirror each other, and comment on the dramatic significance of these settings – the street in Venice and the bedroom in Cyprus. You might also choose to discuss how Shakespeare narrows the focus of the play to provide a sense of claustrophobia by locating Act V Scene 2 in Desdemona's bedroom.

Othello the automaton

Othello is little more than an automaton in this scene. Yet again he is an onlooker who fails to see the truth. **Ironically**, it is a misunderstanding that spurs Othello on to his own act of violence. He believes 'brave … honest and just' (line 31) Iago has killed Cassio. It is horrible that Othello acts in direct response to the treacherous example he believes has been set by Iago. Shakespeare is linking Othello's murder of Desdemona with Iago's cowardly wounding of Cassio. Othello's language also links him with the atmosphere of treachery: Othello speaks of blood and lust, blotches and stains. Othello's violent words foreshadow his violent deeds. He talks like a villain, announcing his evil intentions in a dramatic way: 'strumpet, I come' (line 33). But Othello is not taking responsibility for his actions, claiming it is Desdemona's 'unblest fate' that he is fulfilling (line 33). Othello's melodramatic speech style detracts from his heroism but also reminds us how completely his mind has been corrupted by Iago.

A04 KEY CONNECTION

The language Othello uses when he prepares to kill Desdemona is violent and bloody. During Acts IV and V, Othello sometimes sounds like a villain in a **revenge tragedy**. Does this prevent an audience from sympathising with him?

Progress booster: Bianca the victim

Shakespeare uses Bianca to keep Desdemona in our minds in this scene. Bianca's love for Cassio is honest, but she suffers for it. Like Desdemona before her, she tries to defend herself, but fails to make her voice heard. Notice how Bianca's abuse and suffering mirrors Desdemona's downfall. Here Bianca is in danger because of her love for Cassio. By the end of this scene she is falsely suspected of being involved in a murder plot. It could be argued that love makes women helpless victims in *Othello*. Do you agree?

Key quotation: Roderigo's death

Roderigo is the first to recognise Iago's villainy. His dying words are 'O damned Iago! O inhuman dog!' (line 62).

- Iago has used animal imagery to his own advantage and is now recognised as a villain using similar language.
- The imagery of dogs reminds us of how Iago's inhumanity has dehumanised Othello.
- Ironically, Roderigo sees the truth too late, just as Othello will in the next scene.

ACT V SCENE 2

Summary

- As Desdemona sleeps in her room, Othello explains he will kill her, then kisses her, thus waking her.
- Desdemona weeps when Othello tells her Cassio is dead and, believing Desdemona loved Cassio, Othello smothers her.
- Emilia is horrified when Desdemona revives briefly and says she caused her own death.
- After Othello explains why he killed Desdemona, Emilia insults him and summons Montano, Gratiano and Iago.
- Iago denies Emilia's accusations of villainy, stabs her and leaves her to die on the bed next to Desdemona.
- Guards return with Iago; Othello wounds him but Iago will not explain his actions.
- Iago's plots are revealed and, realising his folly, Othello kills himself.

Analysis

Death

There are three violent deaths in this scene: of Desdemona, Othello and Emilia. There are other 'deaths' too, most notably the death of Othello's reputation. The 'valiant Moor' (I.3.48) destroys his good name when he murders Desdemona. Othello's suicide is both retribution and rehabilitation. Othello is destroying the villain he has proved to be, while at the same time trying to resurrect his reputation. Desdemona tries to preserve Othello's good name when she says that she is responsible for her own death. However, Emilia's voice prevails. She insults Othello in language which highlights his race: 'most filthy bargain', 'As ignorant as dirt' (lines 153, 160). Emilia is correct in her allocation of blame for the death of Desdemona: Othello has proved to be a bad bargain as a husband. The reference to Brabantio's death from grief reinforces this idea. The other fitting 'death' is Iago's unmasking as a villain. Desdemona's and Emilia's sacrificial deaths are clearly undeserved. However, their reputations are enhanced when they die. In death, Desdemona and Emilia prove their honesty and loyalty.

Study focus: Justice

Othello uses the language of justice and the law to justify killing Desdemona ('it is the cause', line 1) and demands that she 'deny each article' (line 54) of his accusations before he smothers her. When he realises the truth, Othello takes justice into his own hands and commits suicide. This is **poetic justice**: he kills himself with the sword he used to kill enemies of the Venetian state, which is what Othello proved to be when he took the life of Desdemona. Iago gets his just deserts when his villainy is revealed by Emilia. It is appropriate that one of the women he treated so badly causes his downfall. It is also fitting that Cassio, whom Iago sought to destroy, will be responsible for Iago's torture. But Iago gets away with a great injustice when he refuses to explain himself.

 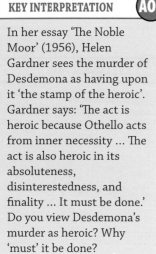

Tragic imagery

The **tragedy** of Desdemona's death is heightened by references to light and religion. These allusions are ominous in the first part of the scene and emphasise the enormity of Othello's crime. Othello enters carrying a light, which **ironically** makes him seem like a priest officiating at a religious ritual. Othello speaks about the 'heavenly' (line 21) sorrow he feels, suggesting he is reluctant to begin the ceremony of death. He repeats the word 'light' several times as he prepares to kill: 'once put out thy light … I know not where is that Promethean heat/ That can thy light relume' (lines 10–13). The words Othello uses to describe Desdemona's body can be linked to the **imagery** of light as her paleness suggests her innocent purity (lines 4–5). Even before she is dead, however, Othello sees her as a funeral monument. When she wakes Othello urges Desdemona to pray because he does not want to 'kill thy unprepared spirit … I would not kill thy soul' (lines 31–2). Still obsessed with his masculine reputation, Othello wants to be 'an honourable murderer' (line 291).

When he confronts his crime, Othello again uses religious imagery, but he no longer uses it to justify his actions. Instead he invites God's punishment. Othello addresses Desdemona's dead body: 'When we shall meet at compt [the Day of Judgement]/ This look of thine will hurl my soul from heaven/ And fiends will snatch at it' (lines 271–3). Othello is tortured by what he has done and recognises his guilt: 'Whip me, ye devils,/ From the possession of this heavenly sight!' (lines 275–6). He believes he deserves the torments of hell.

Love and self-love

While the constancy of the women's love heightens the tragedy of Desdemona's death, the male characters do not emerge so well from this scene. Othello and Iago can both be accused of excessive self-love. Determined to preserve himself, Iago kills Emilia to silence her. His final lines are gloating and selfish: 'Demand me nothing. What you know, you know./ From this time forth I never will speak word' (lines 300–1). Iago's silence is as cruel as his poisonous words have been and in keeping with the villain's egotism.

We may judge Othello less harshly than we judge Iago. Othello still loves Desdemona. He weeps and kisses her before he smothers her. But his self-love will not allow her to live. Othello insists that he has done nothing 'in hate, but all in honour' (line 292). Throughout the play Othello has been torn between his love for Desdemona and his regard for his own honour. It is perhaps a combination of overwhelming love for Desdemona and self-love that made his jealousy so extreme. Othello himself says he was 'one that loved not wisely, but too well' (line 342). Unlike the villain, Othello atones for his excessive self-love by destroying himself. Like Desdemona, his last words and actions are loving: 'I kissed thee ere I killed thee: no way but this,/ Killing myself, to die upon a kiss' (lines 356–7). By linking kissing and killing, Othello is suggesting that he cannot live without Desdemona. Cassio's description of Othello is a fitting epitaph. Othello was 'great of heart' (line 359).

A05 KEY INTERPRETATION

The philosopher Stanley Cavell asserts that Othello's opening speech in Act V Scene 2 is 'part of a ritual of denial'. Do you agree? Does Othello deny he is responsible for his actions?

A05 KEY INTERPRETATION

Dr Johnson found Act V Scene 2 so moving as to be unendurable. What aspects of the scene do you find moving?

Progress booster: A tragic ending **A02**

If you are asked to write about the ending of *Othello*, you should consider the dramatic methods Shakespeare uses to ensure Act V Scene 2 is an effective ending to the play as a **tragedy**. For example, you could write about the imagery Shakespeare uses and the language of Othello's final speeches. You could also consider whether we are encouraged to view Othello's death as inevitable, stoical and heroic, referring to the conventions and expectations of the hero's death in the genre of tragedy. Does Othello's death create pathos, as **Aristotle** said tragic endings should?

EXTRACT ANALYSIS

Act V Scene 2 lines 222–79

The confused physical violence that occurs at the beginning of this extract **mirrors** the confusion of the opening scene. There is a sad **irony** in the fact that Othello the great soldier is now reduced to a failed attempt on the life of Iago, the 'notorious villain' (line 237). Emilia has revealed the truth about the handkerchief, the device that the whole plot has hung on. It is appropriate that 'honest' Iago (e.g. I.3.295) is destroyed by his wife's real honesty. Iago is unmasked as a despicable creature. He curses Emilia before wounding her and running off. This act of unnatural cowardice is the perfect physical expression of Iago's values; yet again he abuses a woman to preserve his own honour. Iago's defiance is unsurprising and typical of him. Even when he is captured Iago remains evasive and selfish: he will not speak.

Emilia's role is to give voice to the audience's outrage at Desdemona's murder. She speaks plainly and passionately, defending Desdemona and guiding our responses to the heroine's death. The repetition in her lines is affecting. Emilia's echoing of Desdemona's willow song as she dies is designed to add to the **pathos** of the scene. Her righteous anger moves Othello towards recognition of his crime. The wretched hero accepts Emilia's harsh words because he knows he deserves them.

The responses of Gratiano and Montano to Othello provide another view of the **protagonist** and his actions. These two characters will provide a sense of closure at the end of this scene. Here they begin to reassert the common-sense, masculine values of the Venetian state by insisting that wicked deeds are punished. The tragic hero has been reduced to the status of base villain. Montano and Gratiano treat Othello like a common criminal: 'let him not pass/ But kill him rather' (lines 239–40). The disarming of Othello is symbolic. Othello is reduced to a nonentity; he is no longer a husband, and now the Venetians have taken his weapon, he is no longer a soldier. In this extract Othello has been degraded. This is fitting given his crime.

But we also see that Shakespeare means to rehabilitate the tragic protagonist. Othello rises above Emilia and the Venetians' reductive versions of him because he readjusts his perception of himself. Othello's desire to be punished (rather than run away from the consequences of his actions as Iago does) goes in his favour. And Othello clearly feels that he deserves not just punishment, but torture: 'Whip me, ye devils … Blow me about in winds, roast me in sulphur/ Wash me down in steep-gulfs of liquid fire!' (lines 275–8). Othello knows he deserves to die. 'But why should honour outlive honesty?' is a key question which needs careful consideration (line 243). We may doubt Othello's conception of himself as honourable at this moment, but not for long. When we realise Othello has another weapon at line 250 we know that he will use this weapon on himself, and inflict the punishment he feels he deserves.

Shakespeare makes Othello impressive again in Act V Scene 2, but his speech at line 257, which begins, 'Behold, I have a weapon', suggests remorse and misery above all else. Othello's desolation comes across strongly in his fatalistic question 'Who can control his fate?' (line 263) and his use of the third person – 'Where should Othello go?' (line 269) – does not so much suggest egotism as dislocation. Othello is lost: he has no wife or profession to sustain him, and as a murderer he is a condemned man. So he turns his weapon on himself and takes control of his own fate, just as he used to determine the fates of his enemies. Othello sees himself in a new and reduced light. He speaks of his 'little arm' and describes the 'impediments' he has made his way through on the battlefield not to boast, but to show that he is diminished (lines 260–1). It is appropriate for Othello to refer back to his earlier life; Shakespeare wants to remind us how far this mighty, noble man has fallen.

The fact that Othello is confined to his bedchamber by others (and by his own actions) shows how he has been reduced. The once great warrior is now a prisoner. The location of this scene suggests claustrophobia and isolation. Although there are other characters on stage we feel that Othello is really alone. He speaks to others briefly, but mostly speaks to himself, to prepare for his self-inflicted fate. If we accept that Othello is speaking of himself and not Iago when he calls out 'O cursed, cursed slave!' (line 274), we have further proof that Othello now feels himself unworthy. He feels the loss of Desdemona agonisingly. Looking at her body Othello is overcome by woe: 'O Desdemon! dead, Desdemon. Dead! O, O!' (line 279). These lines echo Othello's earlier despair. Throughout the play the hero has been inarticulate in moments of extreme pain. When he refers to his wife as an 'ill-starred wench' (line 270) and himself as a man unable to control his own fate we realise that the hero is moving closer to Desdemona and her romantic values again. As in his final speech, Othello's last thoughts here are about the wife he has loved and lost.

This extract prepares us for Othello's final speech: it is the step he must take before killing himself. It is necessary that he explain his thoughts, feelings and remorse so that we will view him as a tragic hero when he dies. The differences between Othello and Iago need to be reasserted. During Acts IV and V, Othello spiralled downwards, becoming more and more like Iago in his words and actions. When he begins to speak in verse with some of his former nobility it is a relief: we know that Iago's spell has been broken. Othello's measured calm is deeply affecting, especially given the hysteria and emotional tension of the earlier part of the scene. The 'cruel' Othello whom Emilia describes has died with Desdemona; now we know the hero's cruelty will be directed against himself because he has acknowledged his folly. Although Othello confronts Iago and will say that he feels he is not entirely to blame for his actions because he was 'Perplexed in the extreme' (V.2.344), we know that the hero accepts responsibility for his crime and will pay for it.

A05 KEY INTERPRETATION

T. S. Eliot criticised Othello for trying to dramatise himself in a self-aggrandising way in the final scene. See this assessment of Othello in 'Shakespeare and the Stoicism of Seneca', *Selected Essays* (1932). For a further negative reading of Othello's character, see F. R. Leavis's comments about the hero in 'Diabolic Intellect and the Noble Hero', *The Common Pursuit* (1962). For a reading of Othello as noble hero, see A. C. Bradley's *Shakespearean Tragedy* (1992 edition).

A03 KEY CONTEXT

Although suicide is a sin in Christianity, the Ancient Greeks and Romans often saw suicide as patriotic or noble because it was a way of avoiding disgrace and preserving one's honour. In many Greek and Roman **tragedies** the protagonists commit suicide for other reasons as well: to avoid further suffering, end grief or sacrifice themselves for the greater good. Do you feel any of these motives apply to Othello's suicide at the end of the play?

PROGRESS CHECK

Section One: Check your understanding

These short tasks will help you to evaluate your knowledge and skills level in this particular area.

1. Make a list of 3–4 examples of betrayal that occur in Act I.

2. What aspects of Iago's behaviour in Act I Scene 1 prepare us for the events he sets in motion in Cyprus?

3. What is the dramatic significance of Othello and Desdemona's elopement? Write a paragraph explaining your ideas.

4. Make a list of 3–4 reasons why we sympathise with Othello and Desdemona in Act I Scene 3.

5. Write a paragraph summing up Desdemona's relationship with Brabantio.

6. What are the 3–4 key differences between Othello as a soldier and a husband?

7. Write a paragraph summing up Iago's motives, which he outlines in Acts I and II.

8. Make a list of the 3–4 key events which occur in the drinking scene, Act II Scene 3.

9. Write down at least 3 methods Iago uses to poison Othello's mind in Act III.

10. Write a paragraph about the disturbing aspects of Act IV Scene 2, focusing on the three central characters – Othello, Desdemona and Iago.

11. What aspects of the willow scene, Act IV Scene 3, prepare us for the tragic ending?

12. In what ways is Iago responsible for the events of Act V Scene 2?

13. Make a table of the deaths that occur or are referred to in Act V in chronological order, commenting on whether the death is tragic, deserved and/or appropriate.

14. Violence is a key issue in the presentation of male–female relationships in this play. Make a table of at least 3 examples of verbal or physical violence, including textual evidence.

15. What evidence is there that Iago is misogynistic? Make notes listing at least 3 examples.

16. In what three ways does the Roderigo subplot contribute to the tragedy of the play?

17. Write a paragraph summing up Desdemona's relationship with Emilia.

18. Write a paragraph summing up the significance of reputation in *Othello*.

19. Make a table comparing Othello, Cassio and Iago as lovers/ husbands, supporting your points with textual evidence.

20. Write a paragraph summing up the ways in which the tragic ending is both satisfying and unsatisfactory for the audience. Argue both points of view.

Section Two: Working towards the exam

Choose one of the following five tasks which require longer, more developed answers. In each case, read the question carefully, select the key areas you need to address, and plan an essay of 6–7 points. Write a first draft, giving yourself an hour to do so. Make sure you include supporting evidence for each point, including quotations.

1. 'Othello is a supremely romantic figure.' To what extent do you agree?
2. 'The play presents a pessimistic view of marriage.' To what extent do you agree?
3. Referring to Iago's soliloquy at the end of Act II Scene 3, discuss how evil is presented in this scene and the tragedy as a whole.
4. Explore the significance of Emilia's exchange with Iago in Act III Scene 3 when she gives him the handkerchief. How does this episode contribute to the tragedy of the play?
5. Focusing on Othello's soliloquy which opens Act V Scene 2, explore Shakespeare's portrayal of Othello as a husband here and elsewhere in the play.

Progress check (rate your understanding on a level of 1 – low, to 5 – high)	1	2	3	4	5
What the key events of each act are					
How the key male–female relationships develop and change during the course of the play					
How Othello's and Iago's relationships with the other male characters are portrayed					
How the key themes e.g. deception, love, jealousy are established in Act I					
The different factors that contribute to Othello's downfall.					

CHARACTERS

Othello

Who is Othello

- Othello is a Moor, and a successful mercenary general who works for the state of Venice.
- He is a middle-aged bachelor who elopes with and marries a wealthy young Venetian, Desdemona.
- Othello is posted to Cyprus as governor during the Turkish conflict.
- In Cyprus, Othello believes Iago's false tales of his wife's adultery and smothers her, afterwards killing himself.

Othello: first impressions

Before he appears on stage we are led to believe by Iago that Othello is bombastic, conceited and personally lascivious. But Othello's appearance in Act I Scene 2 contradicts Iago's assessment. Instead we see an impressive figure who displays a number of fine qualities: openness, sincerity and a natural authority. Unlike Shakespeare's other tragic **protagonists**, Othello is not a monarch (King Lear), an aspiring monarch (Macbeth) nor a displaced prince (Hamlet). However, he is a worthy figure and Shakespeare stresses his nobility. The Moor is the descendant of a royal line of kings (Othello refers to his birthright when he defends his right to marry Desdemona) and has been an impressive military commander.

'Valiant Othello' (I.3.49) commands the respect of figures of authority (the Duke of Venice, Governor Montano and even Brabantio). Although we do not see much evidence of his leadership in Cyprus, we know Othello is a conscientious soldier. He attempts to ensure that the carousing at his wedding festivities does not get out of hand and inspects the fortifications in the town in Act III Scene 2. Othello speaks and acts powerfully and in a way that inspires confidence in his character throughout the first two acts of the play (for example his dignity in front of the senate in Act I Scene 3). Othello's positive attributes indicate that we should view him as a hero, as does his customary mode of speech. (Othello speaks in **blank verse** early in the play and is a fine rhetorician, despite his protestations to the contrary.)

Study focus: Othello and opposition

Othello is a play about opposites and opposition, and the many contradictions contained in the play are embodied in the tragic hero. All the characters hold specific, and often opposing views of the Moor. We have to judge Othello in the light of the evidence they present, whilst also taking into account the hero's words, actions and idea of himself (which change). The hero's two contradictory roles also need to be considered. Othello is both military man and lover-husband. There are other contradictions to think about. Othello occupies contradictory personal and political positions. He is a trusted foreign servant (an outsider), wielding power on behalf of the Venetian state, who seeks to become an equal member of and participant in that society through marriage. He is also, of course, a black man in a white world.

Othello's tragedy: a domestic tragedy?

The focus in this play is, as has often been suggested, domestic. Othello's previous history, the Turkish invasion and machinations of the Venetian state provide the backdrop to an essentially private **tragedy**. However, while the play focuses on the tragic consequences of sexual jealousy, we must not ignore the wider worldly or political dimension of Othello's tragedy. Othello is proud of his profession and his reputation as a soldier is an essential part of the hero's conception of himself. Othello's desire for revenge is prompted by his need to recover his reputation. A **Jacobean** audience would have understood the weight Othello attaches to his reputation: a man's honour was important and his wife's chastity was an integral part of it. When Othello fears that he has been cuckolded the hero doubts himself and is forced to accommodate a new role, that of duped husband, which his pride will not allow him to accept. It is possible to argue that Othello's marriage is a political act; a black soldier marrying a white aristocrat cannot be viewed in any other way, according to the views of the time.

Othello's race

Othello's race is a significant part of his **characterisation**. Othello is not the stereotypical immoral, lustful Moor of much Renaissance drama. He is portrayed as such by other characters – notably Iago – but we realise that we cannot trust the judgement of those who make negative comments about Othello's race. Shakespeare encourages the audience to view the Moor's race positively, as Othello does himself in Acts I and II. Race is not an issue for the heroine: as Othello reminds Iago, 'she had eyes and chose me' (III.3.192). Does Othello's race trouble him later in the play? It may make a modern audience uncomfortable, but it seems so. When his mind is poisoned by Iago, Othello comes to doubt his attractions. Othello mentions his blackness, his unsophisticated manners and his advanced age in a speech which suggests diminishing self-confidence as a husband (see III.3.262). Has Iago's prejudice infected the noble hero? Even if it has, we will never feel that Othello becomes jealous and murderous because he is black. His negative emotions and actions are a result of being 'Perplexed in the extreme' (V.2.344) by Iago, whose discrimination is a part of his evil, just as Othello's blackness is portrayed by Shakespeare as part of his nobility. (For further comments on Othello's race, see **Part Four: Language**.)

Study focus: Othello and slavery (A02)

Critics have suggested that Othello became 'tawny' rather than black in stage productions in the 1800s. This was to prevent the role from being linked to the idea of slavery. At the time that *Othello* was first performed, the African slave trade was already established. In the 1550s, Elizabethan adventurers had set out to the coast of Africa, where they raided the villages and kidnapped some of the inhabitants, bringing them back to England. Othello himself describes how he was briefly imprisoned as a slave.

Othello: lover and husband

The difficulty for an audience comes in accepting Othello as a perfect wooer, lover and husband, partly because Othello married Desdemona in secret – a covert act that sits uncomfortably with Othello's protestation that he has nothing to hide after the marriage. However, we are not encouraged to dwell on the elopement itself because it becomes clear that Desdemona was 'half the wooer' (I.3.176) and the couple speak clearly and honestly

---

(A05) KEY INTERPRETATION

The philosopher Stanley Cavell says that 'tragedy is the place we are not allowed to escape the consequences or price'. How does this statement apply to *Othello*?

(A05) KEY INTERPRETATION

Ania Loomba ('*Othello* and the Radical Question', 1998) says that '*Othello* is both a fantasy of interracial love and social tolerance, and a nightmare of racial hatred and male violence.' To what extent do you agree with her interpretation of the play?

about their love, to the council and to each other. Their meeting in Cyprus reveals the intensity and sincerity of their mutual affection, and we are also assured of their sexual attraction.

The Duke of Venice recognises Othello's suitability as a wooer when he says, 'I think this tale would win my daughter too' (I.3.172). He then seeks to reassure Brabantio, 'Your son-in-law is far more fair than black' (I.3.291). However, there are tensions and contradictions that must be considered, as Desdemona's need to live with her husband conflicts with Othello's intention to keep the marriage separate from his duties. We gradually come to question Othello's self-knowledge on this point. He may be a capable general, but the events of the play suggest that Othello is out of his depth in matters of the heart.

Progress booster: Othello's love

It is important that you can track the course of Othello's love for Desdemona, and how it is gradually overcome by darker emotions. When Othello greets Desdemona in Cyprus we get the first hint that the hero is overwhelmed by his love for his wife – he is almost too happy. Then in Act III Scene 3 he says that he fears chaos when he is away from Desdemona: 'perdition catch my soul/ but I do love thee! and when I love thee not/ Chaos is come again' (III.3.90–2). It seems Othello cannot master his powerful romantic and erotic feelings. Is Othello in the grip of emotions that he cannot control, even before Iago sets to work on him? The successful soldier becomes a blind lover. The qualities that served Othello well as a soldier contribute to his downfall. Othello's decisiveness leads him to seek 'ocular proof' (III.3.363) and then when he is presented with that proof his decision to pursue a bloody course is made swiftly.

But it is not as simple as this. Othello suffers acutely from Act III Scene 3 onwards and does not give into his feelings of jealousy as swiftly as William Hazlitt suggests when he describes Othello as having 'blood of the most inflammable kind'. Othello tries many times to persuade himself that Desdemona is honest; he has second thoughts about murdering her as late as the final scene. And we cannot ignore Iago's presence. Iago is immensely plausible and cunning and Othello has no reason not to trust him. There is a good deal of evidence to indicate that Othello is pushed towards tragedy by a ruthless 'demi-devil' (V.2.298), who takes advantage of his noble nature, and is not simply a jealous 'booby', as Thomas Rymer claims. We know just how powerful Iago's influence is because Othello begins to speak and think like the ensign when his imagination is polluted. We are forced to come to terms with the idea that Othello is not wholly noble; he is also capable of savagery and crudeness.

Othello's transformation?

The transformation of Othello is troubling. Why does Othello trust Iago more than he trusts his beloved wife? Why does he believe the worst of Cassio, who has been a trusted friend and colleague? We have to understand that Othello's conception of himself has been challenged. Iago cruelly reminds him that he is an outsider and addresses him as an ordinary, foolish cuckold (see IV.1.65–73). Given his pride, the hero finds this intolerable.

F. R. Leavis has suggested that Othello's readiness to believe Iago is a sign that the hero is rather 'simple minded', inferring that lack of intellect contributes to Othello's **tragedy**. But Othello is much more than a weak fool. By the time Othello descends into murderous jealousy we are well acquainted with his noble character and recognise that he has been 'ensnared'

(V.2.299). Surely Othello's preoccupation with honour and chastity are the obsessions of a virtuous, moral character? We might also feel that his desire for revenge is the result of Othello's failure to combine his roles as soldier and lover. When Othello fears that he has been betrayed by Desdemona he says woefully, 'Othello's occupation's gone!' (III.3.360). It is as if Desdemona was the prize Othello earned for his military victories. She has perhaps replaced his career as the source of his pride and honour. No wonder Othello feels her loss so keenly.

Othello's final scene

It is possible to argue that his insistence on the importance of his honour both redeems and damns Othello. His concern for his reputation in the final scene can diminish Othello in the eyes of the audience. Nonetheless, Othello believes he is saving other men's honour and redeeming his own when he smothers Desdemona, calling himself an 'honourable murderer' (V.2.291). Shakespeare reminds us that the hero was a worthy man before he was ensnared by Iago, in order to create **pathos**. When Othello commits suicide he courageously takes his own life to pay for the crime of killing Desdemona. In his final lines and final act Othello is perhaps able to reconcile his two contradictory roles: the soldier kills the faulty lover. So, while it is impossible to condone Othello's actions in Act V Scene 2, it is possible to sympathise with and pity the fallen hero, whose suffering has been extreme.

Readers and critics of *Othello* have responded in many different ways to the **protagonist**. One popular view is that the character of Othello disintegrates psychologically and morally through the play and that this disintegration can be followed in his changing speech style. For example, he uses more oaths in the second half of the play, perhaps indicating moral corruption. Others, such as the scholar Muriel Bradbrook, see Othello as the descendant of the medieval stage devil, a corrupting influence throughout the play. She suggests that Othello should be considered a 'bogeyman'.

Caryl Phillips, on the other hand, believes Othello to be fundamentally 'an impulsive and insecure man', a vulnerable human being who reacts under pressure ('A black European success', *The European Tribe*, 2000). Some critics go even further and praise Othello's decision to commit suicide, reading it not as a mark of weakness but as a sign of a Stoic hero. Stoics, who followed the teachings of the Greek philosopher Zeno (335–263 BC), were supposedly indifferent to pain, and bore suffering without complaint.

A03 KEY CONTEXT

Africans of both sexes were a visible minority in seventeenth-century London. It has even been suggested that Shakespeare knew a black prostitute who lived in the Cripplegate area of the city. However, in the theatre, Othello would have been an unusual tragic hero because of his race.

A05 KEY INTERPRETATION

For a negative reading of Othello's character in the final scene of the play, see T. S. Eliot's 'Shakespeare and the Stoicism of Seneca', *Selected Essays* (1932). Eliot says that Othello's last speech is a 'terrible exposure of human weakness'. Othello turns himself into 'a pathetic figure'. Do you agree with these comments?

Key quotation: Othello's concept of himself   **A02**

Othello is proud of his career and character. He says, 'My parts, my title and my perfect soul/ Shall manifest me rightly' (I.2.31–2).

- Othello defends his character and actions in Act I. He feels that he is a worthy husband for Desdemona and that he has acted honourably. Has he?
- Some critics suggest that Othello's downfall is caused partly by the sin of pride. Do you agree?
- Compare the positive **imagery** that Othello uses to describe himself in Act I with the imagery in his final speech in the play, where he compares himself with a 'base Indian' and 'circumcised dog' (V.2.345 and 353).

Desdemona

Who is Desdemona?

- Desdemona is a wealthy young Venetian woman, the daughter of Brabantio.
- She elopes with Othello the Moor and accompanies him to Cyprus.
- Desdemona is falsely accused of adultery and murdered by Othello.

Brabantio's Desdemona

Early in the play Brabantio defines Desdemona as his 'jewel' (I.3.196). He says she is 'A maiden never bold,/ Of spirit' (I.3.95–6), modest and opposed to marriage, afraid to look on Othello. She emerges from her father's descriptions as an innocent, girlish figure. This version of Desdemona proves inaccurate when she speaks in Act I. However, by the end of the play Othello's abusive treatment has turned Desdemona into the fearful girl Brabantio described. This is horribly **ironic**. Desdemona has been silenced and it seems her final role is to be a sacrifice to masculine pride.

Desdemona the wife

Desdemona asserts her rights as a married woman and insists that she is ready for a sexual relationship. There are other exchanges in the play that suggest Desdemona's sexuality, for example Desdemona's participation in the crude talk with Iago in Act II Scene 1, and her admiring reference to Lodovico in Act IV Scene 3. But the heroine's active sexuality is necessary to the play. Iago is able to make a great deal out of the fact that Desdemona deceived her father in order to choose her own husband, and is therefore untrustworthy.

It is important to remember that although Desdemona has disobeyed her father, she expects to submit to Othello's authority. She states this explicitly when she says, 'My heart's subdued/ Even to the very quality of my lord' (I.3.251–2). When Desdemona urges Othello to reinstate Cassio, she believes she is acting in Othello's best professional interests. Desdemona's 'nagging' can be portrayed on stage as playful and loving, her anxiousness about Othello's health touching.

But Desdemona is not faultless. She lies to Othello about the handkerchief (understandably, for he frightens her with his serious talk about its magical properties). When Othello strikes her publicly Desdemona reproaches him briefly: 'I have not deserved this' (IV.1.240). She then accepts – and defends – his authority over her, as we see from her discussion with Emilia at the start of Act IV Scene 3. Desdemona asserts her loving loyalty and questions Othello bravely in Act IV Scene 2 (see lines 30–89) but is reduced to dumb misery when her husband calls her 'that cunning whore of Venice' (IV.2.91): 'nor answer have I none' she says woefully (IV.2.105), remarking – girlishly – that she is 'a child to chiding' (IV.2.116).

Study focus: Desdemona's final words

A02

Ultimately Desdemona refuses to blame Othello for her unhappiness: she declares it is her 'wretched fortune' (IV.2.129). Marriage teaches Desdemona that 'men are not gods' (III.4.149) and this is a disappointment to her. But while Desdemona submits willingly to the man she chose to marry, she dies valiantly, fighting to be allowed to live and asserting her honesty. Her final words are intriguing and contradictory. Why does Desdemona take the blame for her own death? Is she trying to protect Othello in death as she sought to defend him in life? Or is she simply a victim asserting her own innocence? However we interpret Desdemona's final words, we will probably feel that the heroine's passivity in Act V Scene 2 contradicts her earlier assertiveness.

Desdemona: Iago's victim

While we will certainly blame Othello for killing Desdemona, we will also blame Iago. An audience may wonder how he feels about the woman whose reputation he so brutally destroys. In Act II Scene 1, Iago says that he 'love[s]' Desdemona, 'Not out of absolute lust' but 'Partly to diet mine own revenge' (II.1.289–92). He wants to be even with Othello 'wife for wife' (II.1.297). So Iago decides he will 'turn her virtue into pitch' (II.3.355).

Does Iago ever regret what he does to Desdemona? E. A. J. Honigmann argues that Iago finds it difficult to respond to Desdemona in Act IV Scene 2 when he sees how miserable she is. There is one line of Iago that could be delivered with a hint of regret: 'Do not weep, do not weep: alas the day!' (IV.2.126). However, you may feel this is another example of Iago's ability to dissemble and further proof that Iago enjoys turning Desdemona into a victim.

Key quotation: Desdemona's bravery

A02

Desdemona defends her own honour throughout the play, shown when she says to Othello, 'By heaven, you do me wrong' (IV.2.82).

- Desdemona is still brave and assertive, even when Othello attacks her verbally and physically.
- The reference to heaven reinforces Desdemona's virtue.
- This is an example of irony and **foreshadowing**; Othello will refer to heaven just before he murders Desdemona.

Further key quotations

- Desdemona actively chose Othello and sees him as a hero: 'I saw Othello's visage in his mind/ And to his honours and his valiant parts/ Did I my soul and fortunes consecrate' (I.3.253).
- Love of Othello makes Desdemona submissive: 'my love doth so approve him/ That even his stubbornness, his checks, his frowns … have grace and favour' (IV.3.17–19).
- Desdemona loves Othello to the bitter end. Her final words are: 'Commend me to my kind lord – O, farewell!' (V.2.122).
- For Othello there are two Desdemonas. She is firstly his 'soul's joy' (II.1.182) but when he thinks she is unfaithful she becomes 'that cunning whore of Venice' (IV.2.91).
- Desdemona is Iago's victim. His intention is to 'out of her own goodness make the net/ That shall enmesh them all' (II.3.356–7).

Iago

Who is Iago?

- Iago is Othello's ensign. He has served with Othello in a number of military campaigns.
- Eaten up by jealousy and hatred, Iago seeks to destroy Othello by poisoning his mind against Desdemona.

Iago the villain

Iago is a compelling and sophisticated villain. He is part **vice**, part **Machiavel** and, like many villains in Renaissance drama, seems to be inherently evil. Shakespeare presents Iago as cynical, quick witted and opportunistic – all qualities of stage villains in **revenge tragedies**. Iago revels in his ability to dissemble and destroy, but while he enjoys having an audience and outlines his plots clearly, he is also rather mysterious, especially when he refuses to speak at the end of the play. Iago's silence led Romantic poet and critic Samuel Taylor Coleridge to conclude that the ensign is an example of 'motiveless malignity'. Coleridge also viewed Iago as a 'being next to the devil'. In more recent times, Iago's role has been reassessed. Iago is no longer considered the epitome of evil. Instead he can be seen as an example of an emotionally limited man, driven by petty professional jealousy and class consciousness. Like many stage villains, Iago is a source of **irony** and humour, which makes him appealing to audiences.

Iago's motives

Critics are divided about whether or not Iago's motives are adequate or plausible. Many also question whether he believes in them himself. One school of thought suggests that Iago knows the things he says about others are not true, but that his desire for revenge demands that he has an explanation for his actions. Iago claims that professional jealousy is his initial motive for disgracing Cassio. He is certainly also envious of the 'daily beauty' in the lieutenant's life (V.1.19). In addition, Iago says that he believes Cassio has committed adultery with his wife, Emilia. Iago's relationship with Roderigo is driven by callous greed and when his 'purse' (I.3.381) becomes a dangerous inconvenience, he kills him. His motives for destroying Othello's happiness are driven by negative impulses. Iago holds a grudge against Othello for promoting Cassio over him. Iago is also eaten up with sexual jealousy. He says he hates Othello because he suspects the general has "twixt my sheets … done my office' (I.3.386–7). There is no evidence in the text to suggest he has been cuckolded, either by Othello or Cassio. It is tempting to add misogyny and racial prejudice to Iago's motives. Although he never says explicitly that he hates women or foreigners, his low opinion of them is clear in many of his speeches. Iago wants to degrade those he despises.

Progress booster: Iago's success

It's important that you are able to discuss why Iago is so successful. He is self-contained, egotistical and confident, and successful because he can play different roles. He enjoys his ability to hoodwink others into believing he is honest. With Cassio, he is coarse and genial when offering plausible practical advice. He adopts a similar sympathetic approach with Desdemona in Act IV Scene 2. With Montano and Lodovico he makes a point of stressing that he has Othello's and the Venetian state's best interests at heart. There seems to be an absence of ego in his dealings with these characters, who are socially and professionally superior to him. But this is deliberate and false. Iago can afford to be less cautious with those who are dependent on him. Pay close attention to his exchanges with Roderigo, and what they reveal.

PROGRESS BOOSTER **A03**

When writing about Iago's evil it is important to be able refer to it in relation to the literary and historical context of the play. For example, Iago demonstrates several characteristics of a typical **Jacobean** stage villain.

KEY CONNECTION **A04**

It is worth considering the view of women expressed by Iago in relation to all the female characters in *Othello*. Do they provide proof that they are weak minded, foolish, petty or inconstant? There is a strong sense that the women in this play are hapless victims. Bianca, the least powerful figure in the play, is – ironically – the only female survivor.

Iago and Othello

Iago's dealings with Othello reveal his real skill. It is possible to argue Iago seeks to replace Desdemona in Othello's affections. Although this is debatable, Iago certainly sets out to prove that he is true to Othello, while Desdemona is false. Gradually, the ensign assumes the control and power we associate with Othello. He is so successful that Othello begins to speak and think like the villain. How does the 'inhuman dog' (V.1.62) destroy the mind, soul and body of the noble, valiant Moor? Iago makes Othello believe that he is loyal, conscientious and noble minded (these are of course – ironically – Othello's best qualities). Iago pretends that he would like to cudgel Othello's detractors in Act I Scene 2 and appears hesitant to describe his 'friend' Cassio's part in the drunken brawl. Iago's show of reluctance in Act III Scene 3 is devastatingly effective. Iago's role-playing enables him to become stage manager and dramatist, controlling his victims' fates.

Iago on stage and screen

Iago has been played by a number of famous actors, including the Victorian actor Henry Irving, who covered his face with his hands at line 393 in Act I Scene 3 when he said 'let's see'. Irving took a long pause before slowly withdrawing his hands to reveal a face which was, according to one spectator, 'all alive with the devilish scheme which had come into his mind'.

Iago's facial expressions are also key in the 1989 and 1995 TV/film productions, in which he speaks directly to camera in close-up, drawing the viewer in. Many **soliloquies** are whispered coolly and ferociously, through clenched teeth. The line 'I hate the Moor' (I.3.385) is emphasised slowly and very bitterly by the Iagos of Ian McKellen and Kenneth Branagh. In a 1995 film, the director Oliver Parker chose to emphasise Iago's brutality towards his wife. During the scene when Emilia gives Iago Desdemona's handkerchief, the villain is lying on top of, and hurting, his wife.

Study focus: Iago's limitations (A02)

Does Iago's crude world view indicate that he is a petty character whose cleverness is superficial? The end of the play proves that you cannot hoodwink everyone all of the time: Iago is foolish to believe that he can. An assessment of Iago must acknowledge his terrible achievements as well as his ultimate failure. The villain succeeds in destroying a marriage and two noble characters, as well as his wife and Roderigo. On the other hand, we must also take into account Iago's refusal to speak at the end of the play. When he takes refuge in silence does Iago reassert his power one last time despite his inevitable fate?

Key quotation: Understanding Iago's abuse of Desdemona (A02)

Iago's plan is to use Desdemona's virtue to destroy Othello. He says 'out of her own goodness [he will] make the net/ That shall enmesh them all' (II.3.356–7).

- The **imagery** suggests that Iago is setting a trap for his prey.
- The imagery here also suggests Iago has contempt for innocence and goodness.
- Iago's intended exploitation of Desdemona's goodness prepares us for his abuse of the other female characters, Emilia and Bianca, later in the play.

(A05) KEY INTERPRETATION

For a detailed discussion of Iago as alienated, triumphant villain, and an exploration of the villain's motives, see W. H. Auden's essay 'The Joker in the Pack' in John Wain (ed.), *Othello* (1971).

(A04) KEY CONNECTION

A Freudian interpretation of the play might suggest that Iago is subconsciously in love with Othello. This is how Laurence Olivier played the part of Iago. At the line 'I am your own forever' (III.3.482), he kissed his Othello (Ralph Richardson) on the lips. Do you think this is a plausible reading of Iago's character?

(A05) PROGRESS BOOSTER

The theatre critic Susannah Clapp reviewed a production of *Othello* in 2007. She said that Iago was portrayed as 'the thinker' while Othello was a 'feeler'. Is this how you see these two characters? The actor Dominic West, who played Iago in 2011, said that 'it's much easier to make a devil interesting'. Do you agree that Iago is more interesting than the other characters in *Othello*?

Cassio

Who is Cassio?

- Cassio is a Florentine soldier, who is promoted by Othello to the post of lieutenant.
- He acted as go-between during the courtship of Othello and Desdemona.
- Cassio is disgraced when he is involved in a drunken brawl, but is made governor of Cyprus at the end of the play.

Cassio the soldier

In Act I Scene 1 we are offered a belittling portrait of Cassio by Iago. Iago presents Cassio as an inexperienced soldier, a mere 'arithmetician' (I.1.18) who has been promoted beyond his deserving. Perhaps this is a case of sour grapes. Iago is jealous of Cassio's promotion. However, there is some evidence that Cassio lacks military judgement. When Othello leaves him in charge, Cassio ends up drunk in a fight. Instead of keeping order and discipline, he creates confusion and alarm. This seems inexcusable, since he has already confessed to having a weak head for drink. Perhaps Cassio's military inexperience is meant to serve as another parallel with Othello, who is an inexperienced lover – despite their inexperience both men take their roles seriously. Because he is made governor of Cyprus at the end of the play, we are encouraged to dwell on Cassio's strengths rather than weaknesses as a soldier.

Study focus: Cassio and Othello **A02**

Michael Cassio's primary function in the play is to offer a point of comparison with Othello. Both soldiers are outsiders who have chosen to serve Venice. Both value their reputations highly. But there the similarities end. Cassio, as an educated Florentine gentleman, is a cultural insider while Othello, due to his race, would have been seen as a cultural outsider. Florence had a reputation as city of culture so, unlike his general, Cassio is a social sophisticate. Othello's relationship with his lieutenant **mirrors** his relationship with his wife. At the start of the play, when Othello is 'well tuned' (II.1.198) with Desdemona, his relationship with Cassio is good. Iago destroys this harmony by creating a fictitious love-triangle. Cassio assisted Othello while he was courting Desdemona but Iago is able to turn this act of loyalty into proof of treachery. At the end of the play Cassio is associated with the restoration of order in Cyprus when he replaces Othello. Cassio's generous tribute to Othello at the end of the play also reminds us how great the hero was. It is fitting that the loyal lieutenant offers the last comment on the 'valiant Moor' (I.3.48).

Cassio and Iago

Cassio's worst qualities are revealed when he is under Iago's influence. This gives us another point of comparison between Cassio and Othello. Iago pretends to be a loyal friend to both men. Iago claims that both men have slept with Emilia, giving him a motive for revenge against both of them. It is to his credit that Cassio is as easy to fool as Othello; to Shakespeare's audience this would have been proof of his honesty.

Iago is able to play on Cassio's frailties in the same way that he exploits Othello. He takes advantage of the lieutenant's courtesy, recognising that Cassio's weakness lies in the fact that he is 'handsome, young and hath all those requisites in him that folly and green minds look after' (II.1.243–5).

By plying him with drink Iago is able to manoeuvre Cassio out of the way and replace him as Othello's right-hand man. From this position of strength, Iago is then able to make Cassio's virtues look like vices. He uses Cassio's courtesy against him and makes his shame look like guilt. Like Othello, Cassio is a puppet in Iago's hands.

Cassio the lover

It is possible to feel that Cassio's gallantry is a little overworked at times. However, an audience can see that the lieutenant's praise of Desdemona is innocent and sincere. Later in the play Cassio's gentlemanly exterior seems to conceal some unsavoury qualities. These are revealed through his interaction with Bianca. Cassio's treatment of his mistress is often callous. While he does show her some affection, Cassio also refers to Bianca contemptuously as a 'bauble' (IV.1.134), and compares her to a 'fitchew' (a polecat, IV.1.145). Polecats were considered smelly and lecherous, so this is a very abusive term. It is hard not to judge Cassio harshly when he tells Bianca to be gone because he does not want to be found 'womaned' (III.4.194). Cassio can be accused of using women in the same way that Iago does. Rather than facing up to Othello he enlists the help of Emilia, then Desdemona to plead his case. Cassio may not 'steal away so guilty-like' (III.3.38), as Iago suggests, but is it not spineless to leave Desdemona to defend him?

It is essential that Cassio hang back for the purposes of the plot. And we cannot blame the lieutenant for relying on female intervention. Iago has persuaded Cassio that his best hopes lie in winning over Desdemona first. To Shakespeare's audience Cassio's casual liaison with a young courtesan would not have been enough to detract from his good qualities. We have to remember the 'daily beauty' (V.1.19) of Cassio's life that Iago detests so much. Overall, we may conclude Cassio's worthiness outweighs his weakness. Writing in 1765, Dr Johnson had a very positive view of Cassio's character. He said that 'Cassio is brave, benevolent, and honest'.

Key quotation: Cassio's loss of honour **A02**

Cassio is full of shame when he is dismissed from his post by Othello: 'O, I have lost my reputation, I have lost the immortal part of myself – and what remains is bestial' (II.3.258–60).

- Cassio's obsession with his reputation mirrors Othello's obsession.

- Cassio's sorrow over losing his profession **foreshadows** Othello's misery when he thinks he has lost Desdemona's love.

- The reference to being 'bestial' foreshadows Othello's downfall – Othello will become 'bestial' himself when he avenges his masculine honour.

Further key quotations

- Cassio's charm and courtesy, welcoming Desdemona to Cyprus: 'O, behold,/ The riches of the ship is come on shore:/ You men of Cyprus, let her have your knees!' (II.1.82–4).

- Cassio's abusive treatment of Bianca: 'I do attend here on the general/ And think it no addition, not my wish,/ To have him see me womaned' (III.4.192–4).

- Cassio's generous tribute to Othello: 'he was great of heart' (V.2.359).

Emilia

Who is Emilia?

● Emilia is Iago's wife and Desdemona's lady in waiting in Cyprus.

Emilia's loyalty

Emilia tries to be a loyal wife and servant but her loyalty is repeatedly tested by the incidents surrounding the handkerchief. Emilia makes the wrong moral choice when she gives the handkerchief to Iago because he 'hath a hundred times/ Wooed me to steal it' (III.3.296–7). Emilia does this in spite of knowing Desdemona 'so loves the token … That she reserves it evermore about her' (III.3.297–9). Will the audience blame Emilia for putting her husband's 'fantasy' (III.3.303) before her mistress's peace of mind? Emilia's loyalty is tested again when Desdemona wonders how she lost the handkerchief. Emilia's lie – 'I know not, madam' (III.4.24) – makes us uncomfortable. Emilia's loyalty is tested for a final time in Act V. Now Emilia puts Desdemona first. She tells the truth about the handkerchief and betrays Iago. She has chosen good over evil.

KEY INTERPRETATION **A05**

Some critics have suggested that Emilia is the most admirable and the strongest woman in *Othello*. They point to her words and actions in the final scene, especially her brave last speech which ends, 'So speaking as I think, alas, I die' (V.2. 249). To what extent do you agree with this interpretation?

Emilia and Iago

Emilia's relationship with Iago is a chilling example of marital disharmony. Whatever love is left is felt by Emilia, who tries to please Iago by giving him the handkerchief. Iago's attitude towards his wife is proprietorial and controlling. Iago is suspicious that Othello has cuckolded him, and dislikes the courtesy Cassio shows Emilia when she first arrives in Cyprus. Iago is jealous not because he loves Emilia, but because he feels his own position is being threatened. We see the couple alone together only once, in Act III Scene 3. Iago treats Emilia contemptuously. He asks her sharply what she's doing alone, implying that her movements should be directed entirely by him. He also insults Emilia as 'a foolish wife' (III.3.308), but when he realises she has the handkerchief, his tone softens: now Emilia is a 'good wench' (III.3.317).

Iago's public treatment of Emilia is as dismissive as the way he speaks to her in private. In Act IV Scene 2, Iago is annoyed when Emilia refers to Iago's false suspicion that Othello cuckolded him. Iago's short lines sound like threats: 'Speak within doors' (IV.2.146) and 'You are a fool, go to' (IV.2.150). In Act V, Iago's verbal abuse intensifies just before he kills her. When she betrays the truth about the handkerchief he calls Emilia a 'Villainous whore!' and 'Filth' (V.2.227, 229). These words encapsulate the disrespect Iago feels for all women. The audience will be pleased that it is his abused wife who brings about her villainous husband's downfall.

Progress booster: Emilia and sexual politics

Emilia is a useful character to focus on if you are discussing the sexual politics of the play. It comes as no surprise that Emilia is cynical about men. Her own match has afforded her little pleasure. Shakespeare gives Emilia a distinctive and increasingly assertive female voice. She uses it to defend herself and her sex. She replies sharply when Iago derides women in Act II Scene 1: 'You shall not write my praise' (II.1.116). In Act III Scene 4 we see that Emilia is more realistic about male–female relationships than Desdemona. Discussing marriage she says, ''Tis not a year or two shows us a man./ They are all but stomachs, and we all but food' (III.4.104–5). The audience will appreciate Emilia speaks from bitter experience. In the willow song scene, notice how Emilia insists that women have the same appetites as men and the same right to 'revenge' if they are badly treated (IV.3.92).

Emilia's judgement

It is difficult not to agree with some of Emilia's harsh judgements of Othello and we know that she is absolutely right to betray Iago. However, you could consider how Emilia's pragmatism about men and women is perhaps not very removed from Iago's cynicism. Look at Emilia's defence of adultery in Act III Scene 4. She speaks theoretically here, but her casual acceptance of sin is perhaps an indication that Emilia is too crude a moraliser to be relied on completely as a judge of Othello's character in the final scene. Should we conclude that Emilia's female voice is trustworthy, but not infallible?

Emilia and Desdemona

Emilia is Desdemona's comforter and protector of her honour. She plays the role that Othello should have played for his wife. As Desdemona becomes less assertive in the second half of the play Emilia's role becomes more important. She becomes her mistress's energetic defender, voicing the audience's outrage at the treatment Desdemona receives. In her role as defender she is selfless and sharp witted. She describes Othello's destructive jealousy accurately. Emilia is also wise without knowing it when she says angrily, 'The Moor's abused by some most villainous knave' (IV.2.141). In the final scene Emilia becomes the voice of truth and stops Iago's evil progress. Her final lines reconfirm her own and her mistress's honesty: 'So come my soul to bliss as I speak true!/ So speaking as I think, alas, I die' (V.2.248–9). It seems fitting that Emilia should die beside the mistress she defended with her dying breath.

Study focus: Emilia's suspicions (A02)

There remain two questions to be asked about Emilia. Firstly, why does she give the handkerchief to Iago when she does not know why he wants it? Emilia regrets giving it to him the moment he takes possession of it, suggesting that she is uneasy about his motives. Secondly, does Emilia suspect her husband before she finally speaks out? Perhaps the answer is yes. When she hears that Iago led Othello to believe Desdemona was false she says, 'I think upon't, I think I smell't, O villainy!/ I thought so then: I'll kill myself for grief!' (V.2.188–9). Her words suggest guilt at keeping quiet about her suspicions. However, Emilia's horrified repeated question 'My husband?' (V.2.138, 142, 145) could be seen as proof that Emilia knew nothing of Iago's villainy. Like Roderigo, whom Iago also brutally silences, Emilia realises the true extent of her husband's evil when it is too late.

Key quotation: Understanding Emilia's comments on jealousy (A02)

Emilia says 'jealous souls … are not ever jealous for the cause, … [Jealousy] is a monster/ Begot upon itself, born on itself' (III.4.159–62).

- These lines describe Iago's jealousy; he takes revenge on Cassio and Othello without a genuine 'cause'.
- These words suggest Othello's jealousy will feed itself.
- The **personification** of jealousy links it to the handkerchief.
- It is **ironic** that Emilia is the wise expert on jealousy, when she seems to have no clue about Iago's villainy.

(A05) **KEY INTERPRETATION**

In *Othello* (1997), E. A. J. Honigmann suggests that Emilia's final actions prove that love triumphs over hate. He says 'Emilia's love [of Desdemona] is Iago's undoing'. Do you agree that love triumphs over hate in this play?

(A02) **PROGRESS BOOSTER**

You need to make precise points rather than sweeping generalisations. This is especially important when writing about language and **imagery**. For example, rather than saying 'there is a lot of imagery of jealousy in the play', try to comment on a specific example: 'In Act III Scene 4, Emilia defines jealousy as … which shows us that …'

(A05) **KEY INTERPRETATION**

For a **feminist** reading of the play, see Marilyn French's essay in John Drakakis (ed.), *Shakespearean Tragedy* (1992).

Brabantio

Who is Brabantio?

● Brabantio is a Venetian senator and Desdemona's father.

Brabantio the senator

Brabantio is an important man used to commanding others. **Ironically**, these are qualities he shares with his son-in-law Othello. We are led to believe that Brabantio is a valuable member of the council, well respected by others. The Duke says that he was missed during the discussions about the Turkish invasion, and takes trouble to reconcile Brabantio to Desdemona's marriage. However, we might feel that Brabantio's professional judgement is questionable. He resolutely refuses to acknowledge Othello's worth, unlike the rest of the Venetian senators. Ironically, like Othello, Brabantio puts his private affairs before affairs of state. Brabantio insists the council put Othello on trial for witchcraft in Act I Scene 3 when they are more concerned with the military fate of Cyprus.

Study focus: Brabantio the patriarch

Brabantio plays the role of the wronged patriarch. Shakespeare's audience may have felt his wrongs more deeply than we do today. They would have recognised Desdemona's elopement as an assault on **patriarchy**. Like Juliet in *Romeo and Juliet*, the treasured daughter denies her father's right to dispose of her in marriage as he sees fit. Brabantio sees this as a 'gross revolt' (I.1.132) against the natural order. He reminds Desdemona that it is her duty to obey him in Act I Scene 3 (see lines 175–9). Brabantio holds what would have been recognised by Shakespeare's audience as traditional, suspicious views of foreigners. These views come across in Brabantio's descriptions of Othello as a 'foul thief' (I.2.62) who has bewitched Desdemona. To a modern audience these views seem racist. Brabantio suggests that Desdemona's marriage to Othello undermines not just his own authority, but the whole social order.

Brabantio's love for Desdemona

Brabantio has not been an unsympathetic parent. Until the elopement his home has been a place of family harmony. Othello has been entertained often and Brabantio has been a friendly host. Any audience would understand Brabantio's desire to find a suitable match for his daughter. His paternal love of Desdemona has been wise. He rejected the unworthy Roderigo, as we see when he sternly reminds the failed suitor that Desdemona 'is not for thee' (I.1.97). Brabantio has also allowed Desdemona to reject suitors herself. Brabantio's descriptions of Desdemona in the senate scene may not fit with the confident young woman we see when she appears, but Brabantio recognises his daughter's virtues and cares for her deeply.

Not all of Brabantio's speeches about losing his daughter are unsympathetic. In Act I Scene 3 it clear that the loss of Desdemona weighs very heavily on his soul. He says 'my particular grief/ Is of so flood-gate and o'erbearing nature/ That it engluts and swallows other sorrows' (I.3.57–9). Brabantio's sense of loss is profound. The intense emotion described in this speech **foreshadows** Othello's outraged feelings when he believes he has been betrayed by

Desdemona. It is ironic that the reluctant father and his son-in-law are linked by the language of loss they use. Like Othello, Brabantio dies grieving for his lost love. We are told Desdemona's marriage was 'mortal [fatal] to him' (V.2.203).

Progress booster: An unsympathetic character

A01

Make sure you can identify the factors that cause us to lose sympathy with Brabantio. His immovable unkindness to Desdemona and Othello prevents us from sympathising with the patriarch wholeheartedly. Brabantio refuses to have anything to do with his daughter after her marriage and he casts Desdemona off. He says cruelly that he would rather 'adopt a child than get it' (I.3.192). Brabantio's final words to Othello are a harsh warning: 'Look to her, Moor, if thou hast eyes to see:/ She has deceived her father, and may thee' (I.3.293–4). The loving, generous father is replaced by a mean-spirited prophet of doom. Brabantio also proves to be too selfishly materialistic. His use of the word 'jewel' (I.3.196) to describe Desdemona suggests that he regards his daughter as a possession. We also come to question Brabantio's judgement when he says it would have been better if Roderigo had 'had' Desdemona rather than Othello. At the same time, it is important to remember that Brabantio is another victim of Iago's manipulation. His unfavourable view of Othello is influenced heavily by the ensign's crude and prejudiced **characterisation** of the Moor.

A05 **KEY INTERPRETATION**

Some critics have argued that *Othello* ultimately teaches audiences that patriarchal society cannot work. Does the fact that Brabantio's point of view and wishes are denied by the senate suggest that this interpretation is valid?

A04 **KEY CONNECTION**

For a comic treatment of a father trying to marry off his two daughters, see Shakespeare's *The Taming of the Shrew*. In this play there are two daughters, Bianca and Katherina. Bianca is outwardly obedient, but secretly arranges her own marriage, while Katherina is a 'scold' who is married against her will to a fortune hunter, Petruchio.

A04 **KEY CONNECTION**

In Oliver Parker's 1995 film Brabantio's bitter lines, 'She has deceived her father, and may thee' (I.3.294), are repeated in flashback late in the play, showing their importance and significance for Othello. How many other examples of deception can you find in the play?

Key quotation: Understanding Brabantio's outrage

A02

Brabantio is outraged by the senate's willingness to accept Othello's elopement with Desdemona: 'For if such actions may have passage free/ Bond-slaves and pagans shall our statesman be' (I.2.98–9).

- Brabantio sees Othello as a threat to social order and stability.
- We are reminded of Othello's history – he was taken into slavery before he became a general.
- These words reveal the social attitudes of many people in Shakespeare's society: Brabantio implies slaves and foreigners should not be treated as equals.

Revision task 5: Male dominance in *Othello*

A02

Make brief notes on what you have learned about male dominance in the play, focusing on Brabantio's role as father and then extending your notes to include Othello and Iago as husbands. Write about:

- Brabantio as a father figure.
- Othello and Iago as husbands.

Roderigo

Who is Roderigo?

- Roderigo is a wealthy Venetian gentleman who had hoped to marry Desdemona.
- He is Iago's first victim, and is exploited for his money and in the plot to kill Cassio.

Roderigo: victim or villain?

As a disappointed suitor Roderigo represents the 'curled darlings' (I.2.68) that Desdemona rejected, providing us with a point of comparison with noble Othello.

Roderigo has extremely poor judgement and his actions are generally despicable. Often he seems villainous – he has no concern for Desdemona's feelings, making him a potential abuser of women. He shares responsibility with Iago for prejudicing Brabantio's view of Desdemona's elopement. In Cyprus, Roderigo participates in the attempt on Cassio's life without feeling convinced that his intended victim deserves to die. However, Roderigo is corrupted by Iago and not wholly bad, merely weak and foolish. He lacks resolution or volition and has to be directed off stage many times. Roderigo is suspicious of Iago, but allows himself to be talked round.

It is possible to see Roderigo as another outsider in *Othello*. Iago keeps him on the fringes of the action, ensuring that he remains powerless. Roderigo's miserable end seems a cruel fate. Like Othello he realises the truth about Iago too late. There is some rehabilitation of Roderigo's character in the final scene when his letters are discovered, revealing the truth about Iago's plots. Perhaps Roderigo, like Othello, is both victim and villain?

Progress booster: The subplot   A01

Notice how the subplot involving Roderigo is linked very closely to the main plot, so much so that they become interwoven. Roderigo's primary role is to enable the audience to gain insight into Iago's methods. In his exchanges with the 'poor trash of Venice' (II.1.301) the ensign Iago's evil nature is revealed. In the subplot Iago exploits Roderigo for his money, promising his victim that he will be able to enjoy Desdemona's sexual favours. In Cyprus, Iago propels Roderigo into the main plot. Roderigo is used as a pawn in two key scenes: the drinking scene where Cassio is provoked, and then the attack on Cassio's life in Act V. It seems appropriate that Roderigo is the first of Iago's victims to die: he was the first to be taken in. What other parallels between the main plot and the subplot can you find?

Key quotation: Understanding Roderigo's death   A02

When he dies Roderigo calls Iago an 'inhuman dog' (V.1.61).

- Roderigo realises the truth about Iago too late, and is **ironically** the first to recognise his villainy.
- The **imagery** of dogs is used repeatedly to describe Iago in Act V; it reinforces the audience's sense of Iago's vicious character.
- It is darkly ironic that Othello will also use dog imagery just before he kills himself, linking his evil actions to Iago's influence.

Bianca

Who is Bianca?

- Bianca is a courtesan, who is in love with Cassio.

Bianca the victim

Bianca is used and abused in *Othello*. She is seen only in relation to the male characters and is always in a vulnerable position. Cassio is prepared to dally with but not marry her. Iago accuses her of involvement in the plot to kill Cassio to distract attention away from himself. Bianca's vulnerability is a result of her social position, as well as her treatment by the male characters. As a prostitute, Bianca's only power lies in her ability to attract customers. If they choose to abuse her, Bianca's voice counts for nothing because her profession makes her morally dubious. Love also makes Bianca vulnerable. As Iago puts it, ''tis the strumpet's plague/ To beguile many and be beguiled by one' (IV.1.97–8). The irony is that Bianca is more honest and true than the outwardly honourable men who abuse her. Bianca's victimisation by Iago in Act V Scene 1 prepares us for the deaths of the other female victims in the final scene.

Study focus: Bianca the lover **A02**

Bianca's relationship with Cassio is less idealistic than the Othello–Desdemona match. However, Cassio is clearly more to Bianca than a mere 'customer'. Cassio tells us that 'she haunts me in every place' (IV.1.132–3), suggesting that Bianca is smitten with him. This explains her indignation about the handkerchief, which Bianca believes must be 'some minx's token' (IV.1.152). Bianca's unfounded jealousy **mirrors** Othello's. However, does Shakespeare suggest that Bianca has more plausible reasons for her jealousy than Othello? Notice how Bianca uses the word 'cause' when she complains about Cassio's week-long absence from her. She says woefully, 'To the felt absence now I feel a cause' (III.4.182). Her words **foreshadow** Othello's opening line in the final scene, when he repeats 'It is the cause' (V.2.1) to justify killing his wife. It is worth thinking about why Shakespeare links Bianca and Othello linguistically?

Cassio and Bianca make up, unlike the tragic central couple. We know this because Cassio is dining with Bianca before he is wounded in the final scene. In Act V, Bianca's genuine love for Cassio is seen when she discovers her lover has been stabbed: 'Alas, he faints! O Cassio, Cassio, Cassio!' (V.1.84). Her constancy in love links Bianca to Desdemona. Unlike the stereotypical crude and aggressive prostitute of much Renaissance drama, Bianca is a faithful lover.

Key quotation: Bianca's powerlessness **A02**

When Cassio sends her away because he doesn't want to be seen with her Bianca says: ''Tis very good: I must be circumstanced' (III.4.202).

- Bianca's words reveal how powerless she is.
- Bianca has to be content with the way men treat her, just like Desdemona.
- Bianca's acceptance of Cassio's authority over her foreshadows Desdemona's words and actions in Act IV Scene 2.

A03 **KEY CONTEXT**

Venice had a reputation for its courtesans. In Renaissance Venice there were two classes of courtesan: the *cortigiana onesta* (the intellectual courtesan) and the *cortigiana di lume* (lower-class prostitute who lived and practised her trade near the Rialto Bridge). Guidebooks were available, which gave the names, addresses and fees of Venice's most prominent prostitutes. Some courtesans were married women, some were single. Iago jokes with Cassio about his marrying Bianca, so we can assume she is single.

A05 **KEY INTERPRETATION**

Some critics have argued that Shakespeare criticises the double standards applied to male and female sexuality in *Othello*. Consider Bianca's defence of herself in Act V Scene 1 when she says 'I am no strumpet/ But of life as honest as you that thus/ Abuse me' (lines 121–3). To what extent do Bianca's words here support this interpretation?

THEMES

Jealousy

Jealousy and destruction

Jealousy is a form of tyranny in *Othello*. It destroys love, honour and nobility in those it afflicts. It makes both male **protagonists** murderous and violent. It also seems that it is the nature of jealousy not to be satisfied. Iago continues plotting against Cassio after he has disgraced him and is not content with disturbing Othello's peace of mind: he must continue until Desdemona is dead. Othello's jealous thoughts are characterised by references to acts of violence against Desdemona. He says he will 'tear her all to pieces!' (III.3.434) or 'chop her into messes' (IV.1.197). Othello also wants to torture and kill his supposed rival Cassio. Once his jealousy has been proved false, Othello turns his sword on himself. Jealousy has destroyed him. It also destroys Iago, whose torture is fitting punishment for his jealous crimes.

The imagery of jealousy

The **imagery** associated with jealousy suggests it is an all consuming, irrational emotion. It is 'the green-eyed monster, which doth mock/ The meat it feeds on' (III.3.168–9), 'a monster/ Begot upon itself, born on itself' (III.4.161–2). There is a strong sense of devouring and being devoured in these images, which fits in with Iago's description of Othello as being 'eaten up with passion' when he believes Desdemona is unfaithful (III.3.394). Shakespeare explores the monstrous power of jealousy again in *The Winter's Tale*, where King Leontes becomes convinced his wife, Hermione, has been unfaithful. Unlike Othello, whose mind is poisoned by a villain, Leontes's jealousy is fuelled by his own thoughts.

Study focus: Jealousy and madness

A02

Iago makes explicit connections between jealousy and madness. When Othello is overcome by jealous thoughts he falls down in a fit. Iago observes how 'he foams at mouth, and … Breaks out to savage madness' (IV.1.54–5). Later Iago feeds Othello's jealousy as Othello watches Iago's conversation with Cassio. Othello believes he is watching Cassio describe his adulterous liaison with Desdemona. Iago comments, 'As he [Cassio] shall smile, Othello shall go mad' (IV.1.101). Emilia also makes a connection between madness and jealousy when she describes how husbands 'break out in peevish jealousies' (IV.3.88). If jealousy is associated with madness, to what extent is Othello responsible for the actions he commits when he is under its influence?

Professional jealousy

Iago's professional jealousy, which can be linked to the sin of envy, sets the tragic events of the play in motion. Iago envies Cassio primarily because he is promoted to a post Iago has coveted. Iago is also envious of Cassio's superior manners and social status. As late as Act V, Iago is still motivated by jealous thoughts about Cassio. Iago says Cassio must be destroyed because of the 'daily beauty in his life/ That makes me ugly' (V.1.19). Ask yourself whether there is an element of professional jealousy in Iago's treatment of Othello. Does the ensign wish to destroy Othello's military reputation, as well as his marriage?

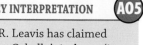

KEY INTERPRETATION A05

F. R. Leavis has claimed that Othello's jealousy 'is unassociated with any real interest in Desdemona as a person'. He says Othello 'slips ... readily into possessive jealousy because he is "self-centred"'. To what extent do you agree with these comments?

PROGRESS BOOSTER A03

For the best grades you must take into consideration different ways of looking at the text. For example, you might make a **feminist** interpretation of the play, exploring the presentation of gender roles. Or you could take a **New Historicist** approach and look at the way ethnicity is presented, taking into account Elizabethan ideas about race (see **Part Five: Historical Context**).

Sexual jealousy

There are three examples of sexual jealousy in the play, all of them unfounded. Bianca, Iago and Othello all believe that they have been betrayed by those they love, and they are all wrong. Does sexual jealousy turn Iago into a villain? Iago's aim is to make Othello and Cassio suffer as he suffers because he fears he has been cuckolded. Unlike Othello, Iago is cool and calculating when he chooses to act on his suspicions, suggesting jealousy follows on naturally from hatred in his characterisation. This is not the case with Bianca and Othello. Their sexual jealousy is a response to feelings of genuine love when they believe their partners have been unfaithful. Perhaps Othello's insistence on proof might suggest that this jealous husband is a nobler man than Iago.

Iago's sexual jealousy is prompted by rumours that 'the lusty Moor/ Hath leaped into my seat' (II.1.293–4). These words suggest sexual jealousy is prompted by competitiveness, as well as possessiveness. This is something we see again when Othello's overpowering jealousy takes hold. Othello cannot bear the idea of Desdemona's 'stolen hours of lust' (III.3.341). He feels he has been 'robbed'. In *Othello* sexual jealousy seems to be the 'flipside' of boundless love. What Othello shares with Iago is covetousness: both men feel jealous because they have lost possession of something that they held dear.

Finally, *Othello* suggests jealousy is ridiculous and humiliating, as well as terrifying and corrosive. Iago's motives for revenge are inadequate, and the proofs he provides flimsy. It is horribly humiliating that Othello, a renowned and experienced soldier, should kill his wife and himself because of a handkerchief, which has absurdly come to symbolise his own and Desdemona's honour.

A04 KEY CONNECTION

Sexual jealousy is an important theme in other plays by Shakespeare. In the comedy *Much Ado About Nothing* the young lover, Claudio, believes his fiancée, Hero, has been unfaithful with another man and rejects her at the altar. His suspicions are proved false and the couple are reunited at the end of the play.

A05 KEY INTERPRETATION

There are several indications in the text that we should not view Othello as a naturally jealous man. When Brabantio warns him that Desdemona may deceive him, Othello is dismissive. He replies, 'My life upon her faith' (I.3.295). Othello trusts his wife completely. It seems that Iago's cunning, Othello's trust in his ensign, and his quick decision-making all conspire to make a jealous man out of him.

Key quotation: Jealousy **A02**

Emilia's definition of jealousy suggests how irrational and corrosive it is: 'jealous souls will not be answered … They are not jealous for the cause,/ But jealous for they're jealous' (III.4.159–61).

- Emilia's words can be applied to both Iago and Othello – neither has a just 'cause' for his actions.
- Iago's jealousy 'will not be answered': Iago's professional grudge against Cassio and Othello turns into a multiple murder plot.
- Othello's jealousy 'will not be answered': he refuses to believe Desdemona's protestations of her innocence.

Revision task 6: Jealousy and Othello's marriage **A02**

Make brief notes on what you have learned about the way in which jealousy contributes to the destruction of Othello's marriage. Write about:

- The contribution of Iago's jealousy to the destruction of Othello's marriage.
- The qualities and consequences of Othello's jealousy.

Love and relationships

Double standards

At the heart of *Othello* is the idea of double standards, a concept which still exists today. Codes of conduct for men and women are very different in this play, as they were in Shakespeare's society. Men have more personal freedom, and women are judged by them and in relation to them. Bianca's vulnerable status as 'strumpet' (IV.1.97) reminds us of the double standard. It is socially acceptable for Cassio to consort with a courtesan, but it is presumptuous for Bianca to expect him to marry her. Iago pretends to help Roderigo in his adulterous pursuit of Desdemona because it enables him to keep hold of his 'purse' (I.3.381). Men toy with and discard women as they choose. Iago's successful vilification of Desdemona is the key example of this. Iago uses the double standard to his advantage when he blackens Desdemona's name. The masculine code of honour is threatened by the idea of active female sexuality, so Iago destroys Othello by making the hero believe his chaste wife has strayed. There are two types of women in Othello's world: chaste wives or whores. If Desdemona is not one, then she must be the other. If she is a whore, she has to be punished.

Progress booster: Gender and power

It's important that you can discuss how power is a key factor in all the relationships portrayed. To begin with we are presented with a picture of powerful womanhood: Desdemona has deceived her father and asserted her independence from **patriarchy** by choosing her own husband. The example set by Desdemona shows that male–female relationships are the focus of conflict in this play; they are about opposition and power. Throughout the play we see further power struggles between couples and friends: Iago competes with Desdemona for Othello's ear; Desdemona and Emilia defend themselves against their husbands' suspicions; Bianca tries to assert her rights as Cassio's mistress. The women lose these power struggles. By the end of the play all the female characters are silenced, their fragile power negated. That they ever had any power is debatable. They are only ever seen in relation to the male characters, who have the power to describe, define and kill them.

Couples

Initially, Desdemona and Othello stand apart from the other couples because they have a harmonious relationship. There is no disillusionment or dissatisfaction here. The relationships of Bianca and Cassio and Emilia and Iago are not happy. The former is an unequal match between a 'customer' (IV.1.120) who feels a limited affection and a 'bauble' (IV.1.134), whose genuine love makes her unhappy. Cassio reveals the limitations of this relationship – which he clearly feels is unworthy in some way – when he tells Bianca to be gone because he would not be seen in her company. Emilia and Iago are a chilling match. Marriage has made Emilia cynical about male–female relationships. She knows she is merely 'food' (III.4.105) for Iago, acceptable until she disobeys him and refuses to be silent, at which point her husband tries to kill her.

The misogyny of Iago casts a dark shadow over Othello's relationship with Desdemona, which seems so full of optimism and delight at the start of the play. Despite their different social, cultural and racial backgrounds the hero and heroine symbolise a meeting of two minds in Acts I and II. Othello loves Desdemona for her feminine grace and sympathy; she loves him for his masculine heroism. Essentially, Othello and Desdemona love each other harmoniously because of the differences they perceive in each other. These differences become distorted by an interloper, a man who cannot bear to see two lovers 'well tuned' (II.1.198). The envious, unhappily married Iago destroys true love.

A love triangle?

In some ways it is possible to see the Othello–Desdemona–Iago relationship as a warped kind of love triangle. Iago seeks to displace Desdemona. What is it that he objects to so strongly when he looks at Othello and Desdemona together? Why does Iago wish to get between them? The text suggests that there is something very complicated going on. Iago's responses to the feminine reveal a mixture of fear and loathing. Part of his contempt for Othello is located in his fear that Desdemona has power. Iago has been sidelined. We know from his mocking reference to Desdemona as Othello's 'general' (II.3.310) that he cannot bear the fact that a female exerts influence. Iago despises Othello for giving into love, which he sees as a feminine, unworthy emotion. Iago's derision of love and the female is also illustrated when he sneers about Desdemona being able to 'play the god' with Othello (II.3.342). Iago loathes the idea of a man being in thrall to a woman, believing Othello is weakened and trapped by love. Othello's soul is 'enfettered' to Desdemona's love, so much so that 'she may make, unmake, do what she list … With his weak function' (II.3.340–3).

Iago responds to this by denigrating Desdemona and by making her voice seem unreliable. The power struggle comes into sharp focus when we consider the vow Iago makes to Othello at the end of Act III Scene 3: 'I am your own for ever' (line 482). Iago's fake love destroys Othello's real love. Othello begins to assert his masculine power in an overbearing way because he believes that Desdemona has begun to assert herself sexually. To any Renaissance husband, this would be unacceptable. We might see the events of Acts IV and V as an attempt by Othello to reassert his own power over Desdemona. Because of this we come to associate masculine love with violence. Iago's misogyny triumphs.

Key quotation: Emilia on marriage   **A02**

Emilia has a disillusioned view of marriage: ''Tis not a year or two shows us a man./ They are all but stomachs, and we all but food' (III.4.104–5).

- These words remind us that the female characters are powerless in *Othello*; they are 'food' for their men.
- Emilia's cynical comments undermine the romance of the marriage of Othello and Desdemona.
- Emilia reminds us of the importance of not judging by first impressions and appearances.

Revision task 7: Women as victims   **A02**

Make brief notes about the extent to which you believe the women in the play are portrayed as powerless victims. Write about:

- Whether Desdemona, Emilia and Bianca have any power in their relationships.
- How and why the female characters lose control over their fates.

A05 PROGRESS BOOSTER

If you are asked to write about the ways in which love and marriage are presented in *Othello* you need to link these themes to the cultural and historical context of the play in order to get the best grades. For example, you could consider the status of women in a patriarchal society when commenting on the ways in which Desdemona, Emilia and Bianca are treated by the male characters.

A05 KEY INTERPRETATION

In 'The Noble Moor' (1956), Helen Gardner suggests that Desdemona is 'love's martyr'. By dying she wins Othello's love again. Do you find this reading of the end of the play plausible?

A03 KEY CONTEXT

In the Renaissance, men expected to command and control their wives. Desdemona submits willingly to Othello's authority. On her marriage day she says, 'My heart's subdued/ Even to the very quality of my lord' (I.3.251–2). Later she obeys Othello even when he strikes her, saying 'I will not stay to offend you' (IV.1.246). Desdemona proves that she is a good Renaissance wife, even if she does deceive her father.

Race and colour

Othello's race

It is not possible to define Othello's race exactly. There have been suggestions that he is a Negro, Arabian, Berber or that his Spanish name makes Othello a 'Morisco', a descendant of the Moors of Granada, whose famous palace at Alhambra was built in the fourteenth century. It can be argued that Othello's race is irrelevant. If this is the case, why did Shakespeare break with dramatic tradition and present a Moorish hero? Before Othello black characters in Renaissance drama were usually villains. The wealth of **imagery** of black and white and light and dark suggests that colour is significant in this play (see **Part Four: Language**). At the time *Othello* was written there were various stereotypes of the black man, most of them negative. From the medieval period onwards the devil was often depicted in art as a black man surrounded by the flames of hell. Other traditions associated the black man with lust, sin and death. Prior to *Othello*, 'blackamoors' in plays and pageants were usually sinister figures.

Contrasting views of Othello's blackness

There are opposing views about Othello, and his race is at the heart of the way he is perceived. Early in the play positive descriptions of Othello's blackness come from the Moor himself, the Duke of Venice and Desdemona. The fact that Othello has risen to the important and powerful position of general and is accepted as a distinguished member of Venetian society suggests that the state he serves is prepared to see good in foreigners and accept that they have a useful role to play.

However, it is noticeable that even Desdemona, who never regrets marrying Othello, is forced to explain her choice. She defends her marriage by saying she 'saw Othello's visage in his mind' (I.3.253). This suggests either that Desdemona looked past his colour or that Othello's stories and origins excited her. Is Shakespeare suggesting that Othello is the exception to the rule that black is usually bad, or urging us to see that racial differences do not matter in love? If this is the case, Desdemona holds a radical point of view for a **Jacobean** heroine. She is probably the only character in the play who does not view mixed marriages with anxiety. Do the Duke's words to Brabantio suggest caution or racial tolerance? Consider the line, 'Your son-in-law is far more fair than black' (I.3.291). Is this an attempt to excuse Othello's blackness? Does it mean 'Try to accept your daughter's marriage because Othello is virtuous, even though he is black'? Or is this an example of another 'colour blind' white character dismissing race as an irrelevance?

Even when Othello doubts his attractions as a middle-aged black husband, we will recognise that the hero is more noble and impressive than any of the other male characters in the play. Othello is compelling because he is different. His history is fascinating and heroic. It is important to remember that the heroine made an active and positive choice. Othello stresses this when he says 'she had eyes and chose me' (III.3.192). It is Desdemona who insists – publicly – on being allowed to enjoy her marital rights, not Othello.

KEY INTERPRETATION A05

In '*Othello* and the Radical Question', 1998, Ania Loomba notes that, 'because Othello is needed in order to combat the Turks, the Senate is willing to regard him as "more fair than black" but for Desdemona's father such colourblindness is not possible. Here we see a tension between the state and the family.' Loomba wonders, 'How might an English audience have reacted to the Senate's pronouncements?' What do you think? Would a seventeenth-century theatre-goer respond to Othello's race differently from a twenty-first-century audience?

KEY INTERPRETATION A05

The famous black actor Paul Robeson, who was a notable Othello, said the play was 'a tragedy of racial conflict; a tragedy of honour rather than of jealousy ... [It] is because he is an alien among white people that his [Othello's] mind works so quickly, for he feels dishonor more deeply'. A victim of racial prejudice himself, Robeson saw Othello as an underdog. How do you respond to Robeson's reading of Othello's situation?

There is a negative view of Othello's blackness, which is undermined because we are not encouraged by Shakespeare to respect the speakers, or we at least question their judgement. To Iago, Roderigo and Brabantio, Othello's colour and racial background – particularly in relation to his marrying a white female – are alarming. Their references to a 'sooty bosom' (I.2.70), 'the thicklips' (I.1.65) and 'an old black ram' (I.1.87) who practises witchcraft construct a negative racial stereotype of Othello. This stereotype would have been very familiar to Shakespeare's audience, even though it makes us uncomfortable today. It is important to remember that the negative racial descriptions of Othello, which dominate the play at times, are inaccurate. The Othello they describe does not exist, although it is possible to argue that the hero begins to display some of the negative aspects of the stereotype when he is persecuted by Iago. Othello is superstitious (the handkerchief), he is passionate (he weeps many times) and he does become violent.

Study focus: Othello the outsider (A02)

New Historicist critics have argued that Othello's tragedy comes about because he can never be anything except an outsider. Othello is in an impossible position as a black man serving a white **patriarchy**. Is Othello foolish to expect his adopted society to accept his marriage to a white woman? There are other ideas of dislocation to consider. We might feel that the hero is dislocated because he marries, turning his back on his profession to become a husband. Othello becomes further dislocated when he views his own race negatively, giving in to Iago's prejudice. Consideration of Othello's dislocation must include an assessment of his final speeches, which suggest he is not his noble self because he has become a villain. Gratiano and Montano never mention Othello's race when they take him prisoner; they simply want to punish the 'rash and most unfortunate man' for his crimes (V.2.280). References to the devil are reserved for Iago at the end of the play, linking him firmly to the theme of dislocation. In the final scene race is not the cause of Othello's dislocation: his murderous actions are.

(A03) **PROGRESS BOOSTER**

To get the best grades it is important to consider a range of contextual factors when writing about the play. One of the key contexts you should consider in relation to Othello is the way in which the tragic **protagonist** conforms to and challenges Renaissance stereotypes about race.

Key quotation: Race and colour (A02)

Desdemona views Othello's origins positively. When asked if Othello is jealous she praises her husband's character: 'I think the sun where he was born/ Drew all such humours from him' (III.4.30–1).

- Desdemona's positive view of Othello's race provides a clear contrast with the negative Renaissance racial stereotype of Othello as a cruel, savage black man, which comes across in Iago's speeches.
- Desdemona's positive view of Othello's origins echoes Othello's own early positive descriptions of himself, showing how well matched the couple are, in spite of their racial difference.
- **Ironically**, Desdemona is wrong about Othello: he does become jealous, although Shakespeare does not suggest Othello has a propensity to jealousy because he is black.

(A03) **KEY CONTEXT**

England and Morocco were closely linked in the late sixteenth century through trade. Elizabeth I set up the Barbary Company, and an embassy of Moroccans was received at court in 1600. At the same time, Elizabeth was responsible for a decree that tried to expel foreigners, specifically Negroes and 'blackamoors', from England in 1601. English attitudes to 'foreigners' were clearly contradictory. We see similar contradictions in *Othello*. The Duke accepts Othello's marriage to Desdemona, while Brabantio cannot.

PROGRESS CHECK

Section One: Check your understanding

These short tasks will help you to evaluate your knowledge and skills level in this particular area.

1. Make a list of 3–4 key reasons why you think Othello's tragedy is inevitable.
2. Write a paragraph explaining why you think Roderigo is important to the play.
3. How is Bianca treated in the play? Make brief notes on what happens to her.
4. What aspects of Cassio's character are appealing?
5. Write a paragraph summing up the relationship between Othello and Iago.
6. Race is a key issue in the play. Create a table comparing the ways the different characters feel about race.
7. Write down at least three ways in which the play explores the theme of love.
8. Write a paragraph explaining the significance of Emilia's role.
9. What evidence is there that Brabantio is a good father?
10. List 3–4 ways jealousy plays a part in the events of the play.

PROGRESS BOOSTER

For each Section Two task, read the question carefully, select the key areas you need to address, and plan an essay of 6–7 points. Write a first draft, giving yourself an hour to do so. Make sure you include supporting evidence for each point, including quotations.

Section Two: Working towards the exam

Choose one of the following five tasks which require longer, more developed answers:

1. 'In Act III Scene 3 Othello gives into jealousy too easily.' Do you agree?
2. Discuss the presentation of idealised love in *Othello* in Act I Scene 3.
3. 'In Act V Scene 2 Emilia is the only truly impressive and honourable character.' Do you accept this view of Emilia?
4. 'In Acts IV and V Desdemona's passivity in her relationship with Othello makes her unappealing to modern audiences.' To what extent do you agree?
5. 'The male characters are unworthy of the women who love them.' To what extent do you agree?

Progress check (rate your understanding on a level of 1 – low, to 5 – high)	1	2	3	4	5
How the main characters contribute to the main action, themes and ideas					
How the minor characters contribute to the main action, themes and ideas					
The different ways each character can be interpreted in terms of Shakespeare's presentation of them					
What the key themes of the play are					
How the key themes reflect wider ideas about society both at the time and today					

GENRE

Tragedy

The origins of tragedy

Greek tragedy is based on conflict and depicts the downfall of high-ranking characters, who make fatal errors of judgement (**hamartia**) because of their overweening ambition and pride (**hubris**). They are destroyed swiftly by the disastrous consequences of their errors. There is a strong element of fate determining the outcome in Greek tragedy, which the tragic hero dies fighting against. At the end of Greek tragedies justice and order are restored and a new status quo is established. **Catharis** – a purging of the emotions – has taken place. **Aristotle** suggested that tragedy should evoke pity and fear (**pathos**) in an audience.

Greek tragedy and *Othello*

Othello fits into the classical mould in a number of ways. Othello is a high-ranking general and is descended from a line of kings. Many believe that he suffers from hubris. What do you think? Is Othello overambitious when he marries Desdemona? Does he overreach himself when he tries to combine the roles of soldier and husband? Is the hero too proud and self-satisfied? It is possible to argue that there is a sense of inevitability about Othello's downfall from the moment he arrives in Cyprus and declares he feels 'too much joy' (II.1.195). Undoubtedly, the tragic denouement in Act V evokes feelings of fear and pity. Emilia performs some of the functions of a Greek **chorus** when she comments on Othello's folly.

Conflict and suffering in tragedy

Conflict lies at the heart of all Shakespeare's tragedies. Driven by negative impulses and emotions – envy, hatred, lust and personal ambition – characters in **tragedies** find themselves embroiled in disputes with each other. Often these disputes lead to disorder and division. They also cause great suffering to the tragic protagonist and those around him. In *King Lear*, Shakespeare explores what happens when Lear selfishly divides his kingdom, and the terrible consequences of his disputes with his daughters. In this play the whole nation is affected by the king's foolish actions. In *Othello*, Shakespeare presents a different type of conflict. The focus is narrower. The conflict we witness is in Othello's mind. Othello becomes divided against himself, conflicted about whether he loves or hates Desdemona. His conflict causes him great suffering and anguish, which intensifies as the play moves towards the tragic outcome. Shakespeare does not suggest that Othello deserves to suffer, but the audience knows that the consequences of the hero's conflict will be terrible. In tragedy, conflict and suffering end in violent death. When Othello's internal conflict drives him to murder, we know that the resolution of the play must include the tragic **protagonist's** own demise.

However, *Othello* is a highly original tragedy. Shakespeare presents the first black hero in English drama, departing from theatrical convention. Shakespeare also subverts tragic conventions by keeping the evil revenger Iago alive at the end of the play. In most **Jacobean** tragedies the villain dies as part of the process of catharsis so that order can be restored. Iago's dominance in this tragedy is also unusual; the villain and hero have equivalent stage time and are equally powerful speakers.

A03 **KEY CONTEXT**

A chorus is a group of characters, featured in the tragedies of Ancient Greece who represent the ordinary people in their attitudes to the action. They witness and comment on events, but do not participate in them.

A02 **PROGRESS BOOSTER**

In classical tragedy, the hero's tragic end is inevitable. Make sure that you can comment on this aspect of genre in relation to *Othello*.

A01 **PROGRESS BOOSTER**

To get the best grades you must use terminology accurately when commenting on the language, form and structure of the play. When you are writing about *Othello* as a tragedy, you may find it useful to include some of the Greek terms associated with the genre, e.g. hubris, hamartia, pathos. Be sure that you understand what they mean.

A05 **KEY INTERPRETATION**

Although in 'Diabolical Intellect and the Noble Hero' (1963), F. R. Leavis accepts Othello is a tragic hero, he does not believe that Othello learns anything in the course of the play. He claims that Othello realises his folly but there is 'no tragic self-discovery'. As a result, Othello 'is now seen as tragically pathetic'. Is this how you view Othello at the end of the play?

Study focus: Shakespearean tragedy and *Othello*

In his **tragedies** Shakespeare explores the nature of good and evil, the disintegration of families and the breakdown of law and order within states or countries. In *Othello*, Shakespeare pits good (Othello) against evil (Iago) and we watch as the tragic hero's new family unit is destroyed against the backdrop of the Turkish conflict. As well as observing some of the conventions of Greek tragedy, Shakespeare makes effective use of the theatrical conventions of his own age. By the time he came to write *Othello*, it was usual to present tragedies in five acts, with a climax or turning point in Act III and a tragic outcome in Act V.

Love and pity in *Othello*

Othello is a tragedy preoccupied by the nature of love. In Act I we are presented with a couple whose deep mutual love makes them appealing to the audience. We side with Othello and Desdemona in the Senate scene in Act I Scene 3 because their love is threatened. As the play progresses our admiration for the couple is turned to pity, as we watch Iago destroy their relationship. From Act III love is undermined by mistrust, uncertainty and jealousy. However, in spite of the violent deaths in Act V, it is possible to argue that love reasserts itself at the end of *Othello*. Desdemona defends her love for Othello with her dying breath, and the tragic protagonist dies 'upon a kiss' (V.2.357).

PROGRESS BOOSTER A02

A key theme in tragedy is isolation. Think about how the villain Iago works to isolate the characters from each other in *Othello* and why he does this. You might also consider to what extent Iago's success lies in his own isolation. Or does Iago need others for his plans to succeed?

The power of the villain in *Othello*

In *Othello* the tragic hero becomes a victim because of the evil schemes of the villain, Iago. The suffering of the central couple is a direct result of his malicious plotting. The audience will recognise that Othello has faults, but that he is a noble man brought low by a very powerful adversary. The play is extremely painful to watch because we know how untrustworthy the villain is from the very first scene, and can see how expert Iago is at exercising his power.

The influence of comedy

PROGRESS BOOSTER A02

If you are asked to write about genre you need to be able to discuss whether *Othello* is a domestic tragedy. In Renaissance drama a domestic tragedy is a tragedy in which the protagonists are ordinary middle-class or lower-class individuals. This contrasts with classical tragedy, in which the central character is usually a king or of noble rank and his downfall not simply a personal matter, but also an affair of state with consequences for the whole nation he rules.

Shakespeare makes use of a number of theatrical conventions that his audience would have recognised as belonging to comedy. These borrowings reveal Shakespeare's ability to work innovatively with the tragic form. The central focus in the play – the jealous husband who fears he has been cuckolded – is more often associated with comedy than tragedy. Iago is a descendant of the cunning slaves of Roman comedy, who delight in outwitting their masters. The foolish father Baptista and his wily daughter Bianca, who chooses her own husband in Shakespeare's early comedy *The Taming of the Shrew*, are ancestors of Brabantio and Desdemona. Both – deceived father and deceptive daughter – are stock characters from comedy.

Revision task 8: *Othello* as tragedy

Write brief notes about what you have learned about *Othello* as a tragedy. Write about:

- How *Othello* conforms to the conventions of classical tragedy.
- Whether *Othello* is simply a domestic tragedy.

STRUCTURE

Dramatic structure

The use of settings

There is a narrow focus in *Othello*. There are two principal locations, Venice and Cyprus, but gradually our attention becomes fixed on a single bedroom, creating a feeling of claustrophobia that is unique in Shakespeare's tragedies. The outer world becomes insignificant as Othello becomes obsessed and jealous. The use of Venice as a location is significant. At the end of the sixteenth century, dramatists began to use Italy as a suitable location for **revenge tragedies**. The Italians were thought to be worldly and Venice in particular was associated with everything that was culturally sophisticated. It was a location that suggested power, order and wealth.

It is appropriate that the **Machiavellian** trickster Iago should originate and appear in an Italian setting before being transported to Cyprus. Shakespeare's use of a war with the Turks and the uneasy atmosphere of the garrison town in Cyprus – a 'halfway house' between civilisation and the heathen world – is also dramatically significant. The war isolates Desdemona from everything and everyone she knows; similarly, Othello feels his difference and isolation in Cyprus when he is 'Perplexed in the extreme' (V.2.344). Here, in this unfamiliar setting, with the threat of danger lurking, passions are unleashed and order is destroyed. The storm helps to establish and reflect the fear and violence that the characters will experience in Cyprus, while also being a symbol of the love of Othello and Desdemona.

A sense of claustrophobia

The sense of claustrophobia is heightened by the fact that there is no real subplot in *Othello*. The action of the play focuses on Iago's role and Othello's reactions to his 'reports' (V.2.183). Even the characters who seem to have other 'lives' are closely linked to the married couple: Roderigo's foolish hopes and Cassio's relationship with Bianca provide points of comparison with the Othello–Desdemona match. Our sense of claustrophobia is heightened because we are observing a group of characters who exist in a tightly knit social network, where each character has a clearly defined position and a view of every member of the group. Iago threatens the order and harmony of the network because he is able to manipulate the most powerful group member. The single plot intensifies dramatic tension: we are never given a moment's respite to look away from Iago's progress as he pushes Othello towards tragedy.

A04 **KEY CONTEXT**

As well as being a setting associated with sophistication and culture, Venice had a reputation as a place of liberty. In particular, foreign visitors noticed the way in which young men were brought up to have loose morals. In his *History of Italy* (1549), William Thomas noted that the Venetians 'bring up their children in so much liberty that ... by that time he cometh to twenty years of age' a young man 'knoweth as much lewdness as is possible to be imagined'.

A02 **PROGRESS BOOSTER**

When writing about *Othello* it is important to remember that you are writing about a play. Making references to specific dramatic methods Shakespeare uses, e.g. **mirroring**, **foreshadowing**, will help you to demonstrate your understanding of the genre.

KEY INTERPRETATION **A05**

All the main characters (with the exception of his wife, interestingly) call Iago 'honest', and the ensign makes extensive use of the word himself when deceiving his victims. It is as if Shakespeare is showing Iago's insidious power to 'enmesh them all' (II.3.357) through his ability to get his victims to think of and describe him in the same way. For comments about the fifty-two uses of the word 'honest' in the play, see William Empson in John Wain (ed.), *Othello* (1971).

Study focus: Long and short scenes **A02**

The construction of scenes is extremely effective in *Othello*. Long scenes of painful discussions or confrontation are punctuated by short scenes or moments of violence – verbal and physical. Act III Scene 3 is a good example of how Shakespeare structures a scene for maximum theatrical impact. It is the longest scene in the play, and painful to watch. Iago takes full advantage of the awkwardness that already exists between the married couple. His relentless assault on Othello begins after Desdemona has tried and failed to get Cassio reinstated. When he knows he has hooked Othello, Iago exits. It is safe to leave because Othello has just asked him to set Emilia spying on Desdemona: Iago's poison is working. Othello's first moment of isolation shows his agony. He asks wretchedly, 'Why did I marry?' (III.3.245). After further awkward exchanges between the major characters, Othello is back in Iago's clutches. From line 331 to the end of the scene, 130 lines later, Othello's speeches become explosive and bloodthirsty. By the end of the scene Othello's 'fair warrior' (II.1.179) has become 'the fair devil' (III.3.481). Iago has won the battle of words.

Reversal and repetition

The structure of the play relies on reversal and repetition. In the first three acts Iago comes to dominate. In Act I he is the underdog, overlooked and irrelevant except as an escort for Desdemona. In Act II, Iago forms his plans and sets up his revenge, so that in Act III he is able to 'triumph' over Othello. Conversely, Othello is at his most secure in Acts I and II, when he defends and then consummates his marriage. In Act III he struggles to resist the jealousy that threatens to overpower his reason, succumbing to it in Act IV. In Act V, Othello sinks further when he smothers Desdemona. He becomes what Iago is: a destructive revenger. At the end of the play the tragic **protagonist** is partially redeemed when he recognises his folly and chooses to destroy himself, while Iago's downfall is assured when he is revealed as a scoundrel. Can you find other repetitions and reversals?

Timescale of *Othello*

The 'double time scheme'

The theory of a 'double time scheme' in *Othello* dates from the middle of the nineteenth century. There can be no doubt that there are inconsistencies in the way time is presented in *Othello*. It appears that the disintegration of Othello's mind and marriage occurs extremely fast and Iago recognises that he must move quickly if his plots are to remain concealed; at the  same time the characters make statements that suggest time is moving quite slowly.

'Long time'

In Act III Scene 3, Iago describes Cassio's lustful dream, which we are told occurred 'lately' (III.3.416) when Iago shared Cassio's bed. In Act III Scene 4, Bianca complains to Cassio that he has stayed away from her a week, and Othello himself says that he believes Desdemona has committed adultery with Cassio 'A thousand times' (V.2.210). It seems highly unlikely that Lodovico would be sent from Venice to install Cassio as governor within a week of Othello's arrival in Cyprus. These statements which suggest 'long time' are primarily designed to increase the plausibility of Othello's jealousy. But it is also necessary for Shakespeare to present the poisoning of Othello's mind occurring swiftly, without a substantial interval of time. The play would be less dramatic if Iago loosened his grip on his victim once he was in his grasp.

'Short time'

This brings us to the question of 'short time'. The first act of *Othello* takes place in one night. When the characters have arrived in Cyprus (after a period travelling) time seems to move very quickly, increasing the sense of claustrophobia and heightening the intensity of the drama. The characters land just before 'this present hour of five' (II.2.9–10), the wedding celebrations occur that evening, Cassio is dismissed from his post the same night and we see Iago packing Roderigo off to bed at dawn the following morning. On this day Desdemona pleads for Cassio, having met with him earlier in the morning. Iago sees his chance and moves into action immediately. Between Act III Scene 3 and Act IV Scene 1 there might plausibly be a short interval, but thereafter there can be no break until the curtain falls at the end of Act V. It is this relentlessness that grips us in the theatre, where we do not notice the inconsistencies. It might also be argued that an insistence on 'short time' is a deliberate theatrical decision. Perhaps Shakespeare uses his time scheme to show us how powerful and unreasonable jealousy is. We know that Desdemona has not had the opportunity to commit adultery, and yet her husband becomes convinced she has betrayed him often.

A02

Progress booster: Night-time

Notice how the majority of the scenes in the play take place at night. The opening scene occurs in the street in Venice at night, and the play ends in Othello's bedroom in Cyprus at night. Cassio's reputation is destroyed at night after a drunken brawl. In Act V he is wounded by Iago in the street at night. Roderigo and Emilia are also stabbed at night, dying of their wounds. What significance does this have? Because Iago is present or has instigated all the violent events that occur at night, we know that night-time is associated with his evil progress. Iago has been able to use the cover of darkness to conceal his plots, so it is highly appropriate that he is unmasked at night. However, because so much of *Othello* occurs at night, it can be argued that there is never any doubt that evil will triumph over goodness.

A05 KEY INTERPRETATION

Helen Gardner states that the 'terrible end' of Othello has 'a sense of completeness' which makes it 'the most beautiful end in Shakespearean tragedy'. How would you argue for or against Gardner's viewpoint?

LANGUAGE

Styles of speech

Othello's characteristic speech style

From his opening speeches in Act I Scenes 2 and 3 it is clear that Othello's characteristic **idiom** is dignified, measured **blank verse**. This helps establish his heroism and nobility. Othello's speeches demonstrate authority in Act I Scene 2. There is a sense of danger and beauty in Othello's references to 'bright swords' and 'dew' (line 59), when he is confronted by Brabantio and his followers. Shakespeare makes us aware that Othello is an impressive character and a powerful speaker. This power is reinforced in the next scene when Othello uses words not just to defend his elopement with Desdemona, but also to enable him to keep her. If Othello does not speak persuasively the 'bloody book of law' (I.3.68) may deprive him of his wife. Desdemona acknowledges her husband's rhetorical power when she speaks. She was seduced by his storytelling. Desdemona uses the same dignified and purposeful idiom that Othello employs. Through their shared speech patterns Shakespeare conveys the harmony and mutual affection of Othello and Desdemona. The lovers are, as Iago expresses it, 'well tuned' (II.1.198) at this point.

Othello the poet

Many of Othello's long speeches can be compared to poems, expressing the nobility and romance we come to associate with the tragic **protagonist**. Othello is Shakespeare's most 'poetic' hero, which seems appropriate because we focus on his experiences of love in this play. But Othello does not just speak of his love poetically; he speaks of his career as a soldier in the same vein, establishing himself as a great military man. The orderliness of Othello's verse suggests not just his confidence as a lover, but also the fact that the senate are wise to trust in Othello's judgement. Because of his measured speech style, we accept the poetic hero as both soldier and husband in the first act of the play.

Study focus: The power of language in *Othello*

Elizabethan and **Jacobean** dramatists used language to establish and build dramatic atmosphere, to define time, place and character. But in *Othello*, language is not simply the medium by which the drama is conveyed: in this play language is action. Othello 'falls' because he believes Iago, whose every utterance is deceptive. Through language, Iago imposes his will on the hero, and creates opposition within Othello's marriage. When Othello is taken in by false words, **tragedy** is the result. This play shows us the power of words. We watch as characters construct their own and others' identities through language, and exert power either by speaking, remaining silent or silencing others.

Othello's corruption

When Othello is corrupted by Iago's false words, his stately style begins to break down. At his lowest point, just before he falls down in a fit, Othello's words convey his agitation. In Act IV Scene 1 lines 35–43 he asks questions and barks out a series of short exclamations. He exclaims 'handkerchief!' three times. Othello's fractured sense of self is conveyed through the words and syntax. His speech ends with these lines: 'It is not words that shakes me thus. Pish! Noses, ears and lips. Is't possible? Confess? handkerchief! O devil!' (IV.1.41–3).

There is a terrible **irony** in Othello's declaration that 'It is not words that shakes me thus'. The events of the play and the violence of his outburst suggest that words are destroying Othello. Notice the use of disjointed **prose** rather than measured verse: reason has given way to passion. Othello also uses oaths, such as 'Zounds' (II.3.203), which are associated with Iago.

Progress booster: Language and disintegration

A02

Notice how from Act III onwards Othello and Desdemona struggle to understand one another's language. The break-up of their marital harmony is conveyed through the disruption in the lines, and Othello's measured calm gives way to verbal bullying (see III.4.80–98). By this point Othello misconstrues everything Desdemona says. Eventually, failing to see that her words should be taken at face value, Othello smothers and silences Desdemona. When confronted with the truth Othello then recovers, returning to the majestic idiom of his earlier speeches at the end of Act V. His final speech echoes his first speech to the senate, but Othello no longer speaks of himself as a worthy hero. Now he compares himself to 'the base Indian' and 'the circumcised dog' (V.2.345 and 353).

Iago's speech style

Language is the source of Iago's power, but his characteristic idiom is different from Othello's. It is full of **colloquialisms** and oaths, befitting a cynical soldier. But Iago's use of language is more complicated than this. The villain slips between prose and verse, adapting his style to suit his different audiences and purposes. The fast-moving prose of his exchanges with Roderigo conveys Iago's crude nature, but the ensign makes use of a loftier style too, as in his **parody** of Othello's speech style in Act III Scene 3 (lines 465–72). Most worryingly, Othello begins to use Iago's base idiom when he decides to revenge himself on Desdemona, showing Iago's increasing authority over him.

Iago's use of **asides** reveals his cunning, destructive nature. The villain is able not only to direct but also to comment on the action of the play. Iago's use of **soliloquies** reinforces his power. In *Othello*, Iago speaks his soliloquies first (Othello's soliloquies occur towards the end of the play), drawing the audience in as he outlines his intentions. Because we know exactly what his plans are, we might feel that Shakespeare forces us to admire the villain. Iago's soliloquies and asides are also a source of a great deal of the **dramatic irony** of *Othello*, which increases dramatic tension.

Finally, Iago is able to use silence effectively, as in Act III Scene 3 when he deliberately introduces 'stops' (III.3.123) to infuriate and intrigue Othello. By appearing reluctant to talk, Iago gains the opportunity to speak at length and poison Othello's mind. At the end of the play Iago's defiant silence can suggest continued power (the villain refuses to reveal his motives and admit remorse) or power thwarted. It is both ironic and appropriate that Iago is unmasked by Emilia, whose powers of speech he has ignored.

A02 KEY INTERPRETATION

An **aesthetic** critique of the play might consider the ways in which Shakespeare's use of language and imagery contributes to the artistic merit of *Othello*. For example, does the use of prose and vulgar, often sexual, language of the play detract from its aesthetic value, as some critics have argued?

A05 KEY INTERPRETATION

Some critics have argued that Iago's refusal to speak, repent or explain his actions at the end of the play ultimately leaves the audience unsatisfied. To what extent do you agree with this interpretation?

A04 KEY CONNECTION

In the 1981 BBC Shakespeare production of *Othello*, Bob Hoskins's Iago continues to laugh (as he has done throughout the play) after he refuses to speak. The production ends with the sound of Iago's echoing laughter as he is taken away for torture. Iago clearly feels he has triumphed.

KEY INTERPRETATION

Aesthetics is a branch of philosophy which deals with the nature of art, beauty and 'good taste'. An aesthetic approach to *Othello* might focus on the linguistic beauty of the play. For example, you could analyse the imagery and structure of Othello's poetic speeches, comparing the way he speaks when he first appears in Act I and during Act V. What does the imagery he uses in these scenes reveal about the development of his characterisation as a tragic hero?

PROGRESS BOOSTER

Consider the way in which images are used to evoke particular audience responses. For example, how does Shakespeare intend us to feel when we hear Lodovico's comment that the image of the bodies on the bed at the end of the play 'poisons sight' (V.2.362)?

Imagery

Poisoning

There are a number of **images** of poisoning, which we come to associate with Iago. In Act I Scene 1 the ensign says that he wants to 'poison his [Brabantio's] delight' (I.1.67) so that he can make trouble for Othello. Iago's jealousy of the Moor is so strong that it 'Doth like a poisonous mineral gnaw my inwards' (II.1.295). So Iago resolves to 'pour this pestilence into his ear' (II.3.351). These references to poison are appropriate to Iago, whose actions are swift and deadly. Iago relishes the pain he causes, as we can see from his description of his methods in Act III Scene 3. Iago is gleeful as he describes how his poison will 'Burn like the mines of sulphur' (see III.3.329–32).

Othello describes how he feels tortured by jealousy, using images that recall Iago's words, 'If there be cords or knives,/ Poison, or fire, or suffocating streams,/ I'll not endure it' (III.3.391–3). The most chilling reference to poison comes in Act IV Scene 1 when Othello decides to murder Desdemona:

OTHELLO: Get me some poison, Iago, this night. I'll
not expostulate with her, lest her body and beauty
unprovide my mind again. This night, Iago.
IAGO: Do it not with poison, strangle her in her bed –
even the bed that she hath contaminated. (IV.1.201–5)

His mind poisoned with foul thoughts, Othello now seeks to kill Desdemona in the bed that he thinks she has poisoned with her lust. It is particularly chilling that the real poisoner (Iago) suggests the method of killing Desdemona. Iago's power is underlined at the end of the play when Lodovico looks at the 'tragic loading' of bodies on Othello's bed, commenting that it 'poisons sight'. The final image of poisoning in the play emphasises the terrible consequences of infection in *Othello* (V.2.361–2).

Hell and the devil

Shakespeare's use of imagery of hell and the devil subverts the negative stereotype of the evil black man and links Iago firmly to the figure of the **vice** from medieval drama. Iago is associated with images of hell and the devil from the start of the play. He makes the link himself at the end of his **soliloquy** in Act I Scene 3. Outlining his evil intentions Iago says, 'Hell and night/ Must bring this monstrous birth to the world's light' (I.3.402–3). Later there is the **oxymoron**, 'Divinity of hell!', followed by these lines:

When devils will their blackest sins put on
They do suggest at first with heavenly shows
As I do now. (II.3.345–8)

There is delight in these lines. Iago revels in evil. Iago also describes Othello as 'the devil' (I.1.90), but in the context of the play this seems to be a racial slur rather than a comment on Othello's character. Elsewhere Iago comments on the Moor's natural goodness, which makes his (Iago's) work easier. Iago's hellish designs succeed in making Othello see Desdemona as devilish. Othello makes a 'sacred vow' (III.3.464) to wreak vengeance on her 'by yond marble heaven' (III.3.463), convincing himself that Desdemona is damned and must be stopped in her life of sin. In Act IV Scene 2, Othello attempts to force an admission of guilt from Desdemona:

Come, swear it, damn thyself,
Lest, being like one of heaven, the devils themselves
Should fear to seize thee ... (IV.2.36–8)

In this image we see the enormity of Desdemona's crime from Othello's point of view. As he leaves in disgust, Othello turns to Emilia and accuses her too; she 'keeps the gates of hell' for Desdemona (IV.2.94). Emilia turns these words on Othello in the final scene when she discovers Desdemona's murder: 'thou art a devil' she rages, 'the blacker devil' (V.2.131 and 129). But it is Iago who is revealed as the true devil, where he is described as a 'hellish villain' (V.2.366). When he realises the truth about Iago in Act V Scene 2, Othello is bewildered by the ensign's evil. He asks, 'Will you, I pray, demand that demi-devil/ Why he hath ensnared my soul and body?' (V.2.298–9).

Animals and insects

There are numerous references to animals and insects which chart Othello's downfall. In Iago's mouth this imagery is reductive and negative. Several images suggest how much the villain despises his victims. In Act I Scene 1, Iago sets out with Roderigo to 'Plague him [Brabantio] with flies!' (I.1.70). When he describes Othello's match with Desdemona Iago uses crude animal imagery: 'an old black ram/ Is tupping your white ewe!' he informs Brabantio (I.1.87–8); his daughter has been 'covered' with 'a Barbary horse' (I.1.110); the couple are 'making the beast with two backs' (I.1.115). Othello is an object of scorn too. Iago is confident that the Moor will 'tenderly be led by th' nose/ As asses are' (I.3.400–1), and made 'egregiously an ass' (II.1.307). Iago is sure that Cassio can be humiliated too: 'With as little a web as this will I ensnare as great a fly as Cassio' (II.1.168–9).

Othello is infected by this imagery. But the animal imagery in Othello's speeches reveals the hero's misery, rather than sneering triumph. In Act III Scene 3, Othello says:

I had rather be a toad
And live upon this vapour of a dungeon
Than keep a corner in a thing I love
For others' uses. (III.3.274–7)

The image of a toad is repeated in Act IV Scene 2 when Othello describes his sorrow at 'losing' the innocent Desdemona he loved so much. Othello is mortified by corruption. (See IV.2.58–63.)

Iago maintains Othello's jealousy with images of bestial lust. When the Moor demands proof of his suspicions Iago replies sharply:

It is impossible you should see this
Were they [Cassio and Desdemona] as prime as goats, as hot as monkeys,
As salt as wolves in pride ... (III.3.405–7)

We know that Othello has lost all power of reason and can no longer fight off the terrible sexual images his imagination has been polluted with when he yelps 'Goats and monkeys!' (IV.1.263). Othello has become the 'monster, and a beast' he described earlier in the same scene (IV.1.62). It is horribly **ironic** that Desdemona, who we are informed could 'sing the savageness out of a bear' (IV.1.186), cannot convince Othello that his suspicions are false. Appropriately, the last animal images in the play are applied to Iago, whose evil makes him an 'inhuman dog' (V.1.62) and a 'Spartan dog' (V.2.359).

The sea and military heroism

In stark contrast to the imagery associated with Iago, the imagery commonly associated with the noble Othello of the first half of the play is suggestive of power and bravery. Images of the sea and military heroism abound. Othello describes his illustrious career with dignity in Act I Scene 3 (see lines 82–90 and 129–46). Desdemona echoes him when she says:

A04 **KEY CONNECTION**

As well as images of animals and insects, there are references to monsters and monstrous acts throughout the play, which help us to understand Iago's evil and Othello's pain, and how they develop. Do you agree with Othello's assessment of himself as a 'monster'?

A02 **PROGRESS BOOSTER**

Violence is implicit in the sea and military imagery associated with Othello. As he prepares to take his own life Othello refers to his military career, but also recognises that he has reached 'my journey's end, here is my butt/ And very sea-mark of my utmost sail' (V.2.265–6). This final image of the sea is poignant. By reverting to the noble imagery associated with him earlier in the play Othello is able to raise himself again in our esteem.

KEY CONTEXT **A03**

Images of military heroism complement the Cyprus setting of the play. Why is it important to the play's tragic plot that Othello, Iago and Cassio are soldiers?

My downright violence and scorn of fortunes
May trumpet to the world. My heart's subdued
Even to the very quality of my lord ... (I.3.250–2)

By using the terminology of war to describe her love we see that Desdemona is 'well tuned' (II.1.198) with her husband. It is fitting then that Othello describes Desdemona as his 'fair warrior' (II.1.179). Later, when Othello feels their marital harmony has been destroyed, we sense how deeply he feels Desdemona's supposed betrayal as he spurs himself on to revenge, the **imagery** suggesting the violence to come:

  Like to the Pontic sea
Whose icy current and compulsive course
Ne'er feels retiring ebb but keeps due on
To the Propontic and the Hellespont:
Even so my bloody thoughts with violent pace
Shall ne'er look back, ne'er ebb to humble love (III.3.456–61)

Black and white

References to black and white are important. There are also images of light and darkness, heaven and hell (see **Hell and the Devil** above). These images are related to the central paradox in the play: Othello, who is 'far more fair than black' (I.3.291), is the virtuous, noble man, while white Iago proves to be a devilish creature with a black soul. When Iago blackens Desdemona's character, Othello feels his honour is threatened; he expresses his dismay by referring to his own blackness in a negative way. Up to this point Othello has been proud of his race and secure in his love. Now we sense that the 'black' (in the sense of angry, violent) Othello will supersede the 'fair' Othello:

PROGRESS BOOSTER **A02**

Watch out for the imagery of blood in *Othello*. You can relate it to the portrayal of violence and jealousy. For example, Othello repeatedly uses the word 'blood' when his mind is infected and he starts to play the role of revenger.

I'll have some proof. Her name, that was as fresh
As Dian's visage, is now begrimed and black
As mine own face. (III.3.389–91)

We might feel that these lines describe Othello's regret at the corruption of his imagination by Iago. He no longer has a 'fresh' name; instead his mind – as well as his name – is 'begrimed', just as Desdemona's name has been besmirched. Later in the same scene Othello calls for assistance with his revenge: 'Arise, black vengeance, from thy hollow cell' (III.3.450). Here Othello seems to link himself to hell and darkness, even though he also feels that he is serving heaven by making 'a sacrifice' (V.2.65) of Desdemona. The confusion suggested by these images is appropriate: the hero is pulled in two directions for much of the play, wanting to believe that Desdemona is honest, while also believing that she is damned.

KEY INTERPRETATION **A05**

All Shakespeare's **tragedies** include extremely violent acts and deaths. In *Antony and Cleopatra*, another of Shakespeare's tragedies which focuses on doomed love, both the major characters kill themselves: Antony runs himself through with a sword and dies in his lover's arms, while Cleopatra poisons herself with an asp (a snake).

Desdemona is associated with images of light, divinity and perfection throughout the play. The final **metaphor** Othello uses to speak of her suggests her purity and preciousness; she is 'a pearl' he threw away like a 'base Indian' (V.2.345). As he prepares to kill her Othello cannot quite believe that Desdemona was false; the metaphor 'Put out the light, and then put out the light!' (V.2.7) expresses this idea clearly. The drama of the play occurs as Othello moves away from the light of Desdemona's love towards the darkness of Iago and his world view, becoming a black villain in the process. Notice how many of the key scenes or events occur at night (see **The Timescale of *Othello*** above). It might be argued that we associate Othello with darkness from the very beginning of the play: his first entrance occurs at night, and his final act, the murder of Desdemona, also occurs at night. Has the Moor fulfilled his tragic destiny when he snuffs out the light on Desdemona and himself?

Irony

Irony and Iago

There are various types of **irony** in *Othello*, which relies heavily on **dramatic irony** for its effects. There are also examples of situational and verbal irony which help us to understand the action. Iago is the primary source of dramatic irony. He informs us of his intentions, but his victims do not know that they are being manipulated. The audience knows more than the characters, increasing the tension. Will Iago succeed in his diabolical designs or will he be discovered?

It can be argued that the irony that surrounds Iago and his role forces us to reject the villain. We may marvel at his ingenuity and skill but we cannot approve of Iago. We become increasingly worried by the verbal irony of repeated references to him as 'honest'. There is considerable irony in the use of the word 'love' in this play too. Notice how frequently it is on Iago's lips when he is manipulating his victims. Iago's use of the word 'love' is particularly chilling in the scenes in which we watch the true love of Othello and Desdemona being destroyed by the false and empty love Iago pretends to feel.

An audience might also feel that in some ways the joke is on Iago. He thinks that he is a cunning villain, who can arrogantly conceal his true self and remain aloof while all around him 'lose their cool', but is he not driven by passion? Iago's downfall is ironic. He is brought down by two characters he had no respect for and believed he controlled. Emilia destroys Iago's reputation as an honest man and Roderigo's letters condemn him to torture.

Irony and Othello

The many ironies of Othello's situation create his tragedy. The noble warrior is destroyed by his petty-minded subordinate. The great soldier becomes a jealous lover. Othello's military strengths – decisiveness and ruthlessness – are weaknesses in his personal life. The man who roved the world, fighting on its battlefields, dies by his own hand in a bedroom, under armed guard. Othello falls at the very moment that he feels he has reached the height of his success by marrying the 'divine Desdemona' (II.1.73). When his conception of himself is most secure, Othello is undermined. Othello finds that his heroic past counts for nothing: he is forced into the role of villain by the 'inhuman dog' Iago (V.1.62). Having been resolutely sure of Desdemona, Othello finds himself wondering why he has married, convinced that he has united himself with 'the cunning whore of Venice' (IV.2.91). For her own part, Desdemona expects to consummate her marriage in Cyprus, but her marriage bed is transformed into her deathbed. Othello's conviction that his wife has weak morals is heartbreakingly ironic; when he doubts Desdemona, the hero reveals his own weaknesses.

Progress booster: Other examples of irony

Make sure you can discuss other examples of irony in the play. Ironically, other characters reveal their weaknesses when they feel they are on the brink of or have achieved success. Cassio gains promotion only to be disgraced for drunken brawling; Roderigo hopes to kill Cassio and supplant him in Desdemona's affections, but is instead murdered by the man who urged him on to the vile deed, a man whose friendship he believed in. This kind of ironic ignorance is repeated in other relationships in *Othello*. None of the characters truly recognises the real honesty or depravity of those they interact with.

A01

A02 PROGRESS BOOSTER

A comparison of the scenes in which songs are sung in *Othello* will help you to understand Shakespeare's uses of dramatic irony and **mirroring**. In Act II Scene 3, Iago leads the singing of a bawdy drinking song as part of his strategy to get Cassio drunk. The genial mood Iago establishes hides his poisonous intentions. In Act IV Scene 3, Desdemona sings the melancholy willow song. Iago's bawdy singing – ironically – leads indirectly to Desdemona's song about doomed love.

A02 PROGRESS BOOSTER

Dramatic irony is used by many playwrights, but in a play such as *Othello*, in which secrets, lies and people's own words unwittingly condemn them, it is worth mentioning, in relation to AO2, how it is particularly effective in creating tension and tragic momentum.

PROGRESS CHECK

Section One: Check your understanding

These short tasks will help you to evaluate your knowledge and skills level in this particular area.

1. Make a list of 3–4 key reasons why *Othello* is a flawed tragic hero.
2. Write a paragraph discussing whether Othello is responsible for his own tragic downfall.
3. Make a list of 3–4 ways in which the tragic denouement fits in with the conventions of classical **tragedy**.
4. Write a paragraph summing up why Shakespeare sets the first act of the play in Venice.
5. Identify 3–4 examples of **foreshadowing** which contribute to a sense of tragic inevitability.
6. Write down at least three examples of **mirroring**, explaining how they add to your understanding of themes and events.
7. Write a paragraph explaining how Othello's speech style changes during the play.
8. Write a paragraph summing up Shakespeare's use of imagery in relation to Iago.
9. Write a paragraph summing up the significance of the night-time settings in *Othello*.
10. Make a list of 3–4 key examples of **irony** in the play.

PROGRESS BOOSTER (A01)

For each Section Two task, read the question carefully, select the key areas you need to address, and plan an essay of 6–7 points. Write a first draft, giving yourself an hour to do so. Make sure you include supporting evidence for each point, including quotations.

Section Two: Working towards the exam

Choose one of the following five tasks which require longer, more developed answers:

1. 'Iago's use of language is the source of his power.' Explain how Iago uses language to achieve his aims in Act III Scene 3.
2. Using Act II Scene 1 as a starting point, discuss how Shakespeare uses the Cyprus setting to contribute to the tragedy of *Othello*.
3. To what extent is the **imagery** used about women in *Othello* misogynistic?
4. Explain how Shakespeare's use of imagery contributes to the dramatic impact of the tragic denouement.
5. 'Conflict is at the heart of tragedy.' Discuss the types of conflict that Shakespeare explores in *Othello*.

Progress check (rate your understanding on a level of 1 – low, to 5 – high)	1	2	3	4	5
How the speech styles of the major characters change as the play progresses					
How the play is structured so that the tragic outcome seems inevitable					
The ways Shakespeare uses imagery to contribute to your understanding of the play					
What the settings contribute to the themes and events of the play					
How Shakespeare uses dramatic conventions (e.g. irony, mirroring, foreshadowing) to create the tragedy of *Othello*					

CONTEXTS

Historical context

The Renaissance

The Renaissance (literally 'rebirth') saw a revival of artistic and intellectual endeavour, which began in Italy in the fourteenth century. It spread gradually northwards across Europe, and is first detectable in England in the early sixteenth century in the writings of the scholar and statesman Sir Thomas More and in the poetry of Sir Thomas Wyatt and Henry Howard, Earl of Surrey. Its keynote was a curiosity in thought which challenged old assumptions and traditions. There was a new confidence in human reason and in human potential which challenged old convictions. Classical texts and the culture of Greece and Rome were rediscovered and, with this rediscovery, the 'golden age' of English literature began, of which Shakespeare's plays are part.

Shakespeare's drama and the Renaissance

Shakespeare's drama is innovative and challenging in exactly the way of the Renaissance. It examines and questions the beliefs, assumptions and politics upon which Elizabethan society was founded. And although his plays conclude in a restoration of order and stability, Shakespeare subverts traditional values, as we see in *Othello*, where the tragic hero is a black man and the heroine an assertive young woman. Critical, rebellious, mocking voices, like Iago's, are heard in Shakespeare's plays. Are characters like Iago given subversive views to discredit them, or were they the only ones through whom a voice could be given to radical and dissident ideas? Was Shakespeare a conservative or a revolutionary?

Because of censorship, any criticism Shakespeare makes of the way those in authority behave, or questions he asks about race and nobility, had to be muted or oblique. Direct criticism of the monarch or contemporary English court would not be tolerated. This has something to do with why Shakespeare's plays are always set either in the past, or abroad, as is the case with *Othello*.

A03 PROGRESS BOOSTER

Ensure that you have an excellent understanding of the contexts that lie behind *Othello*. On a superficial level you could say that *Othello* is a **tragedy** about love. It is the historical and cultural context that makes the play a complex work. Knowledge and understanding of how Shakespeare uses and challenges the beliefs and values of his day are key.

A03 KEY CONTEXT

In 1600, John Pory published a translation of John Leo's *A Geographical Historie of Africa*, which Shakespeare may have consulted when writing *Othello*. Leo was a Moor who had been brought up in Barbary. He described his countrymen as being honest, credulous, 'proud and high-minded', and wrote that 'no nation in the world is so subject unto jealousy; for they will rather lose their lives than put up any disgrace in the behalf of their women'. Does Othello display any of the traits described by Leo?

A05 KEY INTERPRETATION

In 'Othello and the Radical Question', 1998, Ania Loomba writes, 'England was increasingly hostile to foreigners, both officially and at a popular level, and London had witnessed several major riots against foreign residents and artisans. Would this play have unsettled or reinforced such hostility?' What do you think? Does *Othello* subvert or reinforce negative racial attitudes?

Nationalism and xenophobia

As a student of *Othello*, you need to be aware of the attitudes that existed towards foreigners in Elizabethan England. Italy had what Norman Sanders has called a 'double image'. On the one hand, it was a land of refinement and romance, a model of civilisation. Venice, Europe's centre of capitalism, was a free state, and renowned as one of the most beautiful cities in Italy.

On the other hand, Italy was a country associated with decadence, villainy and vice. Venice itself was suspect, because it was, as Norman Sanders puts it , 'a racial and religious melting pot'. Elizabethans were against mixed marriages and viewed Negroes and 'blackamoors' with suspicion. Elizabeth I issued edicts demanding their removal from England because they were considered an 'annoyance'. What we would now deem racist views were common, and many believed that black people were fit only to be slaves.

Religion in Shakespeare's England

The nationalism of the English Renaissance was reinforced by Protestantism. Henry VIII had broken with Rome in the 1530s and in Shakespeare's time there was an independent Protestant state church. Shakespeare's plays are free from direct religious sentiment, but their emphases are Protestant. Othello has converted to Christianity and the preoccupation with good and evil in the play suggests its religious context. The central figures of many of Shakespeare's plays, including *Othello*, are frequently individuals beset by temptation and the lure of evil. Shakespeare's heroes have the preoccupation with self and the introspective tendencies encouraged by Protestantism. We see an example of Othello's introspection in Act III Scene 3 when he is alone on stage and begins to doubt his attractions as a husband (see his speech at line 262).

Shakespeare's tragic heroes are haunted by their consciences; they agonise over their actions as they follow what can be understood as a spiritual progress towards heaven or hell. This is exactly the psychological journey Othello goes on. We see evidence of Othello's tormented conscience both before and after he kills his wife. Desdemona remarks on Othello's inner torment when she says in alarm, 'Alas, why gnaw you so your nether lip?/ Some bloody passion shakes your very frame' (V.2.43–4).

Female subordination

Although questions were being asked about the social hierarchy, women remained in subordinate roles, their lives controlled by **patriarchy** during the Renaissance. Women expected to be ruled by men, as Desdemona's submission to Othello demonstrates. Women had few legal rights. They were entitled to inherit property, but if they married, everything they owned passed to their husbands. Many men saw women as possessions, and fathers expected to choose husbands for their daughters, as Brabantio does in *Othello*. Intellectually, women were thought to be inferior to men, and incapable of rational thought. They rarely received an education. Assertive and argumentative women were seen as a threat to the social order and were punished for their behaviour with forms of torture such as the ducking stool, the scold's bridle (an iron framework placed around the head) or 'carting' (being carted around town and publicly mocked).

However, European visitors to England commented that English women had more freedom than was the case in many other European countries. Shakespeare's wife successfully managed a home and property, as well as her family, for twenty years while Shakespeare was pursuing his career in London. Shakespeare's audiences included women, and he wrote a large number of parts for strong-minded female characters, like Desdemona and Emilia.

KEY CONTEXT   A03

Renaissance dramatists were heavily influenced by Seneca, a Roman playwright who reworked the plays of the ancient Greek Athenian dramatists. Senecan **tragedy**, characterised by long narrative accounts of events and long reflective **soliloquies**, explores revenge and is full of violence.

PROGRESS BOOSTER   A05

Interestingly, in *Othello*, it is the villain who has the most soliloquies – but is Iago a genuinely reflective character? Rory Kinnear, who played Iago in the National Theatre production of 2013, thought Iago was not reflective. He commented that Iago 'exists in an absence of feeling'. To what extent do you agree?

Shakespeare's theatre

The form of the Elizabethan theatre derived from the inn yards and animal-baiting rings in which actors had performed in the past. They were circular wooden buildings with a paved courtyard in the middle open to the sky. A rectangular stage jutted out into the middle of this yard. Some of the audience stood in the yard (or 'pit') to watch the play. They were thus on three sides of the stage, close up to it and on a level with it. These 'groundlings' paid only a penny to get in, but for wealthier spectators there were seats in three covered tiers or galleries between the inner and outer walls of the building, extending round most of the auditorium and overlooking the pit and the stage. Such a theatre could hold about 3,000 spectators. The yards were about 80ft in diameter and the rectangular stage approximately 40ft by 30ft and 5ft 6in high.

Staging practices

On the Shakespearean stage there was very little in the way of scenery or props – there was nowhere to store them, nor any way to set them up. Anyway, productions had to be transportable for performance at court or at noble houses. The stage was bare, which is why characters often tell us where they are. Location in Shakespeare's plays can be symbolic. Descriptions of places are used to create a specific dramatic mood or situation. The storm in Cyprus that opens Act II of *Othello* is described verbally by the characters on stage, to create a mood of tension for the audience.

During night-time scenes characters may mention they cannot see what is going on to establish a sense of danger, as happens in Acts I and V of *Othello*. Torches, tapers and candles would have been used to signify night to the audience. The main prop for *Othello* would have been the bed on which Othello strangles Desdemona: it would have dominated the stage. Although Othello's violence against Desdemona is shocking, it needs to be considered in context. The Elizabethans lived in a violent world. Domestic abuse was not uncommon and, except in cases of extreme cruelty, not considered unacceptable.

Stage history of *Othello*

Othello has been one of Shakespeare's most frequently performed plays. The first recorded performance was at the Banqueting House at Whitehall in London (see photo) on 1 November 1604. It was attended by James I, patron of Shakespeare's company, the King's Men. The first actresses to play Desdemona would have appeared on the **Restoration** stage. The diarist Samuel Pepys saw the play twice and noted how the audience called out in horror when Desdemona was killed. In the eighteenth century, partly because of the presence of women on the stage and in the audience, it was felt necessary to make refinements to the text so that *Othello* met contemporary standards of decorum. For example, Desdemona's willow song was removed because it was thought unladylike, and Othello's speeches were cut to emphasise his nobility.

A03 **KEY CONTEXT**

No one is quite sure when the tradition of playing Othello as a black man started, although he was certainly played as such by white actors in 'blackface' on the Restoration stage. The tradition of 'blacking up' continued well into the twentieth century. The 1981 BBC TV production of *Othello* features Anthony Hopkins in the title role, wearing black make-up.

A04 **KEY CONNECTION**

The American actor Paul Robeson (1898–1976) played Othello in theatres in America and across Europe throughout his career. One of the productions of *Othello* he appeared in still holds the record for the longest-running Shakespeare play on Broadway, giving an indication of how the play's popularity has endured. For Robeson, *Othello* was 'a tragedy of racial conflict'. To what extent do you agree with this view?

The tradition of cutting the play continued into the nineteenth century, by which time there were two types of Othello on stage: the controlled, dignified Moor or what Norman Sanders describes as the 'blazing portrayal of torrential sexual passion and wild jealousy'. One of the most famous productions of the 1870s involved the Italian actor Tommaso Salvini, who spoke all his lines in Italian while the other characters spoke English. Salvini's Othello was noted for his eroticism and savagery. He prowled around the stage like a tiger, pounced on Desdemona in Act V Scene 2 and 'dashed with her … across the stage and through the curtains … You heard a crash as he flung her on the bed and growls as if of a wild beast over his prey' (see J. R. Towse, *Sixty Years of the Theatre*, 1916). Ira Aldridge, a black American performer who emigrated to England because of racial discrimination against black actors in the USA, was another notable nineteenth-century Othello. He was the first documented black actor to play Othello when he appeared at Covent Garden in London in 1833. He also played Lear, Shylock, Macbeth and Hamlet.

Contemporary productions

In the twentieth century *Othello* remained popular on stage, as it is today. Lenny Henry took on the role of Othello and had a notable success with it in 2009. According to *The Times* (19 February 2009), Henry captured the dignity, anger, bewilderment and pain of Othello. In 2011, Clarke Peters and Dominic West appeared together in Sheffield as Othello and Iago. West played the role of Iago with a Yorkshire accent as 'a bluff, dirty-minded NCO [non-commissioned officer] who is filled with a rancorous, destructive negativity … he has a surface honesty … that yields a lot of laughs' (Michael Billington, *Guardian*, 21 September 2011). Cassio was played as 'a bit of a rake', making Othello's sexual jealousy plausible, while Emilia was 'raunchy' and 'sex starved', 'with an eye for a young lieutenant'.

In 2013 the National Theatre staged *Othello* in a modern war zone setting which revealed 'the play's paranoid mood and uncomfortable humour', according to Henry Hitchings (*London Evening Standard*, 23 April 2013). The director Nicholas Hytner chose to focus on the 'military details and merciless ironies' of the plot, rather than on race. The Cyprus setting was a stark military compound, where, as the *Evening Standard* critic remarked, 'there's not much room for her [Desdemona's] marriage to breathe'. Charles Spencer commented that this production reminded the audience that the tragedy of *Othello* 'is also an intensely painful psychological thriller' (*Daily Telegraph*, 24 April 2013). Adrian Lester's Othello was praised as charismatic and dignified, with Henry Hitchings also remarking on his 'integrity and vulnerability'. According to Hitchings, Rory Kinnear's Iago made deception 'seem creepily amusing'. This Iago was portrayed with 'sickly intensity and occasional bursts of thuggish jubilation'.

KEY CONNECTION

Rex Gibson (see *Shakespearean and Jacobean Tragedy*, 2000) notes how in the twentieth century *Othello* 'proved a significant symbol in the struggle for black emancipation'.

KEY CONNECTION A04

Reviewing the 2013 National Theatre production of *Othello* in the *Guardian*, Susannah Clapp admired Adrian Lester's performance as Othello. She commented that 'the eloquence that breaks out of him as he murders and dies is terrible and marvellous'. Clapp seems to be suggesting that Lester's portrayal of Othello adhered to the classical conception of the tragic hero, whose downfall should evoke pity and fear in the audience.

Settings

Othello is set in Venice and Cyprus. The military events of the play are based on historical fact. Selim the Second launched the Turkish attack on Cyprus in 1570. Act I covers the events of one night in Venice, while Acts II–V are set in Cyprus, which was governed by Venice at the time when the play was set. The two settings are symbolically significant.

Venice

Elizabethan dramatists often used Italianate settings for plays about intrigue, secret love affairs and revenge. This is because foreign courts were stereotyped as being full of villainy and sexual perversion. Venice had a reputation as a city of wealth and sophistication, but was also perceived as a place of loose morals. Shakespeare is able to use the Venetian setting to establish Othello as an outsider. Although he serves the senate, Othello is not Italian, unlike his adversary, Iago. Iago is a typical Italianate villain: scheming, selfish and amoral. Iago is able to make much of Othello's outsider status, convincing him that he does not understand the society he serves.

Cyprus

Cyprus is the 'warlike island' (II.1.43) under occupation. The conflict and danger of the setting are **mirrored** in the tragic events that unfold there. Away from the 'civilisation' of Venice, Iago's evil schemes prosper. Cyprus is threatened by the Turks; Othello's peace of mind and marriage are threatened by Iago. Othello is sent to Cyprus to govern and restore peace. Instead of bringing peace, Othello destroys his wife and then himself. Cyprus is also an isolated setting, which is psychologically appropriate. Secure in their love in Venice, Othello and Desdemona are wrenched apart in Cyprus. It is tragically **ironic** that a once great soldier should die for love in a war zone.

Study focus: Sexuality and setting

The Italian setting is an important backdrop to the way sex and sexual jealousy are portrayed. At the time the play was written Venice was renowned for its large number of courtesans, and was thus a setting associated with sexual sin. Shakespeare's audience would have been familiar with the stereotype of the sexually decadent Italian female from visits to the theatre. Many **Jacobean** plays set in Italy feature courtesans and adulteresses. In *Othello* the perceived immorality of Italian women is neatly encapsulated in Emilia's description of adultery as 'a small vice' (IV.3.69).

Iago makes much of the fact that Desdemona is a sexually sophisticated Venetian noblewoman. He convinces Othello that he knows the 'country disposition' (III.3.204) of Italian women and that it is to be expected that his wife should stray. Iago tells Othello, 'In Venice they do let God see the pranks/ They dare not show their husbands; their best conscience,/Is not to leave't undone, but keep't unknown' (III.3.205–8). Iago is implying that Desdemona is sexually corrupt; she is likely to commit adultery without bad conscience. For the first audiences of the play – and Othello – this is a plausible argument. It makes Othello's sexual jealousy convincing. In Act III Scene 3 Othello becomes sexually insecure, wondering if his wife has strayed because he is 'black/ and have not those soft parts of conversation/ That chamberers have' (III.3.267–9). His words here show how Othello begins to doubt himself as a lover because of his identity as outsider. He is not a gallant Italian gentleman, well versed in the flattery and seduction of women.

A02 PROGRESS BOOSTER

You need to be able to discuss the ways in which the different settings used in the play contribute to the **tragedy** which unfolds. For example, you could discuss the ways in which Iago uses his 'insider' knowledge of Venice and its decadent sexual stereotypes to undermine Othello and Desdemona's love. Or you could analyse the ways in which Iago manipulates events in the military setting of Cyprus to further his plots.

A02 PROGRESS BOOSTER

Iago's relentless focus on Desdemona's bedroom throughout Acts III and IV turns it into a setting of terror and tragedy in Act V. Desdemona seems to have a premonition of her own death when she says she wants her wedding sheets to be her shroud in the willow scene, Act IV Scene 3. It is horribly **ironic** that the tragic heroine makes the link between her marriage bed and death herself. It is also deeply tragic, and degrading, that a military hero should end up killing himself in his wife's bedchamber.

A04 KEY CONNECTION

Bedroom settings are often locations associated with tragedy in Jacobean drama. In *Hamlet* Hamlet confronts his mother Gertrude in her closet or bedchamber, urging her to repent the sin she has committed by remarrying, while in *'Tis Pity She's a Whore*, Giovanni kills the sister he has had an incestuous love affair with in her bedroom.

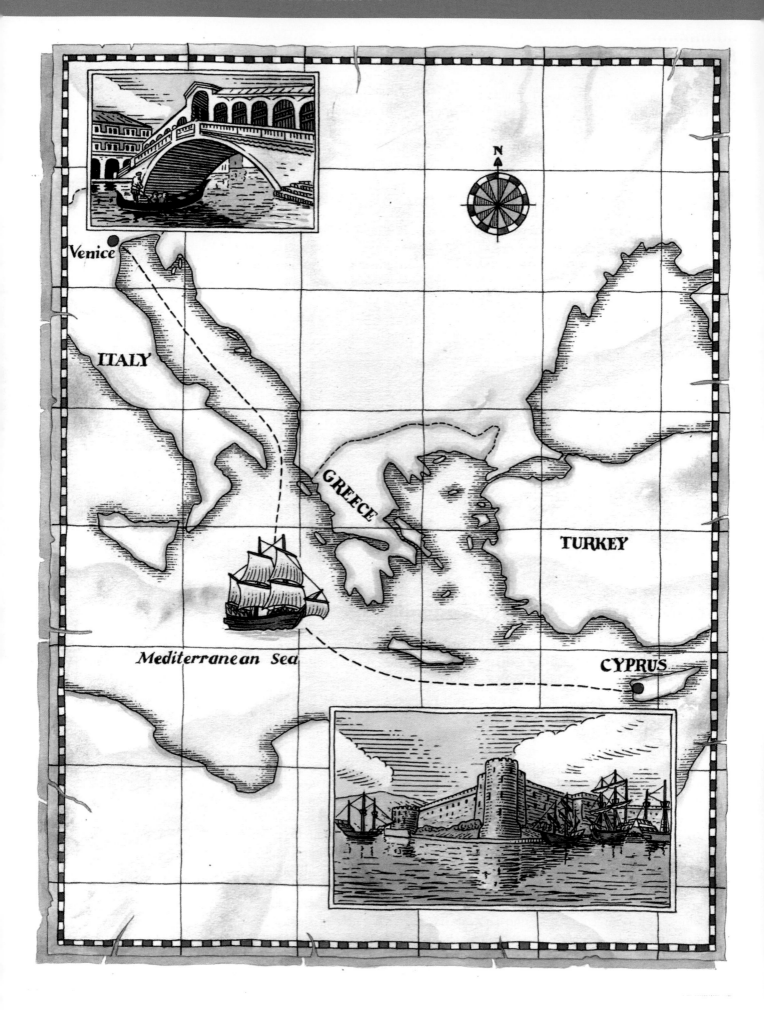

Literary context

Shakespeare and his contemporaries

Shakespeare had previously portrayed a pair of doomed lovers in *Romeo and Juliet* (c. 1595), which features a young couple (Juliet is only 13, Romeo a little older) from rival Veronese families, the Capulets and Montagues. Because of the feud, the love between Romeo and Juliet is as subversive and unacceptable to their families as Othello's marriage to Desdemona. In both *Romeo and Juliet* and *Othello*, Shakespeare explores the tragic consequences of intense love. In each play the tragic heroine is assertive, but the **patriarch** – Capulet or Brabantio – expects his daughter to make a socially acceptable marriage and is angered when she does not.

'Unequal' and socially unacceptable matches are portrayed frequently by Shakespeare's contemporaries, notably in the plays of John Webster. In *The Duchess of Malfi* (c. 1614), a **revenge tragedy**, the Duchess is cruelly tormented and then murdered on her brothers' orders when they find out about her secret marriage to a servant, a steward called Antonio. Like *Othello*, *The Duchess of Malfi* raises questions about the ways in which men dominate and abuse women.

If you are interested in the way in which race is portrayed in other plays by Shakespeare, you could start by looking at the villainous Moor Aaron in *Titus Andronicus* (1593). He fathers a child with a white woman, Tamora. Their baby is described in these terms: 'A joyless, dismal, black, and sorrowful issue./ Here is the babe, as loathsome as a toad.'

There are a number of **malcontent** and **Machiavellian** villains in Renaissance drama who share Iago's cynicism and abuse others to get what they want. In Shakespeare's *King Lear* (c. 1605), the illegitimate son Edmund plots against his brother and father so that he can get their land and titles. Edmund exploits women in the same way that Iago does. Iago can also be compared with the amoral villain Flamineo in Webster's *The White Devil* (c. 1612). In the hope of advancing his career, Flamineo plots a double murder to bring his married sister Vittoria together with the Duke of Brachiano, who is also married.

Study focus: Exploring connections with *Othello* **A02**

Later writers have explored the destructive nature of love in a number of texts that can be compared with *Othello*. Emily Brontë's *Wuthering Heights* (1847), Thomas Hardy's *The Mayor of Casterbridge* (1886) and *Tess of the D'Urbervilles* (1891) and Daphne du Maurier's *Rebecca* (1938) all explore the darker side of obsessive love. Henrik Ibsen's play *A Doll's House* (1879) portrays the disintegration of the marriage of Torvald and Nora Helmer, while Arthur Miller's *A View From a Bridge* (1955) portrays the tragic consequences of Eddie Carbone's possessive love for his niece. Robert Browning's dramatic monologues, *My Last Duchess* and *Porphyria's Lover* (1842), offer poetic depictions of obsessive males, who seek to control the women they love. Many of Elizabeth Barrett Browning's poems depict idealised love, while Sylvia Plath's collections, *The Colossus* (1960) and *Ariel* (1965), include poems which evoke the sinister, destructive qualities of love.

Finally, you might be interested in looking at the work of Caryl Phillips, who explores themes related to race and dislocation. In *The Nature of Blood* (1997), Phillips rewrites Othello's story in the novel's second major story line. The narrative focuses on Othello's attempts to integrate into Venetian society when he is hired by the Doge to lead the Venetian army against the Turks in the late fifteenth century.

A04 **KEY CONNECTION**

Othello can be compared with other **tragedies** where the hero is tempted into evil, for example Marlowe's *Doctor Faustus* (c. 1594), in which Faustus makes a pact with the devil, and *Macbeth* (c. 1606), where Macbeth is spurred on to villainy by his wife and his own ambition.

A04 **KEY CONNECTION**

Love and marriage and gender roles are frequently portrayed in comedy as well as tragedy. Shakespeare's *The Taming of the Shrew* (1593) and *Much Ado About Nothing* (1598) feature strong heroines.

KEY INTERPRETATION

Thomas Rymer was as dismissive of the implausible characters as the plot: Othello was a 'Jealous Booby', Iago too villainous to be believed, and Desdemona a woman without sense because she married a 'blackamoor'.

KEY INTERPRETATION

In 'Diabolic Intellect and the Noble Hero', 1937, F. R. Leavis analyses Othello's final speech, commenting that Othello has 'discovered his mistake, but there is no tragic self discovery'. Leavis says Othello remains 'un-self-comprehending' and that the play 'doesn't involve the idea of the hero's learning through suffering'. To what extent do you agree with Leavis?

KEY CONTEXT

John Russell Brown, in *Shakespeare: The Tragedies* (2001), reminds us of the Christian context of the seventeenth century: 'an audience that believed in devils might see Iago as someone working in close allegiance to an evil power that is greater than any human force'.

CRITICAL INTERPRETATIONS

Early views

Thomas Rymer, one of the play's most negative critics, wrote a commentary on *Othello* in *A Short View of Tragedy* (1693). Rymer was outraged by the idea of a black hero and would not accept that the play was a great **tragedy**, declaring the 'defect' of Othello was that it did not have a moral lesson. Rymer suggested that Othello might serve only as 'a caution' to maidens not to run away with 'blackamoors' without their parents' consent. In contrast to Rymer, Dr Johnson's (1765) response to *Othello* was positive. In Johnson's view Othello was 'magnanimous, artless, and credulous, boundless in his confidence, ardent in his affection, inflexible in his resolution, and obdurate in his revenge'. Johnson also suggested that the play provided a 'very useful moral, not to make an unequal match'.

Nineteenth- and twentieth-century views

At the beginning of the nineteenth century, Coleridge offered a view of Iago's **characterisation** that has been influential. He argued that Iago is 'A being next to the devil', driven by 'motiveless malignity'. Coleridge suggests that Iago operates without adequate motivation; he is bad because he is bad. Many critics have commented on his skill as a 'dramatist'. Other nineteenth-century critics shared Rymer's views about Desdemona's marriage to Othello, suggesting she must be a strumpet who lacks morals because she marries a Moor. At the end of the century Swinburne argued that Othello must be seen as 'the noblest man of man's making'.

In 1904, A. C. Bradley presented a positive analysis of Othello, whom he saw as blameless. For Bradley, Othello was 'the most romantic figure among Shakespeare's heroes'. Bradley's Othello is 'so noble … [he] inspires a passion of mingled love and pity'. Bradley also argued that the newness of his marriage makes Othello's jealousy credible. Bradley believed that Othello never falls completely and suggested that at the end of the play we feel 'admiration and love' for the hero. Two influential critics rejected Bradley's positive analysis of Othello. Commenting on Othello's final speech, T. S. Eliot says the Moor is guilty of trying to cheer himself up and attempting to evade reality. For Eliot this speech is a 'terrible exposure of human weakness'. F. R. Leavis argued that Othello is responsible for his own downfall because he has a propensity to jealousy and a weak character, which is sorely tested by marriage. Othello's love is dismissed. It is 'composed very largely of ignorance of self as well as ignorance of her [Desdemona]'.

Since the 1950s there have been a number of suggestions that Iago is driven by latent homosexuality. Iago has also been considered as an example of the typical stage **Machiavel** who 'personifies … self-interest, hypocrisy, cunning' (Leah Scragg, 'Iago – Vice or Devil?', *Shakespeare Survey*, 21, 1968). Several twentieth-century critics were preoccupied by the Christianity of Othello. Many noted the Christian signification of certain speeches (e.g. V.2.33 and V.2.24). Some critics have suggested that Othello is damned when he commits suicide because he has sinned against God's law; he has also been accused of other soul-destroying sins; murder, despair and entering into a compact with the devil (Iago). Other critics have suggested that *Othello* affirms a morality that is consistent with Christianity; the play presents a positive view of love and faith and shows us that vengeance is wicked and pride dangerous.

Desdemona received a good deal of critical attention during the twentieth century. Some commentators suggested she is a goddess and a saint, others saw her as a representative of goodness and purity. Many critics commented on Desdemona's commitment to love.

Contemporary approaches

Feminist readings of Desdemona

Feminist readings of the play explore the gender politics of *Othello*. A feminist critic would consider the roles of the male and female characters in relation to the **patriarchal** context of the play. Many feminist critics have noted how female characters in **Jacobean** tragedies are victims who have limited power and are punished for their sexuality.

Marilyn French (see *Shakespeare's Division of Experience*, 1982) explores the masculine value system at work in *Othello*. In spite of her assertiveness in choosing her own husband, French suggests Desdemona 'accepts her culture's dictum that she must be obedient to males' and is 'self-denying in the extreme' when she dies.

Lisa Jardine (see *Still Harping on Daughters*, 1983) shares French's viewpoint about the misogyny of *Othello*. She suggests that the stage world of Jacobean drama is wholly masculine and argues that there is only a male viewpoint on offer. Jardine asserts the view that Desdemona proves to be 'too-knowing, too-independent'. Because of her waywardness she is punished by patriarchy. Jardine suggests Desdemona becomes a stereotype of female passivity.

Marxist readings

A **Marxist critic** would be interested in the political context of *Othello* and power structure of the society in which Othello and Iago operate. Marxist critics also examine the relationships between masters and their servants. Dympna Callaghan considers the cultural significance of Desdemona's wedding sheets and the handkerchief, commenting on how these objects had economic and symbolic value in the Renaissance (see Howard and Shershow, eds., *Marxist Shakespeares*, 2001). Callaghan sees the handkerchief as a 'miniature of the nuptial linens' and suggests it is crucially important to the stability of the marriage of Othello and Desdemona.

New Historicist readings

New Historicist critics seek to consider *Othello* in relation to its social and historical context, looking at the play in relation to the ideology and beliefs of Shakespeare's society. New Historicists are particularly interested in whether or not *Othello* reinforces or subverts the values of Shakespeare's society. Commenting on the violence against female characters in drama of the Jacobean period, Leonard Tennenhouse (see *Power on Display*, 1986) asserts the view that 'Jacobean tragedies offer up their scenes of excessive punishment as if mutilating the female could somehow correct political corruption. The female in question may be completely innocent … yet in play after play she demands her own death or else claims responsibility for her murder.' Tennenhouse suggests Desdemona has to be destroyed because she is subversive. Unlike many feminist critics, Tennenhouse suggests that Desdemona is 'the embodiment of power' when she appears in Act I and defends her right to choose her own husband.

Frances Dolan (see 'Revolutions, Petty Tyranny and the Murderous Husband' in Kate Chedgzoy, ed., *Shakespeare, Feminism and Gender*, 2001) considers *Othello* in relation to its historical context. She notes how in Shakespeare's society, murdering one's spouse was considered a threat to the social order. Dolan also comments on how Jacobean drama reflects seventeenth-century anxieties about the racial 'other', the traitor 'inside', the plotting subordinate and abusive authority figures. Dolan says that Othello can be linked to all these 'spectres of disorder'. She defines him as a 'domestic tyrant who murders his wife on spurious grounds'. She also suggests Othello is in an ambiguous position because of his race.

A05 KEY INTERPRETATION

Performance criticism considers the ways in which readers and audiences receive and react to *Othello*. For example, you might consider the ways in which the text or a particular theatre or film production evokes feelings of pity and terror for Desdemona during Act V Scene 2.

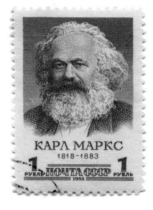

A05 KEY INTERPRETATION

A Marxist reading of Iago may consider whether his subversion of the social order in the play is politically justified. Can Iago be considered a working-class hero? To what extent does he have a legitimate grudge against a bourgeois system that has oppressed him? To answer these questions you need to consider Iago's motives for revenge against Othello and Cassio, and whether or not Othello is a tyrant who deserves to be removed from power.

KEY INTERPRETATION **A05**

In 'Othello's Real Tragedy' (1987), Caryl Phillips offers a reading of Othello informed by **historicist** approaches. Phillips stresses the hero's isolation as a black man in a white world. He says Othello is fully aware of his 'tenuous' position and that his tragedy is caused when he 'begins to forget that he is black'. Do you agree with this view?

KEY INTERPRETATION **A05**

Adrian Lester, who played Othello at the Royal National Theatre in 2013, says that the protagonist is 'very aware of how he appears in front of the Venetians and his appearance is very important to him'. Lester adds that Othello's marriage 'increases his status in Venice'. Is Lester suggesting Othello feels insecure as an outsider?

KEY INTERPRETATION **A05**

Critics who debate *Othello*'s value consider whether it belongs in the canon of great English literary texts. Sean Benson has argued that because it is a 'domestic tragedy', *Othello* is of less worth than tragedies which deal with the fate of nations and state affairs. In the light of this comment, do you think *Othello* is worthy of inclusion in the literary canon?

He cannot hold on to his authority with any confidence or security because he is different from the Venetians. For Dolan, Othello's race would have undermined his heroism: 'By making his protagonist black, Shakespeare prepares his original audience to question Othello's authority, to suspect that he might misuse it groundlessly.'

Nicholas Marsh (see *Shakespeare: The Tragedies*, 1998) considers Iago in relation to his historical context. He suggests that Iago represents a new way of thinking about the world. Iago is a typical **malcontent** or **Machiavel**, a dissatisfied and cynical man who will not stay in his place. He wants to get his own back on a society that thwarts him. Marsh points to Iago's speech in Act I Scene 3, where he outlines his philosophy – ''tis in ourselves, that we are thus, or thus' (line 320) – as proof of his subversive qualities. By way of contrast, Othello 'often conjures the magnificence of a traditional, military order and medieval ideals, such as honour. His love for Desdemona has strong overtones of medieval courtly love where the woman's purity is worshipped and idolized.'

Post-colonial readings

A **post-colonial** critique of the play considers the way in which Othello's race is portrayed, and considers the hero's 'outsider' status in a white world.

In *Gender, Race, Renaissance Drama* (1987), Ania Loomba suggests the central conflict in *Othello* is 'between the racism of a white **patriarchy** and the threat posed to it by both a black man and a white woman'. For Loomba, women and blacks exist as 'the other' in this play. Loomba argues that Othello has a split consciousness and is 'a near schizophrenic hero'; his final speech 'graphically portrays the split – he becomes simultaneously the Christian and the Infidel, the Venetian and the Turk, the keeper of the state and its opponent'. Loomba suggests Othello is an honorary white at the beginning of the play but becomes a 'total outsider' because of his relationship with Desdemona, which ruptures his 'precarious entry into the white world'. Loomba insists, however, that *Othello* 'should not be read as a patriarchal, authoritative and racist spectacle'. Instead the play should be used to 'examine and dismantle' ideas about racism and sexism.

Karen Newman (see '"And Wash the Ethiop White": Femininity and the Monstrous in *Othello*', in Andrew Hadfield, ed., *William Shakespeare's* Othello: *A Sourcebook*, 1987) says the play exposes the 'fear of racial and sexual difference' of Renaissance culture. Newman argues the white male characters in *Othello*, especially Iago, feel threatened by the 'power and potency of a different and monstrous sexuality' which Othello represents. Newman looks at the play in relation to Elizabethan stereotypes of the black male, in particular, worries about mixed marriages. Shakespeare's contemporaries feared 'the black man had the power to subjugate his partner's whiteness'. This makes the black male monstrous. However, Newman suggests 'by making the black Othello a hero, and by making Desdemona's love for Othello … sympathetic', Shakespeare's play challenges the racist, sexist and colonialist views of his society.

PROGRESS CHECK

Section One: Check your understanding

These short tasks will help you to evaluate your knowledge and skills level in this particular area.

1. Make a list of 3–4 key points about attitudes to foreigners in Shakespeare's England, linking them to examples from *Othello*.

2. Write a paragraph summing up the social position of women in the Renaissance, linking your points to examples from *Othello*.

3. Write a list of 3–4 points about how *Othello* would have been staged originally, comparing Elizabethan practices with a production you have seen.

4. Sum up and critique an early critic's viewpoint – for example, Rymer's views on *Othello*.

5. Write a paragraph comparing two twentieth-century critics' views of *Othello*.

6. List 3–4 points which a feminist critic may make about *Othello*.

7. List 3–4 points suggesting how a Marxist critic might view Iago.

8. Sum up and critique a post-colonial critique – for example Karen Newman's – of *Othello*.

9. Using Adrian Lester's comments in the margin box on page 90, make a list of 3–4 examples from the play which support and/ or challenge the actor's views about Othello.

10. Make a list of 3–4 points suggesting why *Othello* is a worthy tragedy which belongs in the canon of English Literature.

Section Two: Working towards the exam

Choose one of the following five tasks which require longer, more developed answers:

1. Dr Johnson has said that *Othello* provides 'a very useful moral, not to make an unequal match'. Explore to what extent you agree that this is the moral of *Othello*.

2. Leonard Tennenhouse suggests Desdemona is 'the embodiment of power' when she first appears in *Othello*. Discuss to what extent you agree with this comment.

3. To what extent can Iago be considered a working class hero?

4. Do you agree with T. S. Eliot that Othello's final speech is a 'terrible exposure of human weakness'?

5. Do you agree with Karen Newman that *Othello* 'challenges the racist, sexist and colonialist views' of Shakespeare's society?

A01 PROGRESS BOOSTER

For each Section Two task, read the question carefully, select the key areas you need to address, and plan an essay of 6–7 points. Write a first draft, giving yourself an hour to do so. Make sure you include supporting evidence for each point, including quotations.

Progress check (rate your understanding on a level of 1 – low, to 5 – high)	1	2	3	4	5
The different ways that the play can be contextualised in its historical background.					
How the conventions of the seventeenth-century theatre shaped the play's presentation.					
How different critics have interpreted the main characters of the play.					
The different interpretations of the play over time.					

ASSESSMENT FOCUS

How will you be assessed?

Each particular exam board and exam paper will be slightly different, so make sure you check with your teacher exactly which Assessment Objectives you need to focus on. You are likely to get more marks for Assessment Objectives 1, 2 and 3, but this does not mean you should discount 4 or 5.

If you are following an AS Level course, check the weightings carefully. Remember, there is no coursework for AS so your response to *Othello* will carry even more weight in your overall result.

What do the AOs actually mean?

	Assessment Objective	Meaning
AO1	Articulate informed, personal and creative responses to literary texts, using associated concepts and terminology, and coherent, accurate written expression.	You write about texts in accurate, clear and precise ways so that what you have to say is clear to the marker. You use literary terms (e.g. '**protagonist**') or refer to concepts (e.g. '**hubris**') in relevant places. You do not simply repeat what you have read or been told, but express your own ideas based on in-depth knowledge of the text and related issues.
AO2	Analyse ways in which meanings are shaped in literary texts.	You are able to explain in detail how the specific techniques and methods used by Shakespeare (e.g. recurrent symbols or motifs) influence and affect the reader's response.
AO3	Demonstrate understanding of the significance and influence of the contexts in which literary texts are written and received.	You can explain how the play might reflect the social, historical, political or personal backgrounds of Shakespeare or the time when it was written. You also consider how the play might have been received differently over time by audiences and readers.
AO4	Explore connections across literary texts.	You are able to explain links between the play and other texts, perhaps of a similar genre, or with similar concerns, or viewed from a similar perspective (i.e. feminist).
AO5	Explore literary texts informed by different interpretations.	You understand how the play can be viewed in different ways, and are able to write about these debates, forming your own opinion. For example, you explain how a critic might view Othello as a noble tragic hero, whilst another might see him as a weak, deluded man, who is responsible for his own downfall.

What does this mean for your revision?

Whether you are following an AS or A Level course, use the right-hand column above to measure how confidently you can address these objectives. Then focus your revision on those aspects you feel need most attention. Remember, throughout these Notes, the AOs are highlighted, so you can flick through and check them in that way.

Next, use the tables on page 93. These help you to understand the differences between a satisfactory and an outstanding response. Then, use the guidance from page 94 onwards to help you address the key AOs, for example how to shape and plan your writing.

Features of **mid-level** responses: the following examples relate to the theme of jealousy:

	Features	Examples
A01	You use critical vocabulary appropriately for most of the time, and your arguments are relevant to the task, ordered sensibly, with clear expression. You show detailed knowledge of the text.	Shakespeare **demonstrates the terrible consequences** of giving in to jealousy in 'Othello'. Othello's jealousy is caused by Iago, who makes him believe that Desdemona is unfaithful to him, but it can be argued that Othello is **ultimately responsible** for her death.
A02	You show straightforward understanding of the writer's methods, such as how form, structure and language shape meanings.	Shakespeare carefully manages the **action of the plot** so that there is no let up in the tension, once Othello's mind has been poisoned against Desdemona. For example, Shakespeare's **dramatic methods** in Acts III to V create a sense of **foreboding**, which is associated with Othello's increasingly destructive **jealousy**.
A03	You can write about a range of contextual factors and make some relevant links between these and the task or text.	Women were seen as the property of men in **Renaissance society.** They were controlled by their fathers and husbands, so it comes as no surprise that Othello's **jealousy** causes him to act tyrannically towards Desdemona. Her reputation is a key part of his masculine honour.
A04	You consider straightforward connections between texts and write about them clearly and relevantly to the task.	Shakespeare presents Othello as a man overwhelmed by **love** as well as **jealousy**. For many critics his weeping proves how much he mourns the loss of his love for Desdemona. Leontes, the jealous king in **'The Winter's Tale'**, is saddened when he believes he has lost his wife Hermione's love. **However, his grief is not as passionate as Othello's**.
A05	You tackle the debate in the task in a clear, logical way, showing your understanding of different interpretations.	**Coleridge has suggested** that Iago' is an example of 'motiveless malignity'. **However, a Marxist critic may view** Iago as being a working class hero, whose grudges against his superiors are justified. **This way of viewing Iago makes his jealousy of Cassio and Othello seem legitimate.**

Features of a **high level** response: these examples relate to a task on the conventions of tragedy:

	Features	Examples
A01	You are perceptive, and assured in your argument in relation to the task. You make fluent, confident use of literary concepts and terminology, and express yourself confidently.	Shakespeare shows there is a **tragic imperative** that drives Othello relentlessly towards his fate. This is coherent with **classical notions of inevitability**; a sense that events collaborate against him to the point that his fall can be seen as ordained from the moment he elopes with Desdemona.
A02	You explore and analyse key aspects of Shakespeare's use of form, structure and language and evaluate perceptively how they shape meanings.	Shakespeare constructs **the sequence of events** so that the swift pace and **dramatic suspense** are maintained throughout, particularly once the characters arrive in Cyprus in Act II. Time seems to favour Iago's plots, which depend upon his 'poison' working swiftly. This creates an effect upon the audience of **spiralling, unstoppable tension,** as we watch Othello hurtling towards **the tragic outcome**.
A03	You show deep, detailed and relevant understanding of how contextual factors link to the text or task.	**Renaissance society** was **patriarchal** and women were controlled by men. Desdemona's elopement is described as **'a gross revolt'**. In **tragedy** there must be a reversion to the natural order at the end of the play, so it can be argued that Desdemona's subversive choice of husband **foreshadows** her tragic death, and the death of Othello.
A04	You show a detailed and perceptive understanding of issues raised through connections between texts. You have a range of excellent supportive references.	Othello possesses a number of **fatal flaws**. Arguably, his worst sin is **hubris**. Even in his dying moments his pride is evident when he says that he has 'done the state some service'. However, we cannot forgive him for murdering Desdemona. We may feel **pathos** when Othello dies, but we know, as he does, that there is 'no way but this'.
A05	You are able to use your knowledge of critical debates, and the possible perspectives on an issue to write fluently and confidently about how the text might be interpreted.	Sean Benson has suggested that Othello is a **domestic tragedy,** of less worth than political tragedies which deal with the fate of nations. However, it can be argued that 'Othello' has a serious political dimension which is highly relevant today. The **tragic protagonist** is an outsider, and the **first black tragic hero in Elizabethan theatre**. That makes 'Othello' highly political.

HOW TO WRITE HIGH-QUALITY RESPONSES

The quality of your writing – how you express your ideas – is vital for getting a higher grade, and **AO1** and **AO2** are specifically about **how** you respond.

Five key areas

The quality of your responses can be broken down into **five** key areas.

1. The structure of your answer/essay

- First, get **straight to the point in your opening paragraph.** Use a sharp, direct first sentence that deals with a key aspect and then follows up with evidence or detailed reference.

- **Put forward an argument or point of view** (you won't always be able to challenge or take issue with the essay question, but generally, where you can, you are more likely to write in an interesting way).

- **Signpost your ideas** with connectives and references which help the essay flow. Aim to present an overall argument or conceptual response to the task, not a series of unconnected points.

- **Don't repeat points already made**, not even in the conclusion, unless you have something new to add.

Aiming high: Effective opening paragraphs

Let's imagine you have been asked about the following question:

'Tragedy is concerned with loss and waste.' To what extent is this true of *Othello*? Here's an example of a successful opening paragraph:

> Gets straight to the point

In 'Othello', Shakespeare explores the tragic consequences of the hero's loss of honour, and the terrible waste of human potential. Othello himself sums up his tragedy in Act V when he asks plaintively before he dies, 'why should honour outlive honesty?' So, how and why does Othello lose his honour, and what exactly is 'wasted'?

> Sets up some interesting ideas that will be tackled in subsequent paragraphs

2. Use of titles, names, etc.

This is a simple, but important, tip to stay on the right side of the examiners.

- Make sure that you spell correctly the titles of the texts, authors and so on. Present them correctly too, with quotation marks and capitals as appropriate. For example, *In Act I of 'Othello'* ....

- Use the **full title**, unless there is a good reason not to (e.g. it's very long).

- Use the term 'text' or 'play', rather than 'book' or 'story'. If you use the word 'story', the examiner may think you mean the plot/action rather than the 'text' as a whole.

3. Effective quotations

Do not 'bolt on' quotations to the points you make. You will get some marks for including them, but examiners will not find your writing very fluent.

The best quotations are:

- Relevant and not too long (you are going to have to memorise them, so that will help you select shorter ones!)
- Integrated into your argument/sentence
- Linked to effect and implications

Aiming high: Effective use of quotations

Here is an example of an effective use of a quotation about jealousy in the play:

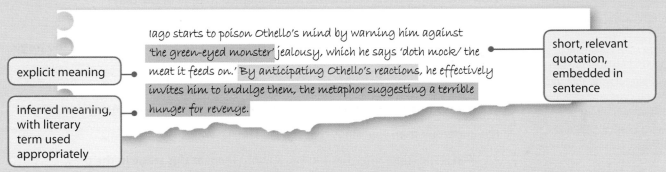

explicit meaning

inferred meaning, with literary term used appropriately

Iago starts to poison Othello's mind by warning him against 'the green-eyed monster' jealousy, which he says 'doth mock/ the meat it feeds on.' By anticipating Othello's reactions, he effectively invites him to indulge them, the metaphor suggesting a terrible hunger for revenge.

short, relevant quotation, embedded in sentence

Remember – quotations can also be one or two single words or phrases embedded in a sentence to build a picture or explanation, or they can be longer ones that are explored and picked apart.

4. Techniques and terminology

By all means mention literary terms, techniques, conventions, critical theories or people (for example, 'paradox', 'archetype', 'feminism' or 'Aristotle') but make sure that you:

- Understand what they mean
- Are able to link them to what you're saying
- Spell them correctly

5. General writing skills

Try to write in a way that sounds professional and uses standard English. This does not mean that your writing will lack personality – just that it will be authoritative.

- Avoid colloquial or everyday expressions such as 'got', 'alright', 'ok' and so on.
- Use terms such as 'convey', 'suggest', 'imply', 'infer' to explain the writer's methods.
- Refer to 'we' when discussing the audience/reader.
- Avoid assertions and generalisations; don't just state a general point of view (such as 'Iago is a typical villain because he's evil'), but analyse closely with clear evidence and textual detail.

Note the professional approach here in the choice of vocabulary and awareness of the effect on the reader:

Iago has some of the typical qualities of the Machiavellian villain of Jacobean revenge tragedy. For example, he is discontented, cynical and self-serving. He is able to disguise his villainous intentions behind a facade of honesty.

QUESTIONS ABOUT A SPECIFIC EXTRACT

One type of question you may have to face is one which asks you to consider a particular idea or aspect in relation to an extract from the play, and then widen the discussion to the play as a whole.

For example, you might be given this extract to write about:

> Act III Scene 3, from Othello, 'O blood, blood, blood!', line 454 to Iago, 'I am your own for ever', line 482

Typical questions might relate to:

- The **dramatic significance** of the extract to the play as a whole, for example:

How does this extract contribute to the tragic outcome of the play?

- A key **idea**, **issue** or **theme**:

What does this extract reveal about the nature and impact of jealousy on the tragic protagonist?

- The way a particular **character**, or **relationship** is presented:

What does this extract show us about the relationship between Othello and Iago?

It is important from your study that you are familiar with:

- **Who** is speaking, and what you know about them **at this stage in the play.**
- **Where** and **when** this passage takes place in the text (is it the ending of a scene or Act? What follows directly before and after it? Where does it take place?)
- What is **significant** about it: even if you are asked about a specific issue, it is important you understand the extract's dramatic significance, even if that is not the main focus.
- How does the **specific language** and **dramatic structure** enable us to understand more about the characters/relationships, ideas/issues or dramatic significance?

So, for example, if you are exploring the way the passage above deals with the impact of Iago's poison on Othello's mind, you might look at:

Key questions to focus your reading and response	Possible answers	Effect (what it tells us about the key idea/issue)
Who is involved/speaking? What do we know about them?	*Othello tells Iago he wants revenge on Cassio and Desdemona. Iago vows to help him. Othello now trusts Iago more than Desdemona.*	*Iago's poison is making Othello violent and destructive. Iago looks as if he has achieved what he wanted: the destruction of Othello's mind and revenge on Cassio.*
Where and when does this take place? What has happened before this scene?	*This extract occurs at the end of Act III Scene 3 in the middle of the play, immediately after Iago has poisoned Othello's mind against Desdemona.*	*Othello is decisive and resolute in this extract, but Iago had to work hard to convince him of Desdemona's treachery earlier in the scene.*
What is significant about the scene?	*This is a turning point for Othello – he commits himself to revenge.*	*Othello's great love has been converted into destructive jealousy by Iago's evil.*
What does the language and structure tell us?	*Othello's speech is full of increasingly violent images, while Iago uses the language of love to urge Othello on to revenge.*	*Othello's language foreshadows the violence he will use against Desdemona in Act V. Iago's false words of love reveal how adept he is at controlling Othello.*

Writing a response

There are two key things you should do when writing about an extract, once you have 'done your thinking' (along the lines suggested in the grid):

- **Focus immediately** on **a specific aspect** from the scene; don't waste time with general waffle
- **Develop your points** succinctly and swiftly but **using inference or insight** to explore them fully

EXAMINER'S TIP

If you have a second question to answer once you have completed your detailed response to the passage, make sure you have left yourself enough time to write fully on the remaining task.

For example, here is an example of an excellent first paragraph:

> *This extract is characterised by images of violence. In the first words spoken by Othello we see how his love has been corrupted by Iago's poison. Othello's exclamation, 'O blood, blood, blood!' signals to the audience that he is now a destructive revenger. Othello says his 'bloody thoughts with violent pace/ shall ne'er look back'. He rejects 'humble love' and sets himself on a course of destruction that will end with Desdemona's violent death. Iago echoes Othello when he tells him he will help in the 'bloody business' of revenge. The impact of the violent language both men use is chilling. We know that the Othello's marital happiness is over and that the play will end in tragedy.*

In subsequent paragraphs, you can work through the extract as it occurs, or take your initial point and link it to a phrase, line, etc. later in the same extract. If you take the latter route, your response may end up moving backwards and forwards within the passage, but it will allow you to make interesting links. For example, you might want to take one particular aspect of the idea/issue being explored and trace one character's words, then move to another character.

For example:

> *Throughout the passage, Othello shows himself to be resolute. He wants revenge, and quickly. We see this in his exchange with Iago in lines 455 and 456, when he says he will 'never' change his mind about wanting revenge. We can infer from this that Othello will act ruthlessly in future scenes.*

Aiming high: Summarising events

Whilst it is important to understand the extract in terms of its plot significance, do not slip into simply retelling what has happened before and then telling the examiner what events are taking place now. Summarise important events swiftly and efficiently in a phrase or two, e.g. 'Following Iago's poisoning of Othello's mind …'

GENERAL QUESTIONS ABOUT THE WHOLE TEXT

You may be asked to write about a specific aspect of *Othello*. These might be on a key issue or idea, or on the way Shakespeare uses language. For example, a 'key idea' question:

Explore how Shakespeare presents evil in *Othello*.

Or:

Explore how Shakespeare uses language to present marriage from a male perspective in *Othello*.

Let us take the first question. This means, you must:

- **Focus** on Iago's evil **motives** and **methods**, and the impact they have on the **tragic outcome**.
- **Explain** *how* Shakespeare **presents** or **organises ideas** about this. Start by discussing Iago's evil motives for revenge, and how Shakespeare uses soliloquies to reveal them early in the play. Then examine Iago's evil methods of manipulation and how they impact on Othello from Act III onwards. You may also want to consider how Iago deceives others. End by discussing **to what extent you believe** Iago is to blame for the tragic outcome.
- Look at the **whole text**, not just one scene or character.
- Consider **context** and **critical ideas** – this means discussing how Renaissance ideas about evil inform Shakespeare's presentation of the theme. You should also consider Iago in his dramatic context as a stage Machiavel. You should examine alternative views of Iago's evil, i.e. discuss whether or not Iago's motives are plausible. You may want to incorporate different critical perspectives, e.g. Marxist, to help you do this.

Structuring your response

You need a clear, logical plan, but it will be impossible to write about every aspect or section of the play. So, you will need to quickly note down 5–6 key points or ideas to build your essay around:

- **Point A**: Iago is implicated in all the deaths that occur in Act V.
- **Point B**: Iago's motives include thwarted ambition and a hatred of goodness.
- **Point C**: Othello becomes evil under Iago's influence; he is corrupted.
- **Point D**: Iago revels in his own evil, like many Renaissance stage villains.
- **Point E**: Some critics view Iago's evil as motiveless, but others feel he has plausible motives for revenge.

Then decide the most effective order for your points (e.g B, E, D, C, A), and draw in supporting evidence *and* reference to context or critical ideas. For example:

Introduction: *Iago is open about his evil motives from Act I Scene 1 onwards, when he tells Roderigo he hates the 'curse of service'.*

Paragraph One (point B, say): *Iago is driven by thwarted ambition. Cassio, 'a great arithmetician' has been promoted over him by Othello.*

Paragraph Two (expand on point B): *Iago hates Othello but follows him 'to serve my turn upon him'. These words reveal that he is scheming, deceptive and self-serving villain.*

Paragraph Three (change direction, now look at Point E, say): *Iago is not an example of what Coleridge calls 'motiveless malignity.' He has entirely plausible motives, having been overlooked.*

... and so on.

EXAMINER'S TIP

If you are following an AS course, you may have less exam time to write than for the A Level – so concise, succinct points with less elaboration than provided here may be needed.

EXAMINER'S TIP

For your conclusion: use a compelling way to finish, perhaps repeating some or all of the key words from the question. For example, either: end with a final point, but add a last clause which makes it clear what you think is key to the answer, e.g.:

Shakespeare's presentation of the evil makes it clear that it is an unstoppable force; Iago succeeds in polluting everything with his destructive jealousy.

Or, end with a new quotation or aspect that is slightly different from your main point; e.g.:

As Francis Dolan says, Othello becomes a 'domestic tyrant who murders his wife on spurious grounds'. This is Iago's fault. His evil has corrupted the tragic protagonist to such an extent that Othello cannot be considered a hero at the end of Act V.

Or you could even combine these two types of conclusion.

Writing about context

Depending on the particular course you are following, you may need to focus on aspects of context that are relevant to the general area you are being asked to explore. In this regard, there are some key things to remember:

Assessment Objective 3 asks you to 'demonstrate understanding of the significance and influence of the contexts in which literary texts are written and received'. This can mean:

- How the events, settings, politics and so on **of the time when the text was written** influenced the writer or help us to understand the play's themes or concerns. For example, to what extent Shakespeare might have been influenced by his society's attitudes towards race and gender.

Or:

- How events, settings, politics and so on **of the time when the text is read or seen** influence how it is understood. For example, would modern audiences brought up in a world of greater racial and gender equality respond differently to the marriage of Othello and Desdemona than Shakespeare's audience?

The table below will help you think about how particular aspects of the time in which the play was written contribute to our understanding now of the play and its themes, as related to the question on page 98.

as related to the question on page 98.

Political	Literary	Philosophical
Military situation in Cyprus; conflict between Christian and Muslim states and nations. The war and the dangerous political situation in Cyprus contribute to the destruction of Othello as Iago is able to take advantage of the uneasy political situation to destabilise his marriage.	Use of Machiavellian villain and Italianate setting; Iago is a cynical malcontent, who, like other Renaissance stage villains, is driven by immoral self-interest.	Beliefs about the nature of evil; Iago is able to hide his villainy in plain sight, like many evil characters in Renaissance drama. Iago delights in his evil and does not seem to possess a fear of the devil or divine retribution. He says men are responsible for their own actions and destinies, rejecting accepted religious ideas.
Scientific	**Cultural**	**Social**
Understanding of medicine i.e. the 'humours' and 'disease' of jealousy. Othello is presented as a man who is controlled by his diseased mind when he is 'poisoned' by Iago. Jealousy has both a physical and mental impact on him.	Attitudes towards mixed-race marriages and foreigners. The Duke is tolerant, but Iago, Brabantio and Roderigo express racially prejudiced views.	Attitudes towards women. Desdemona chooses her own husband, but operates thereafter in a patriarchal world where men have control over what is thought about her and everything that happens to her. The language men use to describe women reveals the patriarchal context.

Aiming high: Making context relevant

It is very important that you do not approach context as something to be 'bolted on' to what you say. You must make fluent links between contextual knowledge and the focus of the task. For example, **don't** just write:

Men dominated their wives in Renaissance society, which was patriarchal. They expected their wives to be submissive and obedient. Women would not participate in the public or political sphere, but would instead focus on their domestic duties.

Do write:

Renaissance society was patriarchal and fathers and husbands expected to control their daughters and wives. Early on in the play Brabantio is horrified when he learns Desdemona has made 'a gross revolt' and was 'half the wooer', suggesting that from the male viewpoint, female assertiveness in marriage is against the natural order of things. However, Shakespeare is not sympathetic to the male viewpoint here. Desdemona is allowed to defend her actions.

QUESTIONS WITH STATEMENTS, QUOTATIONS OR VIEWPOINTS

You may have to respond to tasks which include a statement, quotation or viewpoint which offers a particular interpretation of the text. These might be in relation to the whole text, or with regard to a specific extract, and deal with character, key ideas or. For example:

> **'Othello's virtue and valour ultimately make him admirable.'**
>
> **By considering Shakespeare's dramatic methods, to what extent do you agree with this view?**

The key thing to remember is that you are being asked to **respond to a particular perspective or critical view** of the text – in other words, to come up with **your own** 'take' on the idea or viewpoint in the task.

Key skills required

The table below provides help and advice on answering the question above.

Skill	Means	How do I achieve this?
Consider different interpretations	There will be more than one way of looking at the given question. For example, critics might be divided about Othello's virtue.	Show you have considered these different interpretations in your answer through the way you juxtapose or weigh up ideas. For example: *Othello is a romantic, generous husband in Act I, but he has acted deceitfully in eloping with Desdemona.*
Write with a clear, personal voice	Your own 'take' on the question is made obvious to the examiner. You are not just repeating other people's ideas, but offering what **you** think.	Although you may mention different perspectives on the task, you should settle on your own view. Use language that shows careful, but confident, consideration. For example: *Although A. C. Bradley has claimed that Othello is a romantic figure for whom we should feel 'admiration and love', I believe that Othello is a flawed hero who inspires fear.*
Construct a coherent argument	The examiner or marker can follow your train of thought so that your own viewpoint is clear to him or her.	Write in clear paragraphs that deal logically with different aspects of the question. Support what you say with well-selected and relevant evidence. Use a range of connectives to help 'signpost' your argument. For example: *We might say that Othello is a valiant soldier who has 'done the state some service.' However, he proves to be an unworthy husband. Moreover, his vices outweigh his virtues by the end of the play.*

Responding to a 'viewpoint' question

Let us look at another question:

> **'Desdemona becomes a stereotype of female passivity in the play.'**
>
> **To what extent do you agree with this view of Shakespeare's dramatic presentation of her?**

Stage 1: Decode the question

Underline/highlight the **key words**, and make sure you understand what the statement, quote or viewpoint is saying. In this case:

'To what extent do you agree ...' means: *Consider why you agree and disagree with the statement.*

'stereotype of female passivity' means: *A female character who does not defend herself and accepts her fate without complaining.*

'dramatic presentation of her' means: *The way in which Desdemona's character is presented and developed.*

So, you are being asked whether to agree/disagree with the idea that Desdemona is presented as someone who fails to act to defend herself or her reputation as a woman.

Stage 2: Decide what your viewpoint is

Examiners have stated that they tend to reward a strong view which is clearly put. Think about the question – can you take issue with it? Disagreeing strongly can lead to higher marks, provided you have **genuine evidence** to support your point of view. However, don't disagree just for the sake of it.

Stage 3: Decide how to structure your answer

Pick out the key points you wish to make, and decide on the order that you will present them in. Keep this basic plan to hand while you write your response.

Stage 4: Write your response

Begin by expanding on the aspect or topic mentioned in the task title. In this way, you can set up the key ideas you will explore. For example:

The idea that Desdemona must be seen, ultimately, as someone who is unable or unwilling to act in the face of the violent retribution she endures is interesting given how the play begins. I would argue that far from being passive, Desdemona is an initially assertive character, with a strong will of her own.

Then in the remaining paragraphs proceed to set out the different arguments or perspectives, including your own.

In the final paragraph, end with a clear statement of your viewpoint, but do not list or go over the points you have made. End succinctly and concisely.

> **EXAMINER'S TIP**
>
> You should comment concisely, professionally and thoughtfully and present a range of viewpoints. Try using modal verbs such as 'would', 'could', 'might', 'may' to clarify your own interpretation.

USING CRITICAL INTERPRETATIONS AND PERSPECTIVES

What is a critical interpretation?

The particular way a text is viewed or understood can be called an interpretation, and can be made by literary critics (specialists in studying literary texts), reviewers, or everyday readers and students. Looking at the text from a critical perspective, does not necessarily mean finding what is wrong with it or what you object to, but it is more about taking a position on particular elements of the text, or on what others say about it. For example:

1. Notions of 'character'

- Is the character an 'archetype' (a specific type of character with common features)? (For example, Thomas Rymer, in *A Short View of Tragedy*, suggests Othello belongs in 'a Bloody Farce' because he is the archetype of a foolish cuckold.)
- Does the character personify, symbolise or represent a specific idea or trope (the noble hero brought down by a fatal flaw; how evil preys on goodness)?
- Is the character modern, universal, of his/her time, historically accurate etc? (For example, is Iago the embodiment of Renaissance ideas about evil or, like many modern villains, driven by selfish, petty motives?)

2. Ideas and issues

What the play tells us about **particular ideas or issues** and how we interpret these.

For example:

- Themes and ideas that obsessed **Jacobean** dramatists e.g. the nature of good and evil; the difference appearance and reality; corrupt authority figures
- The role of men/women in Jacobean society and within marriage
- What **tragedy** means to Jacobean audiences
- Moral and social attitudes towards sexuality and race

3. Links and contexts

For example:

- Its influence culturally, historically and socially. Do we see echoes of the characters or genres in other texts? How similar to other stage villains is Iago and why? Does his **characterisation** share features with the **vice** of the medieval mystery plays, for example?
- How its language links to other texts or modes, such as religious works, myth, legend, etc.

4. Genre and dramatic structure

How the play is **constructed** and how Shakespeare **makes** his narrative.

- Does it follow a particular dramatic convention?
- What is the function of specific events, characters, theatrical devices, staging, etc. in relation to the plot?
- What are the specific moments of tension, conflict, crisis and **denouement**.

5. Audience and critical reaction

How the play **works on an audience or reader**, and whether this changes over time and in different contexts. Also, how different types of reader have responded, from reviewers, to actors and directors, to academics and researchers. For example:

- How far do readers or audiences empathise with, feel distance from, judge and/or evaluate the events and characters?
- What ideas do they find compelling and convincing, or lacking truth and impact?
- How far do they see the play as unique and modern, part of a tradition or carrying echoes of other works and ideas?

Writing about critical perspectives

The important thing to remember is that **you** are a critic too. Your job is to evaluate what a critic or school of criticism has said about the elements above, arrive at your own conclusions, and also express your own ideas. In essence, you need to **consider** the views of others, **synthesise** them, then decide on **your perspective**. For example:

Explain the viewpoints

Critical view A about presentation of Othello's race:

> *Frances Dolan feels that Othello's race would have been problematic to Shakespeare's audience and they would have felt suspicious of and mistrusted the hero because he is black.*

Critical view B about the same aspect:

> *Karen Newman does not feel that Othello's race is presented in a derogatory way. She feels that Shakespeare challenges the negative assumptions of his society by making his hero a noble Moor.*

Then synthesise and add your perspective

> *While Frances Dolan's idea that Othello's race is problematic could be considered persuasive given what we know about the negativity of Elizabethan attitudes towards black men, Karen Newman's comment that Othello is 'represented as heroic and tragic at an historical moment when the only role blacks played onstage was that of a villain of low status' provides an alternative angle. However, I feel that, in fact, Shakespeare's presentation of Othello's race is neither problematic nor subversive, but instead is used as a means by which the dramatist can explore ideas about opposition.*

Aiming high: Exploring dramatic conventions

Make sure you have thoroughly explored the dramatic conventions (some of which – such as denouement – are mentioned above). Critical interpretation of drama is of necessity different from critical interpretation of other modes of writing – not least because of audience response, and the specific theatrical devices in use. Key critics are theatre critics – look at what they have to say about recent productions. See the adjacent margin for just two examples of recent reviews of the 2013 National Theatre production of *Othello*. They offer, in fact, different 'readings' of the characterisation of Iago.

EXAMINER'S TIP

Writing in *The Guardian* about Iago in the 2013 National Theatre production of *Othello*, Michael Billington says, 'Rory Kinnear here gives a stunning study of a sociopath whose destructive tendencies have hitherto been held in check only by soldierly discipline.' He adds, 'this Iago burns with a contempt for the human race'.

EXAMINER'S TIP

Writing in *The Independent* about the 2013 National Theatre production of *Othello*, Paul Taylor said that Rory Kinnear's performance as Iago 'may be wonderfully low-key, but you can sense how Iago's revealed "motives" are just a set of disguises that strain to contain the inchoate nihilism that drives him'.

ANNOTATED SAMPLE ANSWERS

Below are extracts from three sample answers at different levels to the same task/question. Bear in mind that these responses may not correspond exactly to the style of question you might face, but they will give a broad indication of some of the key skills required.

> **Read from Act I Scene 3: 'Duke: What would you Desdemona?' to 'Othello: to spend with thee. We must obey the time.' By analysing Shakespeare's dramatic methods, explore the significance of the extract to the tragedy of the play as a whole.**

Candidate 1

Shakespeare uses a lot of dramatic methods in this extract, which comes from the end of Act I, just before Othello and Desdemona go to Cyprus. This is the senate scene and in this extract we see Desdemona and Othello saying how they want to be together. This is significant because the audience can see how in love they are. We know this because Desdemona says 'I did love the Moor to live with him' and Othello says 'My life upon her faith' at the end of the extract. These two lines prove that the couple are well matched and both love each other equally early in the play.

A01 Style is a bit immature. Needs to write more formally

A02 Apt quotations to support the point, but needs to analyse the language in more detail to demonstrate a secure grasp of Shakespeare's dramatic methods

Another dramatic method Shakespeare uses is imagery, which also shows us how Desdemona loves Othello. Desdemona speaks of her 'heart' being 'subdued' to Othello, proving she wants to be a loyal wife who obeys her husband. Othello also speaks of his 'heart' when he says he will go to war 'with all my heart.' Desdemona and Othello are different here. He is putting his career in front of his wife, but she puts him first. This would be expected in Shakespeare's times when wives normally stayed at home while husbands were away on business such as a military campaign. The couple are not presented as completely old fashioned though, because Desdemona refuses to stay in Venice where she would be safe, but instead wants to go with Othello. This may make us worry about what will happen to her in Cyprus.

A03 Some grasp of the social context and gender relations when the play was written

A02 This point is rather vague; needs to analyse dramatic methods and effect

A01 This word isn't really appropriate here – 'traditional' would be a better word to express this idea

Another method Shakespeare uses to make us worry about what will happen to Othello and Desdemona is at the end of the extract. Shakespeare mentions Iago, who we know is not someone Othello should trust. Othello says he will put Iago in charge of Desdemona when he says 'My Desdemona must I leave to thee'. This would make the audience unhappy because now the villain is going to be able to get more control of what happens to Desdemona, which is exactly what happens in Cyprus when he ruins her reputation and makes Othello believe she has slept with Cassio.

A01 This sentence is too long and should be broken up and each point dealt with separately

The dramatic method of using Brabantio to bring up the theme of deception, which is very important, is also in the extract at the end. Brabantio says 'She has deceived her father, and may thee'. He is very bitter about Desdemona here because she deceived him by running away with Othello. This warning is to Othello, but Othello does not listen to him because he trusts Desdemona completely at this point.

A02 Some grasp of the significance of this quotation

The dramatic method of deception is also used in Othello's own long speech in this extract because maybe Othello is deceiving himself. He tells the Duke that he won't be distracted from his job in Cyprus because he doesn't feel lust any more because he's older. The audience may think he doesn't realise what love is really like. This

AO4

Attempt to link this extract to another scene is partially developed and needs supporting quotation

happens again in Act II when he and Desdemona are together again in Cyprus after the storm. Then he says that he feels too much happiness. This extract foreshadows that Othello doesn't cope with love. This will be part of his downfall later.

There are other dramatic methods that Shakespeare uses. The Duke shows us that Othello is a trustworthy character. This is because he allows Othello to take Desdemona with him to war, and also because he makes a positive comment about Othello to Brabantio. He tells Brabantio that he should believe Othello is a good husband for Desdemona. He says 'your son-in-law is far more fair than black.' This is telling Brabantio that Othello's race is not a problem, he is a good man. So Shakespeare is making us believe that Othello is a hero, which will make his tragic downfall more effective later on in the play.

AO1

Moves on to a new dramatic method, showing a grasp of a how to cover a reasonable range of key ideas in a logical way

AO2

Some grasp of how Shakespeare creates meanings, but expression could be more formal – 'not a problem' sounds too much like speech

This extract is significant because it is the beginning of the marriage of Othello and Desdemona and we can see they are united together as a couple. But we can also see that they have got a lot of things to face when they go to Cyprus. The Duke and the senator have lines about war. They make it seem important and something that needs to be dealt with at once. The 1st senator says 'You must away tonight' and the Duke says 'this night'. These lines are showing us that Othello and Desdemona's relationship will always be affected by war, which is foreshadowing bad things to come for them. Iago being on stage with Desdemona and Othello but saying nothing while the senators are speaking, is also foreshadowing of bad things happening to the couple.

AO1

Expression is to casual, and the student needs to explain exactly what is meant by 'a lot of things to face' - this phrase is too vague

AO3

This is a very important point that needs further development to show a grasp of how Shakespeare uses Iago as part of his dramatic methods in this extract

The last dramatic method Shakespeare uses in this extract is some irony. In this scene we find out that Othello's and Desdemona's marriage is going to begin in a war zone. This is ironic because they have already had to battle for their love. They are surrounded by conflict wherever they go. In Venice they had to marry secretly because of Brabantio's disapproval, and now when they are finally allowed to speak up for their love they are being sent to the war zone of Cyprus. The audience will wonder if their love can ever be safe. This uneasiness we feel is typical of tragedy.

AO1

Some grasp of possible audience responses to this extract and the genre of tragedy

MID LEVEL

Comment

The material covered is relevant, but at times the identification of the dramatic methods could be more precise. A limited but accurate range of literary terminology is used, e.g. irony, imagery and foreshadowing are all mentioned. There are apt quotations supporting a number of points and some appreciation is shown of some aspects of language. There is some grasp of Shakespeare's cultural context in the discussion of Desdemona and Othello's marriage for AO3. The student is able to make some connections across the text, linking the extract briefly to other parts of the play for AO4. A sense of a personal viewpoint comes across.

To improve the answer:

A more extensive use of literary terminology e.g. structure, dialogue, dramatic contrast, emotive language would help the student focus more precisely on dramatic methods for AO1 and AO2. In particular, the student needs to develop the point about Iago's silence. The student should make more detailed comments on language for AO2. The student could consider how Shakespeare's audience may have responded to Desdemona's request to go to war with Othello. For AO4 the student needs to include more sustained discussions about the links between this extract and the tragedy as a whole. For AO5 critics could be cited to offer alternative readings; in particular, the characterisation of the central couple and their love.

Candidate 2

A01 Clear signposting and clear topic sentence to introduce first argument

A02 Implicit grasp of structure – but the student needs to develop the point about Desdemona's assertiveness with textual evidence

A04 A fruitful link across the text

A02 Shows a sound grasp of imagery with apt quotations

A03 Implicit grasp of the genre of tragedy – could develop this idea further.

This extract is significant to the tragedy of the play as a whole for several reasons. Firstly, it proves that Desdemona and Othello's love is secure and that they are well matched before Iago's evil plots divide them. We know this because Othello and Desdemona defend their love for each other in this extract. They mirror each other in their language. Desdemona asks the Duke to 'Let me go with him' and Othello asks the Duke to 'Let her have her voice'. These lines suggest they are equally in love, but also hint that maybe the relationship is unbalanced in some way. This is because Othello is echoing Desdemona. He follows her lead, speaking second and supporting her. Even though Othello has more lines than Desdemona, she seems more assertive. This reminds us of their courtship, described by Othello earlier in this scene. Desdemona led Othello to propose marriage to her by dropping hints to him about the kind of man she wanted. This would have been really shocking for Shakespeare's audience in the 17th Century, who expected women to be submissive in courtship and marriage.

The audience may feel that Act I Scene 3 as a whole shows that Othello cannot cope well with love. There will be more evidence of this when the tragic couple are reunited in Cyprus in Act II Scene 1, when Othello will comment that love is 'too much joy'. In "Othello" Shakespeare is interested in exploring what happens to a lover when he is put to the test. His discussion of the theme of love under pressure begins in this scene and extract.

Shakespeare uses other methods to show that Othello is not a very experienced lover. In his speech at line 261 Othello says that he does not want Desdemona to go to Cyprus because he feels lust for her. He claims that 'the young affects' are 'defunct'. He claims he'll not be distracted from his job if he's got Desdemona with him. However, the imagery in the speeches of Othello e.g. 'heat', 'appetite', 'disports' shows he is thinking about Desdemona in a sexual way. The audience may worry about this and wonder if he knows himself. There is irony here because Othello says he cares most about his 'business' (military duties) and 'estimation' (reputation) but he will become obsessed by Desdemona from the moment he arrives in Cyprus.

Iago's silence is important and a source of irony in this extract. The villain doesn't say anything, but he casts a shadow over everything. It is really ironic that Othello addresses Iago directly, bringing him into the plans at the end of the extract, with a speech that begins, 'My life upon her faith'. The linking of Iago and Desdemona is disturbing. This extract makes it clear that Desdemona's reputation is going to be very important. For the audience, it is really painful to think that it is Othello himself who gives Iago the inspiration for his evil plots by saying how much he is in love. There is proof in this extract of one of Othello's weaknesses or fatal flaws – his overwhelming love for Desdemona. In Act III Scene 3 Iago will exploit this weakness very ruthlessly.

Shakespeare makes it clear to the audience that the focus of the next four acts of this tragedy will be Othello's feelings for Desdemona. He does this in the lines spoken by

A05 Beginning to consider alternative readings of the text in a fruitful way

A03 Shows a grasp of historical context and audience reception which could be developed further

A01 This is a good point, but needs further development. At the moment it isn't linked fully to the previous point – maybe it belongs elsewhere?

A01 Good point, but needs to use the terms of the question set to ensure that the response is on track and focused on dramatic methods

AO2

Misses an opportunity to link the senator's speech to Renaissance attitudes towards race and how audiences might respond to his words

the senator and Brabantio near the end of this extract. Both speeches include warnings. The senator seems friendly when he says to Othello, 'brave Moor, use Desdemona well'. However, it is possible to interpret this line in a negative way. Does the senator expect that Othello won't treat Desdemona 'well'? Brabantio gives Othello a direct warning about women. He uses a rhyming couplet, 'Look to her, Moor... She has deceived her father, and may thee.' It is significant that Iago hears these words. Othello may not pay them any attention at the moment, but Iago will make him believe that Brabantio was right. Many critics view Othello as a noble and romantic hero, such as A. C. Bradley. However, in this extract it is easy to say he is foolish because Othello does not recognise the warnings he is given, and because he trusts Iago with his wife. We know Iago is not a trustworthy man.

AO5

Clear recognition that there are different ways of interpreting the text

AO5

The reference to a critic is rather 'bolted on' but the student is again showing an understanding that the text can be interpreted in different ways

AO5

Strong sense of personal interpretation to conclude the essay

To conclude, with the way it links love and war, this extract sums up the tragedy of "Othello". This is the last time in the play when Othello speaks with a lot of self-confidence, and the imagery he uses here shows he is deluded about his love for Desdemona. He is beginning to be overwhelmed by his feelings. It is sad that the destruction of the couple's marriage begins in this extract, where they refuse to be parted. The dramatic methods Shakespeare has used in this extract have all been really effective in preparing us for Othello's downfall.

GOOD LEVEL

Comment

This is a fluent essay with a lot of strengths. There is a grasp of a number of Shakespeare's dramatic methods for AO2, and some perceptive comments about language. The student's own style is coherent for AO1. There is a sound use of literary terminology, used accurately. Arguments are relevant and structured logically, although at times the student could go back to the terms of the question at the start of paragraphs to ensure that everything is linked fully to the task set. Some grasp of Shakespeare's historical/social context is shown for AO3, and a critic is mentioned and assessed briefly for AO5. Connections across the text are consistently made for AO4.

To improve the answer:

For a higher mark the student needs to make reference to and discuss a wider range of Shakespeare's dramatic methods in more detail for AO2 e.g. in particular the dramatic similarities and contrasts between Othello's and Desdemona's speech styles. Further analysis of apt quotations would be needed to do this. The student could also incorporate more literary terminology for AO1. There were opportunities missed to comment on historical/social context in relation to the characterisation of Othello and Desdemona for AO3 e.g. race, women's roles. More could be made of different possible audience reactions to this extract for AO3. The student does offer alternative readings of key moments for AO5, but more examples of different interpretations could add to and support the arguments here.

Candidate 3

AO1
Strong sense of overview to begin with, showing an immediate grasp of the significance of the extract

AO2
Apt use of literary term 'symbol', which is also linked fruitfully to the AO3 context

AO5
Asserting strong individual response to the extract and constructing coherent arguments for AO1

This extract is highly significant because the outcome of this discussion about whether Desdemona should be allowed to accompany Othello essentially determines the tragic couple's fate. Here it becomes clear that Desdemona and Othello's relationship will continue to be characterised by conflict: their married life will begin in a war zone. This ironic foreshadowing is typical of Shakespeare's methods. Even the most passionate speeches in this extract create tension. At the very moment that Desdemona and Othello are united in their love, Shakespeare hints they are vulnerable.

Shakespeare presents Desdemona as sympathetic but potentially subversive. Controversially – for a 17th century audience – she refuses to follow the traditional path of Renaissance wives married to military men. The extract opens with the Duke asking, 'What would you, Desdemona?' suggesting she is free to make her own decision about her future. This is unconventional, as is the sight of a woman defending herself in the Venetian senate, a symbol of male power and authority. However, the whole of Act I Scene 3 has been unconventional. A 'wheeling stranger' has married a Venetian noblewoman. A wealthy patriarch's wishes have been ignored. Desdemona actively wooed Othello. These events have created a lot of dramatic tension.

The language Desdemona uses at line 249 is initially subversive. She says that her 'downright violence and scorn of fortunes/ May trumpet to the world'. Desdemona seems proud of her wilfulness. However, ironically, she uses her rhetorical skills to submit to male authority. She demands her marital 'rites', in order to position herself as a traditional, obedient wife, as a number of historicist critics have noted. Desdemona reminds the Duke she has consecrated her 'soul and fortunes' to Othello: he has total responsibility for her. The language of submission that Desdemona uses makes her forwardness acceptable. Desdemona refuses to be a 'moth of peace' at home. This image suggests her vulnerability; Desdemona cannot live without Othello. I would also argue that her final request, 'Let me go with him', demonstrates helpless dependency, rather than assertive female power.

Shakespeare undermines Othello's conception of himself as an authoritative male, indicating that he is as vulnerable as Desdemona. The structure – Othello speaks second and echoes Desdemona ('Let her have her voice') – hints that he is not in charge of events. His rhetorical skill mirrors his wife's, but Othello's remarks about marriage show a lack of self-knowledge. There is a key example of dramatic contrast. While Desdemona defended her marital 'rites', Othello denies marriage will have any impact on him. He claims that 'the young affects' are 'in me defunct'. Why has he married Desdemona if he has no 'heat' or 'appetite' for her? Shakespeare suggests that Othello suffers from blindness, a fatal flaw which will propel him towards tragedy.

The marriage of sexual imagery with the language of war creates further dramatic tension. Othello claims 'disports' will not 'corrupt' his 'business'. He humorously asserts that his helmet should be used as a 'skillet' if he allows himself to be diverted by sex. This would ruin his 'estimation', implying that his masculine honour is

AO3
Apt and succinct reference to relevant historical context

AO2
Sophisticated grasp of the dramatic impact and significance of Desdemona's language and apt quotation. Shows awareness of critical interpretations for AO5

AO1
Appropriate use of rhetorical question to make an important point

A05

Well-integrated reference to critical viewpoints and apt quote from a relevant critic

highly important to him. This is a theme that Shakespeare will explore further. Critics have argued that it is obsession with his honour which transforms Othello from the loving husband we see here to the 'domestic tyrant' Frances Dolan describes him as.

The line shared between the Duke, Othello and Desdemona in response to the 1st senator's insistence that Othello 'must away tonight' hints at discord and suggests the central couple can be set at odds. Desdemona is dismayed, 'Tonight, my lord?' she asks, surprised (how realistic is she about being a military wife?) In dramatic contrast, Othello's response is automatic and accepting. He says 'With all my heart', quickly returning to the role of cool headed commander we saw earlier in Act I.

A02

Continues to pay close attention to the language of the extract

A03

Shows a good grasp of how the extract works as drama and how an audience might respond

Iago's silent presence is troubling. The audience can imagine how triumphant the villain will feel when he is drawn into events. Othello's unwitting blindness is demonstrated when he puts Desdemona into Iago's care, saying that his 'ancient' is a man 'of honesty and trust'. It is horribly ironic that it is Othello who invites the enemy within the gates. Because we know more about Iago's real nature than the protagonist, Othello can seem complacent and foolish. The theme of deception, which is important throughout the play, is reinforced by Brabantio's rhyming couplet, 'Look to her, Moor...' We will be aware that, ironically, Othello is being warned about the wrong person. There's also a moment of ominous irony when the 1st senator tells Othello to 'use Desdemona well'. This line – and Brabantio's sour note – stand out in this extract because they suggest a less idealised view of love.

A03

Apt reference to another aspect of the play's context

References to Othello's race also create tension. Ania Loomba has said that Othello is treated like an 'honorary white' in Venice, and in this extract there seems to be what many critics have interpreted as an apology for Othello's race. The Duke comforts Brabantio, telling him his 'son-in law is far more fair than black'. These words remind the audience of Othello's noble qualities, but also, in an indirect way, draw attention to the negative 17th century stereotype of the black man. Is Desdemona also apologising for her husband's race when she says she saw Othello's 'visage in his mind'? These are uncomfortable comments for a modern audience. The 17th century theatre goer may have seen them as hints that we cannot trust Othello as a husband.

A05

Shows awareness of critics' responses to a key aspect of the text

A01

Concludes with the same strong sense of overview offered in the opening paragraph

Ironically, the extract ends with Othello in authoritarian mode. He tells Desdemona he can spend 'but an hour' on 'love, worldly matter and direction' with her. However, he also says, 'My life upon her faith'. This sounds romantic, but is troubling. At a moment when he thinks he is focused on war, Othello is actually overwhelmed by love. The seeds of his destruction have been sown here: Othello believes he is in control of events, but Shakespeare makes it clear he is not.

VERY HIGH LEVEL

Comment

Arguments are convincing and coherent for AO1. There is a strong grasp of how Shakespeare uses a wide range of dramatic methods for AO2, with consistently apt quotation and sustained understanding of language. References to the seventeenth-century context are relevant to the extract and show insight into how Shakespeare's methods may impact on the audience for AO3. Connections are made across the text consistently, showing an insight into the play as a whole for AO4. Different critical perspectives are incorporated, with a pertinent use of two specific critics for AO5.

PRACTICE TASK

Now it's your turn to work through an exam-style task on *Othello*. The key is to:

- Quickly read and decode the task/question
- Briefly plan your points – then add a few more details, such as evidence, or make links between them
- Write your answer

Decode the question

> 'Self-destruction and weakness are the main impressions the audience are left with of Othello at the end of the play.'

By considering Shakespeare's dramatic methods, to what extent do you agree with this view?

'Self-destruction'	suggests that Othello is responsible for his own downfall
'weakness'	suggests that Othello is a weak character, who has made poor decisions
'main impressions ... end of the play'	suggests that at the end of Act V the audience will generally feel a particular way i.e. that the tragic outcome is the result of self-destruction and weakness
'dramatic methods'	suggests you must focus on what Shakespeare *does* – but not just language, but also structuring of events, for example.
'to what extent do you agree?'	What is my view? Do I agree with the statement completely, partially or not at all?

Plan and write

- Decide your viewpoint
- Plan your points
- Think of key evidence and quotations
- Write your answer

Success criteria

- Show your understanding of the two key ideas as aspects of character construction
- Draw on a range of critical views or different interpretation as appropriate
- Sustain your focus on the idea of 'weakness' and 'self-destruction'
- Argue your point of view clearly and logically
- Make perceptive points and express your ideas confidently
- Support your points with relevant, well-chosen evidence including quotations
- Use literary terminology accurately and appropriately with reference to the effect on the reader
- Write in fluent, controlled and accurate English

Once you have finished, use the **Mark scheme** on page 120 to evaluate your response.

FURTHER READING

Contemporary criticism

John Russell Brown, *Shakespeare: The Tragedies*, Palgrave Macmillan, Basingstoke, 2001

Written in a style that makes it accessible to A Level students and split into short sections for ease of use, includes a chapter on *Othello* called 'Sexuality and Difference'; covers various aspects of the play

Kate Chedgzoy, ed., *Shakespeare, Feminism and Gender*, New Casebooks, Palgrave Macmillan, Basingstoke, 2001

Includes an essay on *Othello* by Frances Dolan, 'Revolutions, Petty Tyranny and the Murderous Husband'

Rex Gibson, *Shakespearean and Jacobean Tragedy*, Cambridge Contexts in Literature, Cambridge University Press, 2000

An excellent guide to a wide range of tragedies, and their contexts; also covers critical approaches

Jean E. Howard and Scott Cutler Shershow, eds., *Marxist Shakespeares*, Psychology Press, 2001

Contains a **Marxist feminist** essay 'Looking Well to Linens: Women and Cultural Production in *Othello* and Shakespeare's England' by Dympna Callaghan

Claire McEachern, ed., *The Cambridge Companion to Shakespearean Tragedy*, Cambridge Companions to Literature, Cambridge University Press, 2003

Covers ten plays, includes cultural and literary background, the origins of sub-genres of Shakespeare's tragedies, e.g. love, revenge and classical tragedy, critical and theatrical reception of the plays

Lois Potter, *Othello: Shakespeare in Performance*, Manchester University Press, 2002

Traces acting traditions and how they affected interpretations of the central roles in the play; looks at various stage and screen versions of the play. Useful for students who are interested in cultural approaches to studying Shakespeare

Nicholas Potter, ed., *'Othello': A Reader's Guide to Essential Criticism*, Readers Guides to Essential Criticism, Palgrave Macmillan, Basingstoke, 2000

Traces the critical history of the play from the earliest critics up to the present day; also covers the historical context of the play, the most significant themes and recurring critical concerns

Emma Smith, ed., *Shakespeare's Tragedies*, Blackwell Guides to Criticism, Blackwell, Oxford, 2004

Includes an overview of criticism of Shakespeare's tragedies, and two essays on *Othello*, including 'Femininity and the Monstrous in *Othello*' by Karen Newman

Late twentieth-century critics

John Drakakis, ed., *Shakespearean Tragedy*, Longman, New York, 1992

A collection of contemporary criticism with a range of views of *Othello*; includes Marilyn French (a feminist reading), Stephen Greenblatt (a **New Historicist** reading)

Andrew Hadfield, ed., *William Shakespeare's Othello: A Sourcebook*, Routledge, London, 1987

A broad-ranging guide to critical responses and contexts; includes critics Karen Newman and Lisa Jardine, who discuss race and gender roles

Ania Loomba, *Gender, Race, Renaissance Drama*, Manchester University Press, 1987

Explores the sexual and racial politics of *Othello* and Elizabethan attitudes towards race and colour

Nicholas Marsh, *Shakespeare: The Tragedies*, Palgrave Macmillan, Basingstoke, 1998

An accessible guide to Shakespeare's tragedies; includes commentary on several aspects of *Othello* and a chapter on the literary and historical contexts of the tragedies

Virginia Mason Vaughan, *Othello: A Contextual History*, Cambridge University Press, 1996

Examines contemporary writings and explores them in relation to the play, e.g. representations of Africans and 'blackamoors', plus a history of *Othello* in performance

Caryl Phillips, 'Othello's Real Tragedy', *Guardian*, 7 February 1987, p. 19

An accessible piece focusing on Othello as a black man in a white world; also published in a collection of Phillips's essays, *The European Tribe*, Vintage, New York, 2000 under the title 'A Black European Success', pp. 45–51

Leonard Tennenhouse, *Power on Display: The Politics of Shakespeare's Genres*, Methuen, London, 1986

In the chapter 'The Theater of Punishment: Jacobean Tragedy and the Politics of Misogyny', Tennenhouse explores the representation of the female body and female sexuality in Jacobean drama, making some interesting comments about *Othello*

Earlier critics

A. C. Bradley, *Shakespearean Tragedy*, Macmillan, London 1904, 3rd edition by J. R. Brown, Macmillan, Basingstoke, 1992

Focusing on character and motivation, this text was influential in the twentieth century

T. S. Eliot, 'Shakespeare and the Stoicism of Seneca', *Selected Essays*, 1932

Eliot considers Seneca's influence on Shakespeare and comments on Othello's self-dramatisation and weakness in the final scene of the play

Helen Gardner, 'The Noble Moor', *Proceedings of the British Academy*, XLI, 1956

In exploring the heroism of Othello and the nature of his love for Desdemona, suggests that the hero and his love are flawed

R. B. Heilman, *Magic in the Web: Action and Language in 'Othello'*, University Press of Kentucky, Lexington, 1956

Discusses language, symbolism, theme and character in a detailed analysis of the play

G. K. Hunter, '"Othello" and Colour Prejudice', *Proceedings of the British Academy*, LIII, 1967, pp. 139–63

F. R. Leavis, 'Diabolical Intellect and the Noble Hero', *The Common Pursuit*, Chatto & Windus, London, 1962

A response to Bradley's ideas about Othello, arguing that Othello is responsible for his own downfall because of his deficient character

John Wain, ed., *Shakespeare: 'Othello'*, Casebook series, Macmillan, Basingstoke, 1971

Includes comments and essays by Rymer, Johnson, Coleridge, Bradley, Eliot, Leavis

LITERARY TERMS

Aristotle a Greek philosopher (384–322 BC) who discussed tragedy in his *Poetics*. Aristotle observed that tragedy represented a single action of a certain magnitude, that provoked audience reactions of pity and terror which were then resolved by the **catharsis** of the play's climax. **Tragedies** worked on a process of the reversal of fortune, with the **protagonist** making an error of judgement and then learning the truth about his folly, gaining insight into himself and his situation as a consequence.

aside a dramatic convention in which a character speaks in such a way that some of the characters on stage do not hear what is said, while others do. It may also be direct address to the audience, revealing the character's inner thoughts or motives, as is the case with Iago.

Aesthetics Aesthetics is a branch of philosophy which deals with the nature of art, beauty and 'good taste'. It is traditionally associated with literature and the visual arts. So far as literature is concerned, it has led to the delineation of a canon of 'classic' texts which are highly valued for their complexity, use of literary language, aesthetic unity and serious subject matter. An aesthetic approach to Othello might consider the ways in which the play could be considered 'beautiful'.

blank verse unrhymed iambic pentameter: a line of five iambs. One of the commonest English metres, the popularity of blank verse is due to its flexibility and relative closeness to spoken English. It allows a pleasant variation of full strong stresses per line, generally four or five, while conforming to the basic metrical pattern of five iambs. Shakespeare uses blank verse when he wants to convey the intensity of characters' feelings. Heroes generally speak in verse in Shakespeare's plays, so it is significant when Othello speaks in prose.

catalyst a person or thing that brings about an event or change

catharsis in tragedy, the purging of the effects of pent up emotion and repressed thoughts by bringing them to the surface of consciousness

characterisation the way in which a writer creates characters so as to attract or repel our sympathy. Different kinds of literature have certain conventions of characterisation. In **Jacobean** drama there were many stock dramatic 'types' (see **Machiavel**) whose characteristics were familiar to the audience.

denouement the final unfolding of a plot; the point at which the audience's expectations, be they hopes or fears, about what will happen to the characters are finally satisfied or denied

dramatic irony a feature of many plays, it occurs when the development of the plot allows the audience to possess more information about what is happening than some of the characters themselves have. Iago is the source of much of the dramatic irony in *Othello*, informing the audience of his intentions. Characters may also speak in a dramatically ironic way, saying something that points to events to come without understanding the significance of their words.

feminism broadly speaking, a political movement claiming political and economic equality of women with men. Feminist criticism and scholarship seek to explore or expose the masculine 'bias' in texts and challenge traditional ideas about them, constructing and then offering a feminine perspective on works of art. Since the late 1960s feminist theories about literature and language, and feminist interpretations of texts have multiplied enormously. Feminism has its roots in previous centuries: early texts championing women's rights include Mary Wollstonecraft's *A Vindication of the Rights of Women* (1792) and J. S. Mill's *The Subjection of Women* (1869).

foreshadowing a technique used to hint at and prepare the reader for the later events or a turning point in the action

hamartia a Greek term meaning an error of judgement

hubris the self-indulgent confidence that causes a tragic hero to ignore the decrees, laws and warnings of the gods, and therefore defy them to bring about his or her downfall

idiom a characteristic mode of expression for a character

image, imagery in its narrowest sense an image is a word picture, a description of some visible scene or object. More commonly, imagery relates to the figurative language in a piece of literature (**metaphors** and similes) or all the words which refer to objects and qualities which appeal to the senses and feelings. Thematic imagery is imagery which recurs throughout a work of art. For example, in *Othello* Shakespeare's images of the devil and infection underpin the theme of evil.

irony in speech, consists of saying one thing while you mean another (many of Iago's speeches to his victims include examples of this kind). However, not all ironical statements in literature are as easily discerned or understood; the patterns of irony – of situation, character, structure and vocabulary – in *Othello* need careful unravelling. In certain cases the context will make clear the true meaning intended, but sometimes the writer will have to rely on the reader sharing values and knowledge in order for his or her meaning to be understood. Ironic literature characteristically presents a variety of possible points of view about its subject matter.

Jacobean Jacobean drama refers to the plays written during the reign of James I (1603–25).

juxtapose in literature, to place ideas, **images** or events side by side so that they can be compared.

Machiavel a villainous stock character in Elizabethan and **Jacobean** drama, so called after the Florentine writer Niccolo Machiavelli (1469–1527), author of *The Prince* (written 1513), a book of political advice to rulers that recommended the need under certain circumstances to lie to the populace for their own good and to preserve power. Embellishment of this suggestion (which was only one small part of his analysis of political power and justice) made Machiavelli almost synonymous with the Devil in English literature. Machiavels are practised liars and cruel political opportunists, who delight in their own manipulative evil. The topic of dissembling and disguising one's true identity amount almost to an obsession in plays in the early seventeenth century. Iago is one of the most sophisticated Machiavellian villains in Jacobean drama.

malcontent a stage archetype who is disaffected, melancholy, dissatisfied with or disgusted by society and life. Iago is not a true malcontent, but he demonstrates some of these qualities.

Marxist criticism emphasises the role of class and ideology and seeks to establish if a text reflects or challenges the current social order. Marxist critics view texts as products which should be understood in relation to their historical contexts. Marxism began with Karl Marx, the nineteenth-century German philosopher who wrote *Das Kapital* (1867), which is considered the seminal work of the communist movement. Marx was the first Marxist literary critic, writing critical essays in the 1830s on Goethe and Shakespeare.

metaphor goes further than a comparison between two things by fusing them together; one thing is described as being another, thus carrying over its associations. References to Iago as being a dog and a devil help Shakespeare portray the villain's evil.

mirroring in literature, a character or event mirrors another character or event when the two follow similar plots, act in similar ways or contain similar elements or traits. Shakespeare uses mirroring in *Othello* to increase the audience's appreciation of the characters and their situations.

New Historicism the work of a loose affiliation of critics who discuss literary works in terms of their historical contexts. In particular, they seek to study literature as part of a wider cultural history, exploring the relationship of literature to society.

oxymoron a figure of speech in which contradictory terms are brought together in what is at first sight an impossible combination. There are a number of examples in *Othello*, e.g. Cassio is said to be 'damned in a fair wife' (I.1.20); Iago speaks of 'honest knaves' (I.1.48) and also informs us 'I am not what I am' (I.1.64).

parody an imitation of a work or style devised so as to ridicule its characteristics. Iago mocks Othello by imitating his speech style.

pathos moments in works of art which evoke strong feelings of pity are said to have this quality.

patriarchy a community or family under the authority of a patriarch. The patriarchal system places the man at the head of the household or government.

personification a type of metaphorical language in which things or ideas are treated as if they are human beings, with attributes and feelings.

poetic justice Thomas Rymer devised this term in 1678 to describe how literature should always depict a world in which virtue and vice are eventually rewarded and punished appropriately.

post-colonialism criticism explores the ways in which texts carry racist or colonial undertones.

prose the most typical form of written language, which sounds like the natural flow of speech rather than the more formal rhythmic structure of poetry and verse. Prose is traditionally associated with 'low' and comic characters in Renaissance drama, but Shakespeare uses it for other purposes as well. In *Othello*, Shakespeare uses prose when he wants the dialogue to sound urgent and fast moving.

protagonist a main character in a play.

Restoration Charles II was restored to the throne in 1660. The English Restoration (1660–89) refers to the final years of the reign of the Stuart kings.

revenge tragedy a special form of tragedy in which a **protagonist** pursues vengeance against those who have done wrong. These plays often focus on the moral confusion caused by the need to answer evil with evil. The Elizabethan interest in the tragedies of Seneca gave rise to many revenge tragedies. Bloodthirsty scenes and every kind of sensational horror typify revenge tragedy.

soliloquy a dramatic convention which allows a character in a play to speak directly to the audience, as if thinking aloud about motives, feelings and decisions. The use of the soliloquy enables the dramatist to give characters psychological depth. Part of the convention of the soliloquy is that it provides accurate access to the character's innermost thoughts.

tragedy Shakespeare's tragedies concentrate on the downfall of powerful men and often illuminate the resulting deterioration of a whole community. The protagonists in Shakespeare's tragedies are not necessarily good. In *Othello* the protagonist is noble, but becomes cruel and vicious when he is jealous.

vice, the a figure in morality plays of the fifteenth and sixteenth centuries who tempts humankind in a half-comic, half-unpleasant manner. Many critics argue that Iago is modelled on this stock character.

xenophobic fearing or hating foreigners.

REVISION TASK ANSWERS

Task 1: Iago's motives

- Iago hates Othello because he promoted Cassio.
- Iago has a grudge against Cassio because he thinks he is undeserving of promotion.
- Iago is discontented; he is held back by 'the curse of service'.
- Iago's motives are plausible because they are all driven by what seem to be concrete facts about his professional position.
- Iago's motives are plausible because he is a character who is egotistical, envious and manipulative.

Task 2: The couple's loving reunion

- Othello greets his wife first; he is in thrall to Desdemona.
- Othello kisses Desdemona before discussing the Turkish fleet; he now puts love before war.
- Othello seems secure in his love; he calls Desdemona his 'fair warrior' and his 'soul's joy'.
- Othello says he would be 'most happy' to die now because his soul 'hath her content so absolute'; love for Desdemona has made him supremely happy.
- Othello says he feels 'too much joy' when he is reunited with Desdemona; he is beginning to be overwhelmed by love.

Task 3: Iago's poisoning of Othello's mind

- Iago mentions jealousy in general terms and then makes insinuations – his approach is initially indirect, becoming more direct as he sees his method is working.
- Iago uses the handkerchief as proof of adultery, making his insinuations seem plausible.
- Iago promises to serve and help Othello in the 'bloody business' of revenge, making his false love seem more reliable than Desdemona's true love.
- Othello *does not* give in to Iago easily; he demands proof.
- Othello *does* seem to be seized by jealousy quickly –this is convincing because his love for Desdemona is so great.

Task 4: Othello's treatment of Desdemona

- Othello is convinced that Desdemona has been false to him, shown in his bullying words and actions: he tells her she is 'false as hell' and commands her to leave his presence.
- Desdemona pleads with Othello, bewildered. Her questioning between lines 26–71 shows that she desperately wants to find out what has caused the problems between them.
- Othello's verbal abuse of Desdemona becomes more intense: She is an 'impudent strumpet' and then 'a whore.' (lines 82, 88)
- Desdemona insists on her innocence bravely, but when she is called 'that cunning whore of Venice' (line 91) she is overwhelmed, telling Emilia she feels 'half asleep' (benumbed by Othello's accusations). She remains loyal, making no accusations against Othello.
- Desdemona's misery is clear in the exchange with Emilia and Iago. She weeps and blames her 'wretched fortune' (line 130). She remains committed to her love, asking Iago, 'What shall I do to win my lord again?' (line 151).

Task 5: Male dominance in *Othello*

- Brabantio is an indulgent father until Desdemona defies him, when he becomes tyrannical.
- Othello is as loving as Brabantio early on, but becomes domineering when he starts to mistrust Desdemona. He exerts control over her, labelling and interrogating her.
- Othello's murder of Desdemona suggests he believes he has the right to determine his wife's fate.
- Iago is an oppressive husband, who silences Emilia by killing her when she disobeys him.
- All of these male figures treat the women like possessions they have the right to instruct, control and dominate.

Task 6: Jealousy and Othello's marriage

- Iago is driven by professional and sexual jealousy of Cassio and Othello. He seeks revenge on them when he is not promoted.
- Iago's evil schemes suggest he is contemptuous of virtue and happiness and wants to annihilate them. He cannot bear to witness Othello's happy marriage.
- Othello's jealousy is as powerful as his love, and overwhelms him. However, he is torn between wanting to believe Desdemona is faithful and assuming she is false.
- Othello's jealousy causes him mental agony. It makes him irrational. He turns to murder because he cannot be 'satisfied'.
- Jealousy is the most powerful destructive force in this play. It leads to the death of virtue in both protagonist and antagonist. With the deaths of the central couple, love is destroyed.

Task 7: Women as powerless victims

- Desdemona exerts power in her courtship; she chooses Othello and demands the right to live with him. When Othello mistrusts her, her power diminishes and Desdemona is unable to control her own destiny.
- Emilia has little power in her relationship with Iago until the final scene, when she speaks out against him. Until this point, she has unwittingly been his co-conspirator.
- Bianca has no power to command Cassio.
- The women are all vilified by Iago, whose words and actions render them powerless.
- Under Iago's influence Othello becomes a verbal and physical abuser of women. He is the agent of his wife's destruction. Act V shows that all the women are the victims of male aggression.

Task 8: *Othello* as tragedy

- Othello is a conventional tragic hero; he is a noble man whose downfall is brought about by a fatal error of judgment – he trusts Iago more than Desdemona.
- The tragic outcome seems inevitable once Othello's love becomes irrational jealousy.
- The tragic outcome (in particular Desdemona's death) provokes fear and pathos, which Aristotle suggested were the appropriate emotions when watching a tragedy.
- *Othello* is a domestic tragedy because the focus is on the personal life of the protagonist and the destruction of his marriage is a private matter.
- Othello's death represents a military loss for Venice. The theme of race and the mixed marriage of Othello and Desdemona also make this a play about social and sexual politics.

PROGRESS CHECK ANSWERS

Section One: Check your understanding

1. The central couple marry in secret, betraying Brabantio's trust.
- Iago betrays Othello by causing trouble for him with Brabantio.
- Roderigo intends to betray Othello by following Desdemona to Cyprus in the hope of seducing her.

2. Iago manipulates and exploits Roderigo for his own ends; this is a pattern he will repeat with the other characters.
- Iago's use of crude sexually imagery prepares us for his abusive treatment of the female characters.
- Iago's boasting that he is not what he seems prepares us for his treacherous dissembling in later scenes.
- Iago's ability to stay out of trouble is seen when he leaves Roderigo to face Brabantio; he also does this in Cyprus.

3. Othello and Desdemona's elopement is romantic: they have married for love.
- The elopement is also an act of deception, suggesting their relationship will be marred by conflict.
- The elopement reveals seventeenth-century social values: Othello and Desdemona cannot marry openly.
- The uproar caused by the elopement suggests the couple will not be safe from interference in their affairs.

4. Brabantio is cruel and insulting to the couple.
- Othello and Desdemona defend their love with equal passion.
- The descriptions of their courtship are romantic and touching.
- The Duke's respect for Othello suggests he is a worthy husband.

5. Brabantio has been a generous father by Renaissance standards, allowing Desdemona to reject suitors.
- Brabantio loves Desdemona, shown by the depth of his sorrow and bitterness when the Duke supports Othello and Desdemona.
- Desdemona has been deceptive, but she has also been a dutiful daughter, as she reminds Brabantio.
- Both father and daughter show pride and obstinacy in this scene, rejecting each other.

6. Othello is a cool-headed, confident soldier, who commands respect from the senate and Cassio.
- Othello is a dutiful soldier, who puts his work first before his marriage, until his mind is poisoned by Iago.
- Othello needed prompting to woo Desdemona– he is less confident as a lover.
- Othello is out of his depth, overwhelmed by his emotions.

7. Iago is driven by professional jealousy of Cassio who has been promoted over him.
- He is driven by personal hatred of Othello.
- Iago is sexually jealous: he claims Othello has slept with Emilia.
- Iago hates of goodness and wants to destroy it.

8. Iago persuades Cassio to drink too much, knowing he has a weak head for drink.
- Iago persuades Roderigo to provoke a fight with Cassio.
- Montano is wounded in the fight.
- Othello dismisses Cassio from his post.

9. He claims to have witnessed Cassio dreaming about having sex with Desdemona.
- He uses the handkerchief as proof of adultery.
- He torments Othello with descriptions of Desdemona and Cassio having sex.

10. Othello's interrogation of Emilia shows how unreasonable he is becoming: he refuses to accept what Emilia says about Desdemona's honesty.
- Othello bullies and insults Desdemona, trying to extract a confession of adultery.
- Desdemona appeals to Iago for help, unaware that he is the cause of her misery.

11. Desdemona's eyes itch, a premonition of weeping and death.
- The willow song tells the story of a tragic love affair gone wrong.
- Desdemona's request that her wedding sheets be used as her winding sheets foreshadows how she will die.

12. Iago is directly responsible for Roderigo's death.
- Iago is indirectly responsible for the murder of Desdemona. Othello is spurred on to revenge when he thinks Iago has killed Cassio.
- Iago continues to wreak havoc when the truth about his evil is revealed, killing Emilia.

13. Desdemona – tragic, undeserved, inappropriate
- Emilia – tragic, undeserved, inappropriate
- Othello – tragic, deserved, appropriate

14. Othello verbally abuses Desdemona
- Iago physically and verbally assaults Emilia
- Othello physically tries to wound Iago

15. He says women 'rise to play, and go to bed to work', dismissing them as sexual objects.
- He calls his wife a 'villainous whore' because she disobeys him.
- He abuses Bianca in Act V Scene 1, calling her a 'strumpet'.

16.
- The deception and manipulation of Roderigo foreshadows what happens to Othello.
- Roderigo is drawn into violence by Iago, as is Othello.
- Roderigo is brutally killed by Iago; Othello's mind is brutally destroyed by Iago.

17. Desdemona is less worldly and cynical than Emilia, having a more positive view of men and marriage.
- Desdemona confides in Emilia when she is distressed and gains emotional support from her e.g. after Othello calls her a whore.
- Emilia becomes defender of Desdemona's reputation.

18. A woman's reputation is of primary importance –in the eyes of men women are virtuous or whores.
- A man's reputation depends on honourable behaviour in public. Cassio is ashamed when he is demoted; Othello shocks others when he abuses Desdemona.
- An obsession with their honour leads men to abuse women.

19. Othello: a good husband who becomes a domestic tyrant
- Cassio: a faithful lover who can also be abusive
- Iago: a misogynistic and eventually murderous husband

20. Satisfying – Othello deserves to die for his crimes
- Satisfying – Iago deserves to be unmasked and punished
- Unsatisfying – Iago is not killed
- Unsatisfying – Desdemona and Emilia did not deserve to die

Section Two: Working towards the exam

1. Yes – his past is exotic and romantic.
- Yes – his courtship of Desdemona is romantic; the couple find each other magnetic.
- Yes – the poetic imagery Othello uses adds to our sense of him as a romantic figure.
- Yes – his defence of his love for Desdemona is romantic, as is his reunion with her in Cyprus.
- No – he becomes a bully under Iago's influence.
- No – his murder of Desdemona is ignoble.
- Partially – his death can be seen as romantic in some ways; he dies kissing Desdemona.
2. Yes – Iago and Emilia's marriage seems loveless and unequal.
- Yes – Othello becomes a domestic tyrant who abuses his wife.
- Yes – Desdemona is powerless within her marriage.
- Yes – Emilia is murdered by her husband when he cannot control her.
- No – Othello and Desdemona are well matched and their marriage is portrayed positively in Acts I and II.
- No – Othello and Desdemona are driven apart by Iago's evil, not because they are incompatible.
3. Iago despises goodness; he is contemptuous of Othello's 'constant, loving, noble nature'.
- Iago's evil impulses include lust for Desdemona: he feels no positive emotion about women, here or elsewhere.
- Iago wants revenge because he says Othello and Cassio have cuckolded him; his evil thoughts have developed like an infection.
- Iago's evil is driven by jealousy which 'like a poisonous mineral doth gnaw my inwards': Iago is infected with evil.
- Iago's evil demands that he is gets 'even' with Othello, so that Othello feels the same destructive jealousy he feels.
- Iago is proud of and revels in his ability to deceive here and elsewhere: the rhyming couplet that ends the scene is triumphant.
4. The submissive role of married women is exemplified when Emilia gives Iago the handkerchief: she wants to 'please his fantasy'.
- Iago's contemptuous treatment of Emilia until he finds out she has the handkerchief shows a pessimistic view of marriage: Desdemona will be treated with the same brutality Iago uses here.
- Emilia's innocence of her husband's evil designs is established: she does not suspect him of using the handkerchief nefariously.
- Emilia has faulty judgement. She knows Desdemona will 'run mad' when she realises the handkerchief is lost, but still gives it to Iago. She isolates Desdemona by letting her down.
- Iago's command, 'Go, leave me' foreshadows his bullying of Emilia in Act V Scene 2 when she tries to reveal the truth about him.
- The handkerchief is the catalyst that brings about the tragic ending: it is associated with the control and abuse of women.
5. Othello uses the same poetic imagery that he used to defend his love for Desdemona in Act I, but the imagery here is disturbing because it is linked to Desdemona's death.
- Othello idealises his wife still; she is a 'rose' and the 'light'.
- Othello says he does not want to 'scar that whiter skin of hers', suggesting how he is still overwhelmed by her beauty.
- Desdemona's erotic power is shown when Othello leans in to smell her 'balmy breath'.

- Othello's faulty reasoning, which has contributed to his downfall, is shown when he says he will 'love thee after death'.
- Othello's justification for killing Desdemona so that she cannot 'betray more men' suggests he is in the grip of madness.

Part Three: Characters and Themes

Section One: Check your understanding

1. Othello is noble and trusting – he does not suspect Iago.
- Iago's malice is more powerful than Othello's love for Desdemona.
- Othello is resolute – once his mind has been poisoned his powerful love becomes overwhelming jealousy.
2. Roderigo gives us insight into Iago's methods of manipulation.
- Roderigo is a failed lover we can compare Othello to.
- Roderigo is the catalyst in the fight scenes that further Iago's plots.
3. Bianca is powerless in her relationship with Cassio – like the other women in their relationships.
- Iago victimises Bianca, using her to further his plots. He abuses the other women in the same way.
- Bianca is labelled a 'strumpet' and dismissed as an unreliable witness in Act V Scene 1. The same happens to Desdemona. Othello calls her 'whore' and stops trusting her.
4. Cassio appreciates Desdemona's worth and beauty.
- Cassio is a loyal friend to Othello during his courtship and after he is dismissed.
- Cassio's shame at being drunk and losing his post suggests he is not morally corrupt.
5. Othello and Iago share the same obsession with masculine honour. Both have a strong sense of professional pride as military men.
- Othello relies on Iago professionally; his mistake is to trust him in his personal life.
- Iago works very hard to make Othello trust him; he pretends to have his best interests at heart.
6. Brabantio and Roderigo are prejudiced against foreigners and object to mixed marriages.
- The Duke has a tolerant attitude towards foreigners.
- Iago has a low opinion of Othello because of his race.
7. Othello and Desdemona have an idealised love for each other.
- Emilia's cynicism about marriage suggests the limitations of marital love.
- Destructive jealousy appears to be an inevitable part of love where there is mistrust.
8. Emilia is an unwitting catalyst to tragedy when she gives Iago the handkerchief.
- Emilia's unsatisfactory marriage shows us the way in which sexual politics work in the world of *Othello*: women are powerless.
- Emilia becomes the voice of justice, reaffirming Desdemona's honesty and innocence and exposing Iago's villainy in the final scene.
9. Brabantio has not behaved like a despotic patriarch. He has not forced Desdemona to marry to his liking.
- Brabantio has been trusting and generous father, allowing Desdemona the freedom to reject suitors she disliked.
- Brabantio's death from grief shows the depth of his love for Desdemona.

10. Professional jealousy of Cassio is a key part of Iago's motivation.
- Bianca's unfounded suspicions about the handkerchief show how irrational sexual jealousy can be.
- The death of Desdemona shows how destructive jealousy can be.

Section Two: Working towards the exam

1. Agree – Bianca and Emilia are both treated with contempt by their partners, labelled 'a bauble' and 'a foolish thing'.
- Agree – Desdemona is betrayed by Othello, who calls her a 'whore' and refuses to listen to her, putting his masculine honour first.
- Disagree – Othello's love for Desdemona is not unworthy; he idealises her as his 'soul's joy' and is a good husband before he is corrupted .
- Disagree – Othello proves he is worthy of Desdemona's love by killing himself 'upon a kiss'.

2. Agree – he falls under Iago's spell too quickly, moving from a general discussion about jealousy to a desire for revenge ('O blood, blood, blood!') in Act III Scene 3.
- Agree – why would Othello trust Iago over the wife he idealises, never asking her for her version of events?
- Disagree – great jealousy is the 'flipside' of overwhelming love.
- Disagree – Othello's jealousy is convincing because the proofs Iago provides make it so: the handkerchief, Cassio's supposed dream, the eavesdropped conversation with Cassio.

3. Othello's love is sustained by an idealised vision of Desdemona; she is an object for his romantic passion and becomes part of his romantic vision of himself.
- When the romantic vision of Desdemona is destroyed by Iago, Othello becomes destructive: this makes idealised love seem dangerous.
- Desdemona also idealises Othello; but unlike her husband she refuses to allow anything to destroy her vision.
- Even when she is ill-treated Desdemona insists Othello is a not a jealous man, and says 'I myself' when asked who killed her: this makes idealised love seem foolish.
- In spite of the deaths of Othello and Desdemona, Act V Scene 2 suggests idealised love is heroic: Desdemona never gives up on her vision of Othello (her last words are 'Commend me to my kind lord') and he dies 'upon a kiss', for love.

Part Four: Genre, Structure and Language

Section One: Check your understanding

1. Othello is too proud (hubristic).
- Othello is blind/lacking in self-knowledge.
- Othello is obsessed with his masculine honour.
2. Yes – he chooses to trust Iago over the wife he says he trusts absolutely ('My life upon her faith')
- Yes – he is responsible for Desdemona's death, and therefore his own dishonour.
- No – Iago takes advantage of Othello's 'free and noble' nature.
- No – Iago is indirectly to blame for Desdemona's death: he poisoned Othello's mind against the heroine.

3. Hubris is punished: Othello is made to see his errors and suffers for them.
- Order is restored: Cassio is made governor of Cyprus.
- Pathos and fear are dominant emotions during the final scene.
4. Venice is a symbol of power, and Othello has been a success here: the setting suggests his nobility and greatness.
- Venice represents order before the chaos of the war in Cyprus; civilisation is threatened by a barbarian force, mirroring the way Othello is preyed on by Iago.
- Desdemona is secure and assertive in Venice, where she has power and protection; in Cyprus she is as isolated and vulnerable as the island.
- In Venice Othello and Desdemona are united: both are eloquent and passionate in defence of their love in the senate scene. We see how joyful their marriage could have been.
5. Brabantio's bitterness about female deception in Act I Scene 3 foreshadows the destructive negative emotions Othello will feel when he too believes he's been deceived by Desdemona.
- The violent storm in Act II foreshadows the violent destruction of Othello's mind, and his violent words and actions.
- Cassio's obsession with his masculine honour and reputation in Act II foreshadows Othello's own obsession when he believes Desdemona has been unfaithful.
6. Bianca's unfounded but plausible jealousy over the handkerchief mirrors Othello's.
- Iago's possessive and competitive sexual jealousy regarding his wife mirrors Othello's.
- Othello's abusive treatment of Desdemona in Acts IV and V mirrors the way Iago treats women.
7. Othello's speech style is measured, controlled blank verse early in the play. He demonstrates effective rhetorical skills in Act I.
- Othello's speech style mirrors Desdemona's in Act I, showing how well matched they are in Act I Scene 3.
- The poetic images in Othello's early speeches are replaced by imagery of blood, suffering and animals/ insects when he is corrupted by Iago.
- Othello's speech style mirrors Iago's when his mind is corrupted; he begins to use oaths and disjointed prose in moments of agony.
8. Iago is associated with images of hell and the devil, which he uses himself, showing he delights in evil.
- Iago is associated with crude sexual images, which show he understands lust but cannot comprehend love.
- Iago is associated with images of poison and corruption, which illustrate his methods of manipulation.
9. Iago's evil plots depend upon darkness for success in Acts I and V: rousing Brabantio (when he conceals his identity to avoid trouble) and killing/ wounding others (to conceal his crimes).
- A key turning point in the play occurs at night: the drunken drawl in Act II and its aftermath lead indirectly to tragedy.
- Desdemona's death occurs at night, ironically in the bed with her wedding sheets where she consummated her marriage.
- All the other deaths in the play occur at night in Act V as a result of Iago's night-time plotting.
10. When Othello and Desdemona think they are most united and secure in their love in Act I Scene 3, they are sent to begin marriage in a war zone.
- The great, heroic soldier because a crazed, jealous lover.
- A great and noble soldier, who is in command of a large army is brought down by an inferior subordinate officer.
- Iago is brought down by two enemies: Emilia and Roderigo reveal the truth about Iago in speech and writing.

Section Two: Working towards the exam

1. Iago is indirect to begin with – hinting that he does not trust Cassio, to pique Othello's interest.

- Iago leads Othello towards the topic of jealousy and then focuses on it relentlessly.

- Iago uses the language of love to convince Othello that he is 'on his side' e.g. 'I am your own for ever'.

- Iago offers common sense advice to come across as a faithful friend and trustworthy servant e.g. 'Look to your wife'.

- Iago offers proof (Cassio's dream, the handkerchief) to make his story of Desdemona's treachery convincing.

- Iago uses crude sexual imagery of goats, monkeys and wolves when describing Cassio and Desdemona having sex to torment Othello and keep him 'under his spell'.

2. The storm symbolises the conflict to come for the couple.

- Desdemona's anxiety about Othello's safety foreshadows the anxiety she will feel when Othello starts to mistrust her.

- The war zone setting is an ominous sign: it suggests danger and chaos, which will be associated with Iago, who prospers in Cyprus.

- Iago's ability to triumph in this setting is revealed when he arrives before Othello – the storm has helped his progress.

- The heroine's isolation is already apparent in this setting.

- Desdemona says she is 'not merry' and feels 'fear'. She can only wait passively. The bold Desdemona of Act I starts to disappear.

3. Iago's descriptions of women are belittling: women are only good 'To suckle fools, and chronicle small beer' (II.1. 160).

- Brabantio's words about women are not openly misogynistic, but he objectifies Desdemona as his 'jewel' (I.3.196).

- Iago's words to his wife Emilia show contempt: she is 'a foolish wife' (when she says she has something to give him, III.3.308) and then a 'villainous whore' (when she disobeys him, V.2. 226).

- Cassio insults and dehumanises Bianca when he calls her a 'fitchew' (polecat) (IV.1.145).

- Othello's disgust with women and female sexuality is misogynistic; shown when he calls Desdemona 'that cunning whore of Venice'.

- All of the quotations above suggest the language of *Othello* is misogynistic because women are labelled and judged by men.

4. Othello speaks of the events that have led him to murder his wife as 'unlucky deeds'. This phrase suggests tragic inevitability.

- Othello says he has been 'perplexed in the extreme', suggesting the agony he feels in his final moments.

- Othello uses a simile to describe the loss of his wife; 'Like the base Indian' he 'threw a pearl away'. The image suggests Desdemona's value and purity, which have been tragically lost.

- Othello says that he 'drops tears as fast as the Arabian trees' suggesting the depth of his tragic sorrow.

- The image of 'the tragic loading of this bed' which 'poisons sight' heightens the sense of tragic loss.

- The references to Iago in the final moments of the play as a 'Spartan dog' and 'hellish villain' remind us of the depth and cruelty of the evil that has caused this tragic outcome.

5. Internal conflict – Iago is driven by negative emotions –self-love and hatred for others – which make him destructive.

- Internal conflict – Othello is tormented by feelings of love and jealousy; these conflicted emotions are the catalyst for tragedy.

- Military duty versus the domestic sphere – Othello finds it impossible to reconcile the roles of soldier and husband.

- Masculine honour and 'being a man' – Othello is conflicted about his role as a man, and tragically chooses the brutal Iago version of masculinity.

- Marital conflict – the power imbalance between men and women means that women are powerless to influence male behaviour.

Part Five: Contexts and interpretations

Section One: Check your understanding

1. Elizabethans were suspicious of foreigners and 'barbarians', shown by the way the Venetian senate and Othello have negative attitudes to the Turks, who they view as an alien enemy.

- Elizabethans had negative stereotypes of black men, shown in Iago's comments about Othello.

- Elizabethans thought that Venice was a sophisticated but decadent and immoral place, shown by the choice of an Italianate setting for a play about love, sex and revenge.

2. Women were subordinate to men, shown by Desdemona when she says she is 'subdued' to Othello.

- Women were seen as the property of men; Brabantio calls Desdemona his 'jewel'.

- Assertive women were seen as a threat, shown by Iago's treatment of Emilia in Act V Scene 2.

3. The violence of the storm was originally portrayed through language; modern productions can use sound and lighting effects.

- There were few props on the Elizabethan stage, so Desdemona's bed would have been the focal point in Act V Scene 2.

- The violent treatment of Desdemona is perhaps more shocking today than it may have been in the 17th century because attitudes to domestic abuse have changed.

4. Rymer says Othello cannot be a tragic hero because he is black.

- Rymer views the mixed marriage of Othello and Desdemona as socially unacceptable.

- Rymer says that the events and characters are not credible.

5. Bradley – Othello is a noble and romantic figure

- Bradley – Othello's jealousy is credible

- Eliot – Othello is a weak fantasist who is susceptible to jealousy

6. Women are victims of patriarchy in the play.

- Desdemona suffers and is punished because she is too assertive.

- The world of the play is dominated by masculine values.

7. Iago is at the bottom of the hierarchy in *Othello*: he is the proletariat.

- Iago seeks to challenge the bourgeoisie, i.e. Cassio.

- Iago's undermines the existing power structure in order to assert the rights of the oppressed working class.

8. Newman says that the white characters feel threatened by Othello's difference.
- Newman says the play explores Elizabethan worries about mixed marriages.
- Newman says the play does not support racist views, but challenges them.

9. Appearance is important to him – yes – Othello says he 'must be found' in Act I Scene 2, suggesting he does not want to be seen as a deceptive, unworthy character for making a secret marriage.
- His marriage increases his status – he is admired for having married the 'divine' Desdemona.
- His marriage increases his status – no – Iago ridicules the marriage and suggests it diminishes Othello's masculinity.

10. It is a very powerful exploration of the theme of tragic love.
- Iago is one of the most intriguing and complex villains in Elizabethan tragedy.
- The aesthetic beauty of the language – especially Othello's speech – makes the play worthy .

Section Two: Working towards the exam

1. Desdemona is a young Venetian noblewoman, Othello is an older mercenary general: their backgrounds are different or 'unequal'.
- Their differences attract the couple to each other, and they are presented as equally passionate and committed in Act I.
- The couple become 'unequal' only when Iago divides them.
- The effect of Iago's intervention is to make Othello feel he is not Desdemona's 'equal', which makes him doubt his love.
- Shakespeare never suggests the couple's tragedy is caused because they made an unequal match; they die equally committed to each other: both die for love.
- The moral of the play is not to trust false servants, not to avoid an unequal match.

2. Desdemona speaks assertively, demanding her marital 'rites'.
- Desdemona refuses to be parted from Othello, subverting ideas about the military wife's passive role.
- Desdemona is given the power to choose her own destiny by the Duke who asks her 'What would you'.
- Desdemona uses her rhetorical power to keep her husband.
- Desdemona says her 'heart' is 'subdued' to Othello, suggesting she wants to be a traditional, obedient wife.
- Desdemona's 'divided duty' shows that she accepts she is either a daughter or a wife, not an independent female.

3. Yes – he has a legitimate grudge, the hierarchy protects and promotes its own, denying the working class character a chance.
- Yes – Iago's intelligence is ignored because he is not the right 'class' for promotion; Cassio is more acceptably bourgeois.
- No – Iago has no solidarity with others who are oppressed and exploits them e.g. his abuse of Bianca.
- No – Iago is not engaged in a class struggle; he is only interested in personal gain.
- No – Iago has no positive vision of a utopia where the working class get their due; his impulses are to destroy, not to challenge the status quo for legitimate reasons.
- No – Othello is not an evil, bourgeois oppressor who deserves to be overthrown.

4. Yes – Othello is still obsessed with his honour, in spite of the fact that he is a murderer (his 'service to the state' is the first thing Othello mentions).
- Yes – Othello says he cannot control his fate ('unlucky deeds' have overtaken him), yet he has acted brutally to control his wife's fate
- Yes – Othello says he loved 'too well', yet his actions in Acts IV and V have been driven by hatred and jealousy.
- No – Othello compares himself to a 'base Indian' who 'threw a pearl away': he knows the depth of his folly.
- No – Othello kills himself, proving his sense of honour.
- No – Othello knows there is 'no way but this'; he accepts his fate stoically.

5. Yes – the most racially prejudiced and sexist character – Iago – is abhorrent.
- Yes – the presentation of the central couple challenges racist views of mixed marriages.
- Yes – the Venetian senate is not racist or sexist; it supports the central couple.
- Perhaps – Othello does begin to act like the negative stereotype of a lustful, angry black man – although this is under the influence of a lustful, angry white man.
- No – the women are all vilified and sacrificed for male 'honour'.

MARK SCHEME

Use this page to assess your answer to the **Practice task** provided on page 110.

Look at the elements listed for each Assessment Objective. Examiners will be looking to award the highest grades to the students who meet the majority of these criteria. If you can meet two to three elements from each AO, you are working at a good level, with some room for improvement to a higher level.*

> **'Self-destruction and weakness are the main impressions the audience are left with of *Othello* at the end of the play.' By considering Shakespeare's dramatic methods, to what extent do you agree with this view?**

A01	Articulate informed, personal and creative responses to literary texts, using associated concepts and terminology, and coherent, accurate written expression.	• You make a range of clear, relevant points about [whether characters e.g. Othello, have been weak and self-destructive]. • You use a range of literary terms correctly, e.g. **foreshadowing**, **metaphor**, **romance**, **oxymoron**, **dialogue**. • You write a clear introduction, outlining your thesis and provide a clear conclusion. • You signpost and link your ideas fluently about whether Othello is weak and self-destructive within the play. • You offer an overall personal interpretation or conceptualisation of the text which is well argued and convincing.
A02	Analyse ways in which meanings are shaped in literary texts.	• You explain the techniques and methods Shakespeare uses to present Othello's strengths and weaknesses. • You explain in detail how such examples shape meaning, e.g. whether Othello's final speech suggests he is weak and self-destructive. • You comment on how the dialogue e.g. Othello's final image 'to die upon a kiss' represents his weakness or strength as a lover.
A03	Demonstrate understanding of the significance and influence of the contexts in which literary texts are written and received.	• You demonstrate your understanding of tragic tropes and motifs – the 'hero' with a weakness that brings him down; the idea of hubris; the way events combine inexorably to bring about tragedy. • Literary context: Othello as a noble, courtly lover; Iago as an evil Machiavel; suicide in tragedy e.g. is it a noble, stoical act, associated with strong, resolute characters? • Historical context: Renaissance concepts of masculine honour and attitudes to women, and how they can be linked to the themes of weakness and self-destruction.
A04	Explore connections across literary texts.	• You make relevant links between characters and ideas, noting how for example, Othello's strengths become weaknesses as the play progresses and how Iago contributes to Othello's self-destruction from Act III onwards.
A05	Explore literary texts informed by different interpretations.	• Where appropriate, you incorporate and comment on critics' views of the extent to which Othello can be seen as a weak and self-destructive man, or whether he is a strong man brought down by a destructive adversary. • You assert your own independent view clearly.

* This mark scheme gives you a broad indication of attainment, but check the specific mark scheme for your paper/task to ensure you know what to focus on.